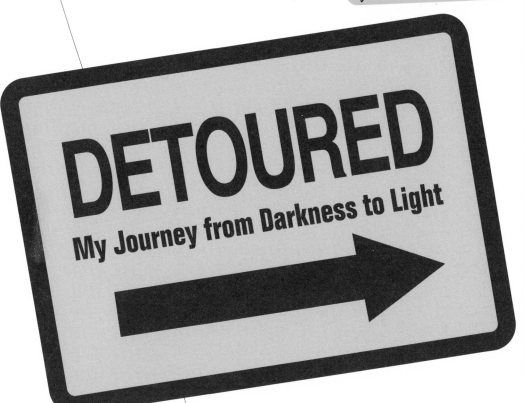

DETOURED
My Journey from Darkness to Light

BY
Jesse De La Cruz

BARKING ROOSTER BOOKS
Los Angeles

ISBN 9780983808800

Book design: Jane Brunette
Cover art: Erin Wells, Rowan Studios, Boulder Creek, CA

PUBLISHED BY:
Barking Rooster Books
PO Box 328
San Fernando, CA 91341

To my Jefita who never gave up on me

*and to my daughter Jessica for touching my heart
in a way that only a child can.*

Naomi — Thank you

INCARCERATION TIMELINE

Year	Age	Facility	Length of Stay
1965	14	Tulare County Juvenile Hall	3 Days
1967	16	Boys Camp	1 Year
1969	18	Tulare County Jail	30 Days
1970	19	Tulare County Road Camp	1 Year
1971	20	Tulare County Jail	7 Months
1972	21	California Rehabilitation Center	3 Months
1972	21	Tulare County Jail	3 Months
1972	21	California Medical Facility	4 Months
1972	21	Deuel Vocational Institution	3 ½ Years
1975	24	San Quentin State Prison	2 Years
1978	27	California Training Facility	3 ½ Years
1985	34	Deuel Vocational Institution	7 months
1985	34	California Men's' Colony	2 Years
1987	36	California Medical Facility-Solano	1 Year
1988	37	Deuel Vocational Institution	1 Year 4 months
1990	40	Mule Creek State Prison	6 months
1991	41	Corcoran State Prison	1 year
1992	41	California Training Facility	1 ½ years
1993	42	Folsom State Prison	3 years

There are times of confinement as a juvenile that are not specified in this timeline simply because I can't remember every time I was incarcerated. I also spent about two and half years going in and out of the Los Angeles County Jail for under the influence of heroin between1982-1985. Additionally, I do not mention the time I spent while awaiting litigation on some of the charges brought against me throughout the course of my criminal involvement. I have also changed some of the names to protect the guilty.

INTRODUCTION

BY JOE LOYA

IN 2005, I received an e-mail from Jesse De La Cruz asking me to read some of his memoir in progress. I told him to send me ten pages. The author Richard Rodriguez read and edited my writings, and introduced me to editors in the early stages of my writing career. He charged me to one day do the same for some other aspiring writer—another Joe Loya—when I had the chance.

I told Jesse that I was on deadline but would read his material and respond within two weeks. Later that day I had an unexpected break, so I decided to read the introduction to his memoir. His story intrigued me. It was clear that Jesse was a natural storyteller. I emailed him and asked him to send me ten more pages. After I read them, I phoned him and told him that I admired his work.

That's how Jesse became my Joe Loya.

We have been friends ever since.

Jesse had written the bulk of his memoir before he approached me. I was impressed. He was madly self-driven and needed to write his story, this much was evident. Like all great memoirists I know, Jesse needed to tell his story. To make us see his life as some sort of text that we could learn from. And why not? His story is a powerfully inspiring one. Both for the way he lived so strongly on the other side of taboo, and also for how bravely he has constructed an honest life for himself and his daughter in daylight, out of the shadows.

In this memoir, you will learn that violence and rage are trained behavior more often than not. Humans are not born monsters, but can learn to behave monstrously after years of pressures on their poise, through the various physical, racial and psychological abuses as are catalogued in so many sociology textbooks. But Jesse doesn't promote victim chic. He accepts responsibility for his actions and therefore his book lacks the sentimentality that so often hurts the writing of folks who lived to write about surviving prison and the mean streets. Jesse is starkly candid about his behavior in the criminal world. And that is the power of the story.

The redemption of Jesse De La Cruz is almost Biblical is scope; an epic story of a life gone wildly astray; a Prodigal Son-like squandering of intelligence and good will. Milton would recognize this story as one of sin and a heroic life regained. St. Paul—an admitted great slave to sin who eventually repented—would know this story of resurrection, and survival of several imprisonments. And of course, there is the 4th century memoirist St. Augustine who confessed his sins and chronicled his spiritual awakening in the most famous memoir in Western Civilization. In my opinion, Jesse De La Cruz's memoir is a 21st Century addition to this long tradition of stories about detours and recoveries.

The question for you the reader, is a riddle: Do you review the life of Jesse De La Cruz through the eyes of a forward-looking boy habituated to hate and violence, who eventually disappeared into the underworld for three decades? Or do we review his narrative from the vantage point of the present, looking back through the eyes of a man, severely mindful as he lives a moral life today? In other words, is Jesse De La Cruz a long time bad man done good in the end? Or is he a good man who acted against his conscience for many years?

I prefer to see him the second way.

But you judge for yourself.

Your journey in the coming pages will reveal Jesse De La Cruz's compelling life confronting every squalid day with the same first intensity that he confronted his sublime and thorough change.

I am ignorant of how I was formed and how I was born.
Through a quarter of my lifetime
I was absolutely ignorant of the reasons
for everything I saw,
and heard, and felt, and was merely a parrot
prompted by other parrots.

VOLTAIRE

CHAPTER ONE

FOLSOM STATE PRISON, *April 2, 1996*:
I had been in prison for the past three years although it wouldn't be long before I was set free again. It was 7:55 a.m., but I'd been awake since 4:00, pacing in my cell, trying to make time move faster. Instead, it seemed to move in slow motion.

It was always like this whenever I was about to be released. The tension would mount each day as the date drew nearer. The nights would seem longer and it would get more difficult for me to sleep. My brain would suffer a persistent dull pain from all the questions that zipped through my mind, making my head hurt like the time Carlos Montes whacked me on my skull with a ball-pin hammer back in '69. Every morning I would suffer unrelenting stomach aches that kept me on the toilet for long periods of time.

Where would I live? How long would I stay out this time? Would I get a life sentence the next time I got busted? After all, the "Three Strikes You're Out Law" had taken effect in March of '94 in California. I had read the language of the statute in the prison library when it had first been implemented, and it clearly stated that anyone with two prior felony convictions who was arrested and found guilty of any type of felony would be sentenced to life. The state was serious too. I had read a newspaper article about a guy from San Diego who had been sentenced to life for stealing nothing more than a couple slices of pizza.

I had five prior felonies.

I really didn't think I could stay out either. The last time I had been cut loose I had been so nervous I had rushed to a liquor store and bought a half pint bottle of Smirnoff Vodka and a pint of orange juice as a chaser to calm my jitters. Even though I hated alcohol, I had guzzled the entire contents of the bottle trying to relieve my anxiety. When the Vodka hit my stomach, it had temporarily eased my fear, but it also tore down what little resistance I'd had about breaking the law. As soon I reached my destination, I quickly located my Homeboy *Babo* and got a free a shot of heroin from him. I started stealing after my $200 release money ran out a few days later.

I didn't want to drink alcohol, use heroin, or steal anymore, but I didn't know how to live in the outside world. Sometimes I wanted to tell someone that I didn't know how I was going to survive on the streets without breaking the law. But there was no way I could tell any of my fellow prisoners I wanted to go straight, or that I was terrified about being outside in the world without sounding weak. The very notion of being afraid of freedom seemed ridiculous—after all, getting out is what every prisoner dreams about.

Suddenly, I heard the echo of the Man's footsteps as he approached to cut me loose.

"*Oralé Hueró*, it's time for me to get going," I said to my cellmate.

"I hear you, homie."

"Come on, De La Cruz, we don't have all day," Officer Miller barked.

Yeah, yeah, I thought, it was the same ole-game of hurry-up and wait.

Officer Miller stuck his big brass key into the lock and in one quick motion turned it to unlock the steel barred door. Everything was deathly quiet in the cellblock and I heard the door squeak as he swung it open. There was no one on the tier when I stepped out of my cell because the entire prison was on lockdown. An altercation between a northern California Mexican (*Norteño*) and a Southern California Mexican (*Sureño*)—violent prison rivals—a few days before had led prison administration to confine all prisoners to their cells 24 hours a day. Walking towards the stairway at the end of the tier, I briefly stopped in front of my road dog *Prieto's* cell.

"Get laid and take a shot for me, Home-Squeeze," he said smiling brightly as he shook my hand through the bars.

"*Simón, Ese*," I replied, as Miller and I continued on.

A guard sitting behind the desk situated inside the cage at the entrance of the cellblock hit a button hidden underneath the counter that unlocked the door leading to the main corridor. Officer Miller pulled the steel door open when he heard a loud buzzing sound, and we stepped into the main hallway, wide and tall enough to drive three eighteen wheel trucks through, side-by-side. Normally, when walking down that corridor at any given time of the day, it was as packed as a crowded state fair at peak hour. You could barely hear the guy standing next to you speak because of the loud chatter created by many men talking and laughing at the same time. But now, Officer Miller and I were the lone two men and hearing the echo of our footsteps in that desolate, cavernous hallway made me feel like we were the last survivors in an abandoned underground nuclear bunker.

It wasn't until Miller unlocked the door to Receiving & Release (R&R) that I saw the other inmates who were being released as well. As soon as I walked into the room, I sensed the underlying nervous anticipation of everyone there. No one said anything, but it seemed as though we all knew we were about to embark on a difficult journey.

An R&R guard stood behind one of those doors that opens the top half, turning the bottom closed door into a sort of counter. He handed me a large brown bag containing the street clothes Mama had sent me two weeks earlier. Mama hadn't forgotten the kind of clothes I liked either. She had sent me a stone gray long sleeve shirt, a pair of black dress slacks, a black belt, matching black socks, some boxer underwear, and a pair of gray-on-black Stacy Adams alligator skin shoes. Taking off my prison suit, I slipped on the clothes and immediately felt that I was no longer a faceless member of the Orange Jumpsuit crowd.

Afterward, I sat down on the long wooden bench bolted to the wall. I tried to sit still as I waited for Officer Miller to call my name so I could sign my walking papers, but my nerves were on edge. I felt sweat run down my armpits underneath my shirt, and my stomach hurt too. It felt like I needed to take a shit. Unable to contain my apprehension, I strolled over to where the other prisoners were waiting to sign their release papers and when my turn finally came, I walked up to the counter where Officer Miller stood. I grabbed a pen and waited to sign my name on the forms he held in his hands. He was reading the paperwork slowly as if something was wrong. After a while Officer Miller looked up over the rim of his glasses, and slowly shook his head.

"I don't think you're going anywhere this morning, De La Cruz," he scoffed.

For a brief moment, I stood there in disbelief. Then a wave of pain moved through my stomach, as if Officer Miller had stuck a knife in my gut and sliced from one side of my body to the other. I tried to keep my facial expression blank, attempting to hide that he had gotten to me, but in that instant, my world came crumbling down. What kind of game was this clown playing? First he tells me I'm going, and then he says I'm not.

"What do you mean, I'm not going anywhere?"

"Well, De La Cruz," Miller smirked, "these documents indicate you have an outstanding warrant."

I wanted to shout "NO!" But my mouth felt dry. I glared at him, thinking that he had to be playing some kind of wicked mind game with me, but the cruel look in his eyes, and the contemptuous grin pasted on his face let me know he was dead serious and that he loved every second of goading me.

Just as I was about to lose my cool and snatch him from behind the counter to beat the life out of him, he smiled at me and said, "Get laid and take a shot for me, Home-Squeeze."

Abruptly, I awoke, gasping for breath, in a cold sweat, disoriented, and realized I'd been dreaming. I shook my head in an attempt to clear my thoughts and remembered that I was going to be released later that morning. And even though I should have been happy that I was finally getting out, I felt a knotted fist in the pit of my stomach.

Looking over at the lighted dial of the small clock sitting on the steel table in the corner of my cell, I saw it was only 4:00 a.m. I wouldn't be escorted to R&R until 8. Not wanting to wake my cellmate, I quietly slid off my bunk, took a leak, washed my face, and brushed my teeth. I filled my tumbler with cold water and plugged the stinger (a device used to heat water) into the electrical socket in order to make myself a cup of instant Tasters Choice coffee.

Waiting for the water to boil, I recalled how at the beginning of my criminal career, and for many years after that, being cut loose from prison had always been like going on a vacation. As soon as I hit the streets, I would hook up with my old friends, start shooting heroin, which led to robbing drug dealers, boosting cigarettes from super markets, breaking into homes to steal the TV's, stereos, jewelry, or guns if there were any. And periodically, if I got angry or drunk enough, I would stab a man. Invariably, I would get caught and sent back to prison.

But things were different now. The last time I had been on the streets had been really tough. I hadn't been able to find a reliable crime partner because most of the guys who had been into crime with me were either dead, serving life sentences, or so sick from Hepatitis C that they couldn't rob or break into homes even if they wanted too. I had ended up homeless.

I remember feeling a sense of relief when I was arrested and ultimately returned to prison. It was as though I had come home. And why shouldn't I have felt relief? I had been shuttling in and out of prison for almost thirty years and confinement was now part of my nature. I had grown accustomed to the State of California telling me when and what to eat, when to move to the yard, when to shower, when to lock up, when to stand for count, when to get strip-searched, and who to live with. In a perverse way, the prison walls had become part of my security.

On the other hand, whenever I was free, I could wake up in the middle of the night with a craving for donuts, walk down to the local 24hour Safeway and get some. During the day I could pick and choose between a Chinese, Indian, or Mexican restaurant to go for dinner. In the evening, I could go to a 16Theater Cineplex and select any movie I wanted to watch. But along with all these choices came the responsibility of having and keeping a job, something I knew nothing about. As much as I hated to admit it, all those street freedoms had meant very little to me. After all, if staying out had been so important why did I always manage to return to the penitentiary? I clearly had become institutionalized.

But I had to stay out this time because it wasn't just about me anymore. Four years earlier I had fathered a baby girl and she needed me now. During this confinement, I had tried desperately not to reflect so much about my baby because thinking about her made me want to cry, and there was no way I would cry in prison. But each day I had been haunted by the image of my little girl's face. She was the first thing I thought about when I woke up, and the last thought that raced through my mind before I fell asleep.

As I sipped on my last cup of prison coffee, I thought about the morning she was born. I had been standing outside the door of the delivery room on the second floor of St. Joseph's Hospital in Stockton, California at 5:58 a.m. when I heard her cry out. A few minutes later I was invited in to see my daughter. I walked into a room and a nurse handed me my baby curled in a pink receiving blanket that was gently scented with baby powder. My baby's fragile pink fingers peeked out from the blanket and waved slowly in the air. Her full head of dark hair was covered with a white beanie, exposing only her rosy face as she slept. For a second, it appeared as though she instinctively smiled sweetly at me. I carefully brought her to my chest with tears streaming down my face. I remember asking myself how in the world I expected to be a father to my child if I was constantly in prison, but I felt powerless to change what seemed inevitable.

I had known lots of guys in the joint who had kids, and I had seen their children end up in prison, too. There was even a guy whose son had been his cellmate. I couldn't understand how he could live with himself knowing he had failed his son completely, but I never asked him how he dealt with it.

What I did know was that I didn't want my child following in my footsteps. Holding her in my arms that day, I made a decision to straighten my life once and for all.

Unfortunately, my old patterns of behavior had been too difficult to change. Within months of her birth, I gave in to my habit of stealing and shooting heroin and had wound up in prison again. So here I was, faced with having to go out to the streets and get straight, or risk being the father whose kid would only see him in prison visiting rooms; if I was lucky.

Lying back down on my bunk, in the dark quiet of my cell, I closed my eyes and tried not to think about all the changes I would have to make if I wanted to stay out. I tried not to think about the Three Strikes Law looming out there ready to snatch me up and take my freedom forever. I wished that I could snap my fingers and live a life similar to the ones I had seen in some of the afternoon soap operas.

Damn, how had I gotten to a place where I was so terrified with something that so many people throughout the world strived for everyday—freedom?

CHAPTER TWO

Jésus Limón is my birth name.
Jesse De La Cruz is my given name.
And Dragón was my barrio name.

I WAS BORN in Edinburg, Texas on April 15, 1951, the il-
legitimate child of Eloisa Sahagun. I wasn't born in a hospital
like other babies. My birth took place in a one-room dilapidated
shack that sat by itself on a slight hill in the outskirts of town
seemingly isolated from the rest of the world. The small house
was next to the canal that separated it from the slaughterhouse
where Grandpa worked. Grandma and her *comadre* delivered
me. A few days later, Mama took me to the county courthouse
to document my birth at the Hidalgo County register's office.
She was only thirteen years old.

Three years earlier, in 1948, my grandparents had moved
to Texas with their seven children Ramon, Jose, Pedro, Mama,
Heriberto, Luz and Chela. Their offspring ranged in age from
two to seventeen. My Grandpa, like many others before him,
had immigrated to the U.S. chasing that dream of providing a
better life for his family. The decision to move had been made
after Grandpa went to visit a friend from his village who had
moved to Edinburg, Texas. Grandpa had been so awed by the
fact that many of the streets in Edinburg were paved and that
the houses there had toilets that he had decided to raise his family there.

In Teocuitatlan De Corona, the small village in the State
of Jalisco, Mexico where Mama's family lived before the move,
most everyone was very poor. Many of the houses were made of
adobe and very few, if any, had running water, electricity, bathrooms, or gas stoves. Wood stoves were used for cooking and
nearly everyone used outhouses, or simply shitted or pissed behind a tree or a bush. A river that ran behind the village served
as a Laundromat to a lot of the people who lived in the town.

The streets were made of dirt and rock, but it didn't matter because at that time there were very few people who owned cars.

Mama's family's first stop on their way to Edinburg was Reynosa, Tamaulipas, a bustling Mexican town bordering the U.S., and a pit stop for many Mexicans on their way to the U.S. While there, Grandpa worked selling blankets, small paintings, and beaded necklaces to the large number of tourists who crossed the border to buy goods at cheaper prices. On weekends, hundreds of students from U.S. colleges crossed the border too. They went to Reynosa to party in *"La zona roja"* (The Red Zone) located on the edge of town, and spent their money on cheap beer and prostitutes, paying less than a dollar to get laid.

During the time he was in Reynosa, Grandpa attempted to obtain the proper documentation to enter the United States legally, but after a few months of frustrating dealings with immigration officials, he was told he couldn't cross over to the other side. So Grandpa acquired the services of a *"coyoté"* (a person who smuggles people into the United States) and under the cover of night, he and his family entered the U.S. illegally by crossing the Rio Grande River into Texas. As planned, they settled on the outskirts of Edinburg, located just twelve miles from Reynosa.

Not long after, Grandpa got a job in a slaughterhouse where he worked as a meat cutter. Eleven-year old Mama helped Grandma with the household chores. She washed the family laundry by hand in a washtub, and helped prepare and deliver lunch to grandpa at the slaughterhouse. My uncle Ramon, who was seventeen, went into the city of Edinburg every morning and waited on the street corner with other men in hopes of getting work in the fields picking fruit. The two other boys, Jose and Heriberto, washed cars, cleaned yards, or swept storefronts for cash.

Juan De La Cruz, a 26-year-old meat cutter my grandfather met in one of the many bars scattered throughout the neighborhood, had helped him get the job. Over time, they became close friends. Juan would pick up Grandpa on Saturday night and they would go party in Reynosa's *"zona roja,"* and not return until Sunday morning. By that time they had obtained illegal identification that allowed them to cross the border easily.

When they arrived home, Grandpa often invited Juan inside for *menudo*, the Mexican equivalent of drinking a Bloody Mary the morning after an alcoholic binge. Mama, who looked older than her age, would serve the hot *menudo* and corn tortillas to Grandpa and Juan.

Juan would smile at Mama in a way no man had ever done before, and he would tell her she was pretty. Mama enjoyed his flirtations. But she worried too because she knew that if Grandpa caught Juan looking at her in that special way they would both be in trouble. In the end, she needn't have worried so much: Grandpa was always too drunk to notice.

My Grandpa and Juan always smelled like women's perfume and alcohol when they walked into the house, but Grandma never said a word to Grandpa. The smell always bothered Mama, for even at her age she understood that in order to smell so powerfully like women's perfume, Grandpa and Juan must have been surrounded by many, many women over the long weekend. Mother would glance at Grandma questioningly, but as long as the two men were in the room, Grandma would keep her lips tightly sealed. It wasn't until later, when the two of them were alone that she would say, "That's the way men are." And leave it at that.

When Mama was 12, Onesimo Mungia began to hang out with my mother's two older brothers, Ramon and Jose. On most Saturday nights, Onesimo and Mama's brothers would often meet at one of the many bars located in their neighborhood. One Saturday, my uncle Jose asked Onesimo if he could take his sister Maria to a dance. Onesimo gave Jose permission, but told him to make sure he brought Maria back before her curfew so Onesimo wouldn't get in trouble with his father. Jose agreed. But instead of bringing Maria back, he took Maria across the border to Reynosa and married her.

It turned out that Jose and Maria had been dating each other on the sly for quite some time without Onesimo's knowledge. Onesimo got really pissed with Jose and to get back at him, he began to date my mother without anyone in Mama's family knowing either. He told Mama that he loved her. That he would make sure she was happy. Mama was ignorant about men's motives, so she often snuck out of her house and met up with Onesimo at his place. One night, in a messy room, with nothing more than a small bed in it, Mama gave Onesimo her virginity.

A few weeks later, Mama woke up and rushed to the toilet where she vomited everything she had eaten the night before. Mama knew something was wrong. She had heard about morning sickness, but for a month or so she tried to pray her pregnancy away. Of course it didn't work.

A month later she got confirmation from a midwife that she was indeed pregnant. She told Onesimo about her pregnancy. He promptly packed up his belongings and left for the state of Washington. When she finally gathered the courage to tell my grandparents, Grandpa beat her as he yelled that he would not have an unwed pregnant daughter in his home. Then Grandpa threw her out of the house.

Mama didn't care so much about the whipping. What truly frightened her was the thought of having to live on her own. The night he kicked her out, she stood outside the house trembling not knowing what to do. Behind the door she could hear Grandma telling Grandpa he couldn't throw her out because she was too young. Grandpa remained silent for a moment and then coldly responded that she hadn't been too young to have sex.

Eventually, after much quarreling, Grandma managed to convince Grandpa to help Mama rent a small shack not too far from where they lived, the place where I was born. Although he had grudgingly agreed to the housing arrangement, Grandfather would not speak to his daughter for the next thirteen years.

Before long, Mama began receiving visits from Juan De La Cruz. Juan knew she was pregnant, but he didn't seem to care. After all, Mama was a young and pretty girl. He enjoyed spending time with her, and was genuinely nice to her. He would bring her groceries and spend time talking with her almost every day, helping to lift some of the burden that was weighing on her regarding my impending birth.

I was born three months before Mama married Juan, who had already been married. Unfortunately, his first wife had died with her child during delivery. He had been left with three children, Delia, Alfredo (later called Dee and Freddy), and Lydia. Ultimately, Juan needed a mother for his children and Mama needed a father for me. So to make living less difficult for each other, they got married.

Becoming an instant mother at any age is not easy, but it was even harder for Mama because she was so young. At thirteen, Mama was a kid, and obviously knew nothing about raising children. Naturally, she had lots of trouble being a parent. She was only nine years older than Delia. No one gave her instructions on what had to be done. Only Grandma came by from time to time to help out and teach mother the secrets to a successful marriage, the main one being that she had to stand by her husband no matter what.

"You made your bed, now you have to sleep in it," she would say.

Juan stopped talking to Mama in that special way he did before he married her. In fact, he began to tell Mama she was lucky he had married her because no other man would want her after she had gotten pregnant at such a young age. According to Juan, Mama was spoiled goods. He never took Mama to a dance, or to the movies, but he made sure he had fun. On Saturday night, after he got off work, he would come home, get dressed, and go party in Reynosa. A lot of times he would only return on Monday morning to change into his work clothes and go to work.

Mama spent her weekends cleaning house, washing clothes by hand using a tin tub and scrub board, and trying not to think about how she was supposed to buy food to feed four hungry kids without money since Father always left to Reynosa without leaving Mama any cash. Sometimes she would have to ask her neighbors for food in order to feed Delia, Alfredo, Lydia and me.

By now father had quit working as a meat cutter. He told Mama that working in the fields gave him more freedom, but the truth was he wanted to keep an eye on her. Father didn't trust Mama. He thought that if he left her alone, Mama would take off with another man. He was right to a certain degree.

She did want to leave him, but not for another man. She wanted to live with her parents again.

One evening, as Mama and Grandma sat on the porch, Mama fearfully broached the subject of leaving Juan, and begged Grandma to let her return home. Grandma had responded with a curt no. Telling Mama that the Catholic Church didn't permit divorce and that was the end of that discussion.

One Saturday night my Grandfather, Uncle Jose, and Uncle Ramon met up with Juan in Reynosa as they usually did to womanize and drink. At one point in the night, and after quite a few beers, Juan revealed to Ramon that he was married to another woman and that he would be leaving Mama.

The following day, Uncle Ramon told Mama that Juan was going to leave her because he had recently married another woman in Mexico. That night, when Mama saw Juan getting dressed to go out again she became suspicious because Juan never went out on Sunday nights after he returned from his Saturday night partying. Although Mama had really wanted to leave him before, she now understood that she was stuck. Divorcing Juan was out of the question because she would bring shame to her family once again. And even though she was angry to learn that he had disrespected her when he married the other woman, she felt as if somehow she had failed him as a wife. This caused her anguish, so Mama got on her knees and begged him not to go.

"What's the matter woman," he chuckled, "I'm just going to the bar for a little bit, but I'll be back."

Mama knew he was lying, because he wouldn't look her in her eyes. She watched as my father finished getting dressed, combed back his hair, splashed on too much cologne, and walked out the door. That night she waited up for him until three in the morning with the four of us kids sound asleep close by her side. Her mind raced. The rent is due soon, how will I pay it? I have to buy groceries, but Juan took all the money. I have to see the doctor soon, and even if I could get there, how will I pay for the visit? She waited all night but father never came back. He didn't come back the next day either, or the next. In fact, a whole week went by without any sign of him. So Mama had to figure out how to survive on her own.

She was fourteen.

Mama asked her neighbors for beans, rice, and the ingredients to make tortillas. The neighborhood wives were willing to help out because they knew she was a struggling young mother. By the second week of Juan's absence, we had to use a kerosene lamp for light because the electricity had been shut off. Although she was concerned about her marriage to Juan, she was too busy every day—with preparing breakfast, getting Dee and Freddy ready for school, making sure they got to school, taking care of me and Lydia, washing laundry, cooking what little food there was for dinner, and putting us to sleep—to dwell on it. It wasn't until Juan got released from jail after being arrested for bigamy that he returned home. Turned out the other woman wasn't as loyal to Juan as Mama. Juan confessed to Mama about what happened, and told her that the other woman had reported him when she found out he was married to Mama.

After his jail release, Father was a changed man. He never talked about that episode in his life after his brief admission to my mother. But I understand about change in jail. For some men, it happens quickly. They consider what they're doing as nothing more than having a good time. They throw caution to the wind for a short period in their lives, partying a lot, cavorting with women. Some of these men, like my father, might even be married, but they are essentially the kind of citizen who keeps a job, pays his bills, and doesn't beat his children. But one day he gets arrested for driving under the influence, or getting drunk and fighting in a bar, or they get caught for traffic warrants and end up spending a night or two in jail among the real lowlifes—the chronic homeless drunks, the robbers, burglars, gangbangers, sadistic guards, and even killers—and he realizes he is caught in a world where he doesn't want to be, a world he doesn't ever want to return to once released. So these men keep their heads low, volunteer to clean the tier, or cook in the kitchen. Sometimes they pick up a Bible and spend a lot of time in the chapel. They do anything they can to get away from the bad men back in their living quarters. And when they are finally cut loose, they forever carry with them the gutter experience of jail and vow never to return. They become family men; dedicated to being workers and providers. In my father's case, he stopped going to bars. Instead, he would take us kids to the movies on weekends, and he started spending time talking to Mama, something he hadn't done much before he went to jail. Father started discussing our future with Mama saying that we should move to California because he had heard life would be better for us there. Mama told him she thought moving to California would be good. After all, Juan seemed truly sorry for what he had done, and was acting really nice to her, and she had learned to care for him.

Juan and Mama continued to work in the fields trying to save as much money as possible. On weekends we would spend time together as a family and for the first time in our lives, Dee, Lydia, Freddy, and I spent time with Father when he took us to the movies, and sometimes to the park.

We lived a fairly peaceful life, until one evening in January of 1954, when I was three years old. I was sitting on the edge of Mama's bed when I fell and hit the floor hard. I tried to get up, but I had lost the ability to move my legs and my muscles hurt terribly. Terrified, I screamed, unable to understand why I was in so much pain. Mama quickly snatched me up and checked my head to see if I had bumped it, but I didn't have any lumps. Thinking that I was crying because I was still frightened because I had fallen, she tried to calm me down.

I wanted to tell her that all my bones ached and that my body felt as if it were on fire, but I was obviously too young to find the words. Mama held me in her arms, and gently whispered "there, there, son," as she softly rubbed my head.

Mama tried everything she could to get me to stop weeping. She rocked me in her arms, bathed me, lay me on her bed next to her because she knew I liked that. But I howled even more. Nothing she did eased my pain. I continued bawling until the next morning. By then, I was delirious with fever and Mama realized something was seriously wrong, so they rushed me to the hospital.

When we arrived I was ushered into a room and given a shot on my butt.

Shortly thereafter the pain miraculously disappeared. Afterward, I was tossed, turned, poked, and prodded by a Caucasian doctor as a series of tests were performed on me.

When he was done, the doctor stepped out of the examination room into the hall where my parents were waiting. In pretty good Spanish, but in a hard tone of voice, he told my mother I had polio. "It's an epidemic without a cure."

The moment the doctor told Mama about my condition, she began to moan like a she-dog that has lost her pup. She wrung her hands and turned to look at my Father for some type of support, but Father was just as shocked as Mama. He stood wide-eyed and pale as a ghost as if someone had stuck a gun in his face. She clearly could not rely on him for comfort. And the doctor seemed oblivious to mother's pain because he turned to a nurse and directed her to admit me into the hospital, and then walked away.

Shortly after the doctor's grim diagnosis, I was wheeled on a gurney to a special ward with other kids who had polio too. There, I was placed into a bed with bars on each side and strapped down so I wouldn't fall off. For the next week or so I was kept under sedation most of the time. When I finally came too, I remembered bits and pieces about the circumstances that had landed me in the hospital. However, the one thing I realized for sure when I fully awoke was that I couldn't walk, sit, or even lay on a bed without assistance. At first I wanted to cry, but as I looked around I saw that there were kids in the unit who had been hit by polio much worse than me. Many had been afflicted, not only in their lower bodies, but in their arms and hands as well. Their hands looked like claws and their arms were twisted like pretzels, and they were so thin that they looked like nothing more than bone covered by a thin sheer layer of skin. As bad as I felt, and the pain was horrific, I could not help feeling sorry for those poor kids who got a more rotten deal than me.

A week or so after my admission into the hospital, I was assigned a physical therapist whose salary was paid by the Crippled Children's Society, an organization established during that time to assist indigent families like mine with the high cost of medical bills brought on by the polio virus. For a long time, my therapist had to do everything for me due to my lack of mobility. I couldn't sit or lie in bed without being strapped down, and I also couldn't control my bladder or sphincter, so I would crap and piss all over myself. I needed to be washed by my nurse several times a day. If a glass of water wasn't positioned in front of me, I was unable to drink the water unless someone handed me the glass. I was helpless in the largest and smallest ways.

My rehabilitation consisted of exercising my waist and leg muscles to rebuild them. My therapist also gave me deep massages and spent hours with me in the hospital swimming pool every day. She told me swimming would strengthen my muscles. She would twist and stretch my body into different positions. At first I would cry because it hurt, but after awhile I got used to it, and gradually pain became part of my everyday life and I wouldn't cry so easily. The first time I didn't cry during one of our exercise sessions, my therapist noticed I was only grimacing and she told me she was proud of me for not crying. I was taken by surprise by what she said. She must have noticed my confusion because she went on to explain that the grimace meant I was now working through the hurt like an athlete works through pain and not just being a crybaby. I became even more determined to regain more mobility in my lower body.

The polio also affected my respiratory system and made it difficult for me to breathe on my own. Part of the everyday routine was for me to be placed in huge, steel, mechanical lung for hours at a time. The first time she put me inside, I cried. I thought the machine was going to swallow me. I would lie motionless in the large tube with its low hum echoing in my ears, while my therapist stood outside the machine where I could see her so I wouldn't be afraid.

After the iron lung came the sweltering towels. Every day, my therapist laid steaming hot towels on my body to ease the pain in my muscles. She would put wet towels in an oven until they were steaming hot. Then she would place them on different parts of my body. When she did this, I would scream my head off because the towels scorched my skin. To this day, I don't know which was worse, the constant ache of my muscles, or the burning sensation of the towels. Sometimes Mama was there when my therapist did this to me. She would hold my hands gently and softly whisper in my ear.

"*Los hombrés no lloran.* You have to be a man, son."

I wanted to please Mama badly, so I held back my tears and stuffed my agony inside, but the truth was that the pain was so unbearable I thought I was going to die. I frequently asked my mother when I would be going home, but she always gave me the same response.

"You're too sick right now, son."

Once, when I wasn't quite asleep, I overheard Mama telling father that she believed it was her fault that I had gotten polio. She went on to tell him she thought God was punishing her for getting pregnant with me out of wedlock. I remember she broke down right there in front of my bed and begged God to spare my life. She told Him that if He let me live, she would go to the city of San Juan where there was a statue of the sacred *Virgen de Guadalupe* and do penance by crawling on her knees until she came to the foot of the figurine. I didn't understand what she was talking about, or whom she was talking to, so I continued to act as though I was asleep until Mama finished. To be honest, it scared me to see Mama cry and talk to someone who wasn't there.

I understood that I wasn't well. But I didn't comprehend the severity of my illness until Mama begged God to let me live. Then I wondered if I was going to die.

During the time I was in the hospital, Mama gave birth to three of my little brothers. The first baby she had was about a month after my admittance. Ramiro was born on February 12, 1954. Juan Jr. was born next on Christmas Day of 1955, and finally Ernesto was born on April 11, 1957. Every time Mama had a baby, she didn't visit me. My Father came to see me every so often, but I had grown accustomed to Mama's daily visits, so her long absence—probably only a week—felt like ten months abandonment to my child's sense of time, and I was lonely for her company. Strangely, nobody explained that she had just given birth. At a certain point in my emotional distress, I would often wonder if I had become too much of a burden to my mother, and whether that was the reason she wouldn't come to see me. Then, out of nowhere, she would show up with a huge smile on her face. I would always be surprised and full of the sappiest joy a little boy is supposed to feel when he's been stuck in a hospital bed, unable to move, desperately missing his mother, and she finally arrives smiling broadly.

During the time I was in the hospital, kids weren't allowed to visit in hospitals. But the nurses felt sorry for me so every once in a while they would let my brothers and sisters sneak into the room for short visits. We would go out onto the balcony while I sat strapped onto a wheelchair because my lower back muscles still weren't strong enough to keep me from toppling over. Compared to Delia, Freddy, and Lydia, I looked pale as a ghost because I was seldom exposed to the sun. Everyone would notice the web of blue veins on my hands and arms. My siblings, with the exception of Dee, would sometimes tease me that I looked like a White Boy. My mother would bring homemade flour tortillas, frijoles, rice, and once in a while, fried chicken. I would sit eating, while my sister Delia combed my hair. My sister Lydia, not knowing how to show her love for me, would playfully tug at my legs and giggle. I always enjoyed their attention, but the whole time they were with me, I felt a secret dread hanging over me because I knew that when the time came for them to leave, I would be left alone again in my hospital bed.

After they would leave, I'd cry silently for hours, as I lay strapped to my bed. I would ask myself why I had been stricken with this virus. I always felt as though I was being punished and often wondered what I had done to deserve all this misery. I didn't understand, and no one ever took time to explain in plain words, why this had happened to me, or why I had to stay in the hospital for such a long time. And I was too confused by the hospital's pace and practices to ask. On countless nights I would lie in bed and cry myself to sleep.

After years of being in the hospital, I went from being paralyzed from the waist down, and unable to breathe well on my own, to being able to sit without being strapped down, to being able to move my right toes, then able to move my right leg, and not having to be placed into the iron lung anymore. For some reason my left leg never completely healed. And finally, in May of 1957, right after my sixth birthday, I was released from the hospital. I could barely walk, and even then only with a seriously pronounced limp. I had been confined to a hospital for more than half of my life.

Mama brought a brand new pair of Levi jeans and a colorful short-sleeved shirt for me to wear on the occasion of my release. She did not bring me any shoes because the shoes I was to wear had been specifically made for me by an orthopedic doctor. I have never forgotten that day. Mama wore a flower print dress and looked beautiful. Her smile seemed brighter, her hair fuller, and her step seemed to have an extra bounce to it. It made me feel special to know she was looking so happy and beautiful just because of me.

"Are you ready to go, son?"

I nodded.

Mama carried me to a wheelchair and placed me in it. My therapist pushed me down the hall, into an elevator, and out of the building. As soon as we were outside, I had to close my eyes because the sun was shining radiantly, and the light blinded me for a few seconds. I lifted my face toward the sun and let the warmth shine on me until my eyes adjusted. When I opened them, I looked up at Mama and saw she was smiling at me. I was happy.

As we made our way onto the parking lot, I spotted Father waiting in the car. When he saw us approaching he climbed out with a wide smile on his face, too. I smiled back at him and got off the wheelchair cautiously. Holding onto Mama's hand tightly, I hobbled the few steps to the car.

When we got home, my month old brother Ernesto was lying on Mama's bed in the spot where I used to sleep. I was jealous. I thought he was trying to take my spot in Mama's heart, so I grabbed his legs and tried to pull him off the bed.

"No mijo," Mama said laughing lightly, "es tu hérmanito."

When I told her why I wanted him to move to another spot, Mama explained that I was a big boy, and that now it was Ernesto's turn to sleep next to her, but that no matter what she would always love us both the same. That night, however, she made an exception, and let me sleep next to her. For the first time in almost 3 years, I slept like a baby.

The following morning she took me with her to keep her promise to God for allowing me to live. I watched her from a distance as she made slow progress towards the statue of the *Virgen de Guadalupe* on her knees while holding a rosary in her hands, praying and thanking God for my safe return home. I could see blood seep out of the scrapes she made on her knees as she inched her way toward the large figurine. I thought she must love me a lot to crawl on her knees for me. It made me feel special because as far as I knew she hadn't sacrificed herself in this way for any of my brothers or sisters.

Following my release from the hospital, my family did everything they could to make life easier for me. Father would carry me in his arms whenever we had to walk long distances. He made me feel exceptional. But it was mostly my sister Delia who was there for me whenever I needed something, since Mama was always working in the fields with father. Delia would bring me water when I was thirsty, so I wouldn't have to walk to the kitchen. She would let me lean on her whenever I had to go to the bathroom.

My bad limp made walking difficult. My doctor had given me a pair of shoes specifically made for me to wear. The left shoe was elevated and connected to a metal brace with leather straps. I was supposed to wear this outer skeleton around my left leg. My doctor told me that the brace had been designed to help me walk better. As far as I was concerned, it just made walking more awkward and certainly unconformable for me to move around. Sometimes when Mama left for work, I would take the brace off and throw it in the closet. I would gimp around all day without it, then; I would put it back on right before she got home. When I couldn't get out of wearing the brace, I would take it off as soon as I left the house, preferring to carry it slung over my shoulder.

I hated that brace.

It kept me from being able to climb trees, or play tag, like every other kid in the neighborhood. Often, I would watch them longingly as they ran around laughing and screaming during a game of hide-and-seek. Like an old man, all I could do was watch from the sidelines.

Sometimes, the neighborhood kids would make fun of the way I walked and their ridicule made me angry, although I never said anything because I was afraid of getting beaten up. And so, I simply put up with their taunting.

I was clearly vulnerable to mockery and even physical attack, but inside I felt like I was the kind of kid who should be doing the teasing instead of being laughed at. Because I had to swallow this aggression, this desire to lash out, it sort of ate at me inside. I hated feeling helpless, unable to really do or say anything to the other kids because of my physical affliction. So my anger at the boys and my helplessness to act began to simmer in me.

In late May of 1957, Father decided to move us to California. He said that in Texas, opportunities for uneducated Mexicans were limited. Father had heard the stories circulating in the neighborhood about the prosperity of California and how anyone willing to work hard could make a good living. I used to hear Father talk about getting ahead, but I didn't really understand what he was talking about. As far as I was concerned there wasn't anything wrong with the way we lived in our Mexican community. Everyone lived the same way. No one had extravagant houses, cars, or clothes and most of the adults worked in the fields picking fruit.

During this period, Texas businesses displayed signs on their storefronts that read: "No Niggers, Mexicans, or Dogs Allowed." Since I was a kid, and stayed in our predominately Mexican community most of the time, I was totally ignorant about this. Until one day when Mama and I rode the bus downtown. We were living in Corpus Christi at the time. I don't remember why we had gone downtown, but somehow Mama got us lost and we ended up in a section of the city where Mexicans weren't allowed. I didn't know anything was wrong until I felt Mama squeeze my hand tightly. I looked up to see what was happening and noticed Mama had a serious look on her face. I didn't say anything as Mama looked one way and then the other trying to figure out where we were. Before Mama could get us out of the area, a White man walked by and said, "Hey Wetback, get out of here! Your side of town is down there."

At first I didn't realize he was talking to us, but Mama did. And she understood what he was saying too. She didn't know how to speak English at that time, so she asked the man for directions in Spanish.

"Look Beaner, this is not your country. Go back to Mexico you don't belong here and you especially don't belong on this side of town, *comprendé?*" The man replied sarcastically.

Mama held my hand even tighter as we quickly walked away silently in the direction the White man had indicated. I struggled to keep up with Mama's fast pace. I don't know if Mama was afraid because she didn't say anything to the man. But I could tell that anger bristled within her because her lips were pressed tightly, and her complexion turned beet red. She didn't speak for hours either. I didn't understand why the man had been so mad at us. We hadn't done anything to him.

Not long after this incident with the rude Caucasian man, we stuffed our meager belongings into the trunk of our family's 1951 Ford, tied two mattresses on top of the roof of the car, and hit the road for California. My sister Dee seemed a bit bothered by relocating, so I asked her why she wasn't excited about us moving.

"While you were in the hospital," she replied, "we moved from San Benito to Harlingen, and then to Corpus Christi to be closer to you. Now here we are moving all the way to California. It's exhausting."

Since I had been confined to the hospital for years, I was thrilled about the trip, but I don't think any of us understood the bold move Father was making, traveling across three states, unable to speak, read, or write English. Yet, there he was, relocating in a strange area with his family and our meager belongings on pure faith.

There were nine of us piled into the car. Ramiro and Juan Jr. sat between my parents. Dee and Freddy, with Ernesto in Dee's arms, sat in the back seat next to the car doors, so Lydia and I wouldn't accidentally open them and fall out onto the highway. Lydia and I fought constantly during the trip, pushing and shoving each other for room.

During the drive, Father told stories about how different life would be once we got established in California. He told us about his friend *Dón* Francisco who had moved to California and had prospered as a crew boss, no longer picking fruits in the field like he did in Texas. He said *Dón* Francisco had bought a big house and that someday we would have one too. As I listened to him, I could almost see the spacious house.

After three days and three nights of travel we finally reached Farmersville, California, the town where *Dón* Francisco lived.

We were all exhausted when Father drove into this small farming community located in the rich San Joaquin Valley. We arrived late at night and slept in the car. Early the next morning, Father contacted *Dón* Francisco who helped him obtain housing at Lineal Camp, an old military base, playing host to families arriving into the valley. Everyone who lived at the camp was Mexican and had come from Texas, Arizona, New Mexico, or Colorado. Just like our family, they were looking for a better way of life.

The camp was relatively large with only one way in and out. There was a large iron gate at the entrance surrounded by a high cyclone fence. Anyone entering the camp came under the scrutiny of the Caucasian men who were the housing authorities. The landscape of the camp was desolate. There were no trees, flowers, or bushes, and the little grass there was between the cabins was dried brown from lack of water. Even though the San Joaquin Valley was one of the most fertile areas in California, the camp looked like the barren deserts sometimes portrayed in the popular Sci-Fi TV show, The Outer Limits.

Father rented two one-room tin cabins for our family. One cabin served as my parent's bedroom and kitchen (where Mama kept our cooking supplies and groceries, and a butane stove to cook our food), while the other housed all us kids. The cabins were one room, corrugated tin square structures with cement floors and long windows on each side. During the summer, when it got too hot, the windows were propped open with a long piece of wood to allow for a draft. Even though it was only hot air that whizzed through the windows, it was better than nothing.

Every cabin was furnished with nothing more than two military canvas cots. At night, my sister Dee would fashion a bed of blankets in one corner of the cement floor where my brothers Ramiro, Juan Jr. and I slept. My brother Freddy, because he was older, would sleep in another corner by himself and Dee and Lydia would share yet another corner. It wasn't so bad, just a little crowded. Mama, Father, and baby Ernesto, slept in the other cabin.

The restrooms and showers were in a large wooden square building located in the middle of the huge camp. Everyone living in the camp had to use them. It would scare me half to death whenever I had to walk to the toilet in the middle of the night. I had heard the Mexican folktale about La Llorona, the story of the Weeping Lady who had drowned her children and had been banished by God from entering the kingdom of heaven until she found them. Our parents often used the story to make us behave, threatening to let La Llorana take us away if we didn't act right.

According to legend, La Llorona could be found wherever there was a river, canal, or lake. Some of the grownups living at the camp claimed to have heard the Weeping Lady howling late at night as she walked aimlessly in search of her children in and around St. John's River which ran near the camp. To make matters worse, the river was surrounded by giant weeping willows, which gave the river an even more sinister look at nighttime. I always woke one of my brothers to go with me whenever I needed to piss, or else I simply pissed in my pants.

During the day, most everyone living at the camp went to work picking oranges, peaches, walnuts, plums, grapes, olives, or whatever other type of fruit or vegetable was in season at the time. Entire families piled into their vehicles early in the morning to go work in the fields and didn't come back until late afternoon. On most days the camp was left empty. It wasn't until the evening that the camp would come alive again. I always got a kick out of watching the parade of cars drive into the camp, rolling slowly to their assigned cabins.

As soon as we got home, Mama and Dee would get busy cooking dinner. They'd cook simple meals of beans, rice, and tortillas, but the food always tasted delicious. After dinner, we kids were ushered outside to play and the camp would become a sea of children screeching and laughing as several games of hide and seek took place. Sometimes I tried to play, but most of the time I simply watched. I couldn't run fast enough to hide so I wouldn't be "it." And of course there was always the ridicule about how I walked.

The mockery had slowed down overtime and I became more competent at walking as my bad leg grew stronger. But there was one particular tall, heavy-set kid who teased me relentlessly.

"Hey," the boy laughed as he pointed at me one afternoon, "look at how he walks." There were other kids standing around too, but none of them said anything. "See how his foot hangs like a wet noodle."

At first I was scared to say anything because the kid was much bigger and older than me. But as he kept saying the same thing over and over, I lost control and punched him right in his nose as hard as I could. I remember that the punch I threw at him seemed to be moving in slow motion, and when it connected, I felt the impact course through my arm. The kid backed away. He grabbed his nose and started to cry.

"Why did you hit me?" he wailed.

I didn't answer. I just stood there shocked at what I had done. But then I felt a rush of energy flow through my body, and the power and control I felt after I hit him made me feel huge. I looked around and saw that the kids who had seen what I had done were staring at me in awe. From that moment on I determined never to let anyone make fun of me again.

That first summer in California, my Father began a yearly routine of following the different harvest seasons. In fact, we had only been living in Lineal Camp for four weeks when he decided to move us to Wasco, California and then Hemet, California to pick potatoes. When the potato season was over in August, our family then journeyed to Fresno, California to pick grapes. We didn't return to Lineal Camp until late October. That's when Dee, Freddy, and Lydia, were able to start school again.

The following year, on April 1, 1958, my sister Gracie was born at the County Hospital in Tulare, California. I went with Father to pick up Mama and Gracie. Mama looked pale and weak as if she'd had a difficult time giving birth to Gracie, but she didn't complain.

Mama had given birth to a child almost every year since I could remember.

With Gracie's arrival there were now eight kids. I knew everyone would have to work harder because there was another mouth to feed. Mama went back to work in the fields only a few weeks after getting home from the hospital.

In late May of 1958, Father pulled Dee, Freddy and Lydia out of school and our family went on the road again. We first traveled to Wasco and then Hemet to pick potatoes. Then we moved to Fresno to pick grapes.

When we arrived to live in the barn behind the farmhouse, the owner Mr. Banas walked out to greet us, with his young daughter Kathy in tow. Kathy walked right over and introduced herself to me as if it was a natural thing to do. I never would have had the courage to present myself the way she did. Her self-assurance amazed me and I thought she liked me because from that moment on we did everything together. We spent hours playing and swimming in the canal that ran through her property. Sometimes, Kathy would let me ride her white horse with her. It was great to sit behind her with my arms around her waist as we rode the horse. I would place my face next to her silky blond hair and smell the tantalizing sense of her cleanliness. She always smelled as if she had just taken a bath.

One day my father and I went to the market to buy food Mama needed to cook dinner. Father always took me with him to reward me for working hard and always let me choose from an assortment of candy on the store shelf. I always enjoyed the indulgence.

Coming around an aisle corner I almost literally bumped into Kathy. She was there with her mother, and one of Kathy's Caucasian friends. I was so happy to see her that I'm sure I must have lit up like a young boy on a Christmas morning with a brand new toy. However, in a split second, before I even had a chance to greet her, Kathy made a strange look on her face, and her complexion turned red. Then, without acknowledging me, she turned her back to me. My smile immediately turned into a frown. I was devastated and didn't understand what had happened. I wondered if I had done something wrong.

After we got into the car and drove off, I wanted to ask Father why Kathy had treated me so coldly. But I didn't say anything. I didn't know how to ask those types of questions. Father noticed I was upset by Kathy's rebuff and told me not to let it bother me. He said White people were different than us, but he didn't explain what he meant. The following day, back at the ranch, when no one was around, Kathy tried to speak to me. She acted as though nothing had happened at the store. I ignored Kathy and never spoke to her again.

In late October we moved back to Lineal Camp. And Dee, Freddy and Lydia, started school again. At this point we had been living in California for over a year, and even though Father had told us how great California was going to be, I hadn't seen any improvements in our living conditions. My parents still worked all the time and we still slept on the floor.

One day, excitement hit the camp. The Martinez family, who had arrived to Lineal Camp a few days before us from Arizona, had bought a TV. I didn't know what a television was because I had never seen one before, but I heard it was some kind of tube in a box that had moving pictures in it. It sounded amazing so that night I rushed over to the Martinez house to see what the excitement was all about. When I got there, there was a long line of kids waiting for the opportunity to catch a glimpse at the TV. Since I knew her son Joey, I was one of the lucky ones *Señora* Martinez let in that evening. From that moment on, I was hooked. I fell in love with TV. Every night I would line up like a soldier with the rest of the kids living in the camp hoping for the privilege of watching the characters on television.

I enjoyed all the shows on the tube except for one, "The Real McCoy's." That show depicted the life of a family who had come from a farm in "Smoky Corners, West Virginia," and moved somewhere in California.

In the sitcom, the McCoy's were portrayed as "salt of the earth" Americans and included as part of their wholesomeness was a certain taken-for-granted condescension to Mexican immigrants. This attitude was portrayed by the manner in which Grandpa, the main character of the show, treated his Mexican ranch hand *Pepino*. Grandpa never even bothered to learn how to pronounce his name. He always called him Pepini. In all the episodes I saw, Grandpa always humiliated *Pepino* by calling him lazy and yelling at him to get to work. It bothered me that *Pepino* accepted Grandpa's demeaning treatment as if humiliation was normal.

Occasionally, *Pepino* would get mad at Grandpa and start talking in bursts of angry Spanish, which Grandpa described as "jibber-jabber."

Every time that sitcom came on, I got mad and would make noise to cause a disruption because I wanted *Señora* Martinez to change the channel. The show angered me because on numerous occasions farmers had screamed and humiliated Father about his work. And like *Pepino*, Father would bow his head and in accented English respond, "Hokay." Although I had seen this happen throughout my young life, there was something about the way Grandpa treated *Pepino* and the way Father's boss treated him that didn't sit well with me.

But as much as I loved watching television, I truly disliked *Señora* Martinez's strict rules. She made everyone sit in straight lines on the hard, cold, cement floor. It was uncomfortable for me because as a result of polio, one of my buttocks was smaller than the other. Therefore, my bigger ass cheek would numb up on me. Of course, I couldn't tell her my ass had gone to sleep and that was the reason I couldn't sit still. It would have opened the door to more mockery. Instead, I would sit trying not to move until commercial time.

Frequently, for one reason or another, *Señora* Martinez would kick me out. I would usually sneak around the side of the cabin and try to watch the tube through the window, but after a while it became too uncomfortable for me to stand for such a long time, so I would just go home. As a result, I hardly ever watched a single program to the end. I suppose she had good reason for being so strict. I should have been grateful that she opened her house to every kid at the camp. Instead, I got frustrated and angry because we didn't have our own television at home.

What I hated most was the fact that we didn't have the kind of family projected on such programs as "Leave it to Beaver" and "Father Knows Best." On those two sitcoms, the parents always spent time with their children. They told their kids they loved them, and took time to explain why things happened the way they did. The families on those sitcoms seemed like total aliens to me. The words "I love you" were never uttered in my family. Love, in fact, was an unspoken topic. We kids were simply supposed to know that our parents loved us. But love wasn't the only thing we never discussed. Talking about the conditions of our life was off limits. No one ever explained why life was so unfair. They never told me why they had to work so much, or why other people never seemed to work at all. My parents never explained anything.

On many nights I would fall asleep thinking that someday I would get rich and be in a position to help my family so that Mama could stay at home like the mothers on TV. I would ponder what I could do to change our living conditions, but always came back to the same conclusion, there was nothing I could do because I was simply too young. I don't know why I always thought about my family and what I could do to make life easier for them. Maybe it was a deep-seated fear that my polio had made me a burden on the family and that at some point they would push me away. That's why I always worked harder, never complained, never asked questions, even when I wanted to. Or maybe it was the same sort of wildly fantastical, yet common, dream that men have while they're in prison about getting out and making a lot of money so they can buy a home with a white picket fence.

A lot of the men in the camp drank heavily, and often partied at the bars in Farmersville a couple of miles away. But my Father, who drank infrequently after he left jail, quit drinking all together once we moved to California. He worked hard and would tell me that in this country anyone could achieve their dreams if they worked hard enough. And compared to where my Father had come from and the conditions in which he grew up, we were now living in luxury.

Father grew up in a small village outside the large city of *Linares*, Mexico. I visited his hometown once right before we moved to California. I saw the house where he was raised. It was a single room square adobe structure (a little smaller than the cabins we lived in at the camp). The shack had a dirt floor and palm branches covering the roof that kept the house cool during the hot summer months. In father's village, none of the houses had bathrooms. They had outhouses. No one living in his village had running water. Most of the dwellings had a small rock insulated pit used to heat water for bathing, but during the summer months, everyone bathed in the river. There wasn't any electricity and petroleum lamps were used to provide light during the night. His father, brother, and my dad worked from sun up to sun down for less than fifty cents a day each. Even though life had been hard for Father growing up, I never heard him complain about his past even though he and Mama came home day after day covered in a white film of dust from the pesticides after picking oranges. He always remained positive and continuously tried to instill in us kids a sense of worth and hope.

CHAPTER THREE

IN NOVEMBER OF 1958 Father decided to move us out of Lineal Camp. He had found a job working as a crew boss for a farm labor contractor where he was in charge of a small group of laborers who made their living picking fruit. Although Father couldn't read, write, and only spoke broken English, he was conversant in Spanish and good at communicating with his workers. The day he told us about his new job, he was beaming with pride.

"You see *Chuy*," Father said, as he drove to our new home, "If you work hard you will have success." I was proud of my Father and for a brief moment, I thought that maybe we would come out of the squalor we had lived in all of my life.

We moved to Woodlake, a small farming community not far from Farmersville with a population of less than 3,000. It was nestled in the foothills of Sequoia National Park, surrounded by mountains and orchards with every single type of fruit in the world. It was a real-life Garden of Eden.

No one who lived in this fertile area ever worried about buying fruit. During the harvest season, all anyone had to do was walk to the nearest orchard and pick as many oranges, peaches, or nectarines as they wanted. Throughout the spring, when the fruit trees were in full bloom, the mixture of the aromas from the different types of tree blossoms produced an exhilarating fragrance that gave the entire *barrio* a smell of abundance.

When we arrived to the neighborhood, Father navigated the car around potholes and breaks in the roadway. I noticed that sidewalks were nonexistent and that the road was a combination of hard dirt, rock, and a little asphalt. There were abandoned shells of rusted, broken-down cars scattered everywhere, which made the barrio look more like a junkyard instead of an actual neighborhood where families lived. Most of the houses were old and in need of repair and fresh paint. And although it was cold, I saw people hanging out in front of their homes as my Father continued driving, and I saw that everyone who lived in the area was Mexican. Later, I learned Caucasian people lived in Woodlake too, but they lived on the other side of town, an area forbidden to Mexicans. I never went to that section of town alone. Having always lived in Mexican neighborhoods and the bad experiences with Kathy and the man who scolded my mother when we got lost in Corpus Christi, I was leery of Caucasian people.

"La Rana," as the barrio was called, was situated in a large hollow at the west end of the small community. The house we moved into was on Antelope Street smack dab in the heart of the barrio, next to a canal filled with green murky water and over grown Tule weeds that ran right through the middle of the neighborhood and emptied into a huge lake on the outskirts of town.

La Rana had gotten its name because there was no central sewage system for the houses in the district, so during the months of January and February, the rainy season, the barrio would invariably flood. That's when the frogs would come out in full force—you could see them bopping up and down on doorsteps, on top of cars, or swimming in the murky water. The incessant croaking sound of frogs always lasted several days until the floodwaters evaporated. Only then would the frogs return to the lake.

Our new home consisted of two bedrooms, a living room, a front porch, and a small back porch. The house seemed huge in comparison to the tin cabins we had left behind at Lineal Camp. The front door hung open attached to the doorframe by one hinge. There was a rickety fence with missing pickets, like a six-year old with missing teeth, and the yard was a combination of dried matted grass and hard clay dirt. In the middle of the yard stood a scraggly elm tree like a tall sentinel protecting its property. The floors of the house were covered with cheap linoleum that was curling up at the seams. The walls were covered with paper worn to the plaster. There was a rust spot in the kitchen sink where water dripped from a leaky faucet, and the stove had a thick coat of grease with embedded tidbits of food. It looked as though it hadn't been cleaned for months. There was a film of green mildew in the toilet bowl, and the tub was covered with a heavy layer of crusted grime.

The backyard was huge, with dense, overgrown weeds everywhere and I vaguely distinguished the outline of an old sofa and mattress hidden in the tall grass. Three long rows of wire stretched from one end of the yard to the other, wrapped crudely around two steel poles, which looked as though they were about to keel over. But as far as I was concerned, the house was great. There was only one drawback. It was brimming with big, dark brown cockroaches. They were everywhere and moved about the house without fear. Oblivious to us as if we were intruding into their world. I didn't like cockroaches. Mama promised to get rid of them as soon as there was enough money to pay for the poison needed to exterminate them.

Later, as we unpacked our belongings, I noticed a group of neighborhood kids nonchalantly watching us from a short distance. There were four of them dressed in tattered clothing. I glowered at them and decided that the first chance I got I would show these guys I wasn't anyone to mess with.

That first night in our home Mama made hot chocolate and served everyone *pan dulce,* Mexican sweet bread, bought at the local Mexican bakery earlier in the day. The entire family sat on the living room floor listening to Father as he told us stories about how things were going to get better. Everyone was in high spirits. I was also excited and even managed to forget about the cockroaches for a little while. However, the true treat came late that night when I woke up to use the bathroom and remembered I didn't have to walk outside to use it. The toilet was a few steps from where I slept with my two younger brothers. No more worrying about *La Llorona* snatching me away.

The next day Father and Mama took my brothers Ramiro, Johnny, and me to Sam's Second-Hand Store on Main Street to buy furniture. The aisles were jammed with used bikes, wagons, huge paintings set in elaborate carved wooden frames, racks of old clothing, and every style of shoe imaginable. Mama picked out two large lamps, a couple of frying pans, a big bed with mattress and box spring, and a black and white television set hidden in one corner of the store. Father told me to ask Sam how much he wanted for the items.

"Twenty dollars for the whole lot," Sam said.

"Tell him I only have fifteen dollars," Father said in Spanish.

Sam went for the offer. He helped Father load the TV, lamps, pots, and pans into the trunk of the car. Father tied the mattress and box spring onto the roof of the car for the short drive home. I was ecstatic about all our acquisitions, but of course, what delighted me most was the TV. As soon as we got home, father screwed the antenna wires to the back of the set, plugged in the electrical cord into the wall socket, switched on the power, and presto! The picture came in crystal clear. That evening, my little brothers and I watched TV until all the stations signed off for the night.

The next day, I decided to explore the neighborhood. I jumped out of bed and headed for the kitchen where I found Dee cleaning. Dee was the best sister ever. She never complained about anything and I never heard her gossip, argue, or curse. Sometimes I felt bad for her because my parents expected her to cook, wash clothes, clean the house, and watch over us younger kids while they were at work even though Dee was only thirteen years old.

Sometimes, on Sunday mornings, my parents had Dee bring coffee to their bed.

"Who do you think you are?" I would ask my mother and father. "She's not your servant."

My father would playfully respond, "Be quiet you crazy kid." Sometimes he would seriously tell me straight-up that she was the oldest and her job as the oldest was to do more.

Dee would simply smile. She sometimes called me her protector.

I found Dee in the kitchen cleaning.

"Good morning," Dee said.

"Hi Dee, is there anything to eat?"

"No, but it won't take long to prepare some breakfast."

She put down the cleaning rag and began to cook. Soon she served me two scrambled eggs, a heap of rice and beans, and two warm flour tortillas. I wolfed down the food and swiped the plate clean with a piece of flour tortilla. Then I placed my dish in the kitchen sink and headed out the door.

When I walked outside, I noticed the same four scruffy boys from a few days before hanging out on the street corner. One of them saw me and nodded his head in my direction. They all walked over to me slowly. As they came, I could see that they were all two or three years older than me. I wondered if I was going to have to fight them to prove I wasn't someone they wanted to start trouble with. Taking a deep breath, I got ready. I was scared, but I made sure I hid my fear the best way I could. When they got to where I stood, the tall, lanky boy, wearing thick glasses, with hair down to his shoulders, spoke.

"Hey," he said as he cracked his knuckles, "I'm Bobby, but everyone calls me Poppers."

In the *barrio*, most everyone was given nicknames according to some physical aspect. For example, if a guy looked like a horse, he was called *Caballo*. Poppers got his nickname because he always cracked his knuckles.

"We saw you moving in the other day," Poppers continued, "but we didn't want to introduce ourselves while you were with your family. That's Frank, over there," he said, pointing to a dark kid in the group, "everyone calls him Claw."

I looked at Frank's deformed hand and noticed it resembled a claw. I knew he had been struck with polio because I had seen many kids with hands like Frank when I was in the hospital. Frank had coarse black hair, a big hooked nose and when he talked, he stuttered to the point that it was difficult to understand what he was saying, especially when he got wound up. The other two kids in the group were named Chris and Jr.

"I'm Jesse. We just moved from Farmersville, and I want all of you to know that I don't want anyone making fun of the way I walk, because if anyone does we're going to have problems."

When nobody answered I became upset.

"You hear what I'm saying, man?" I puffed my chest and balled my fists. I knew I could get hurt by these guys, but I didn't care. By now being ridiculed bothered me so much that I would fight anybody with a quickness to make them stop.

"Hey, man," Poppers replied. "We don't want to fight you. Besides, if you're going to live in the *barrio*, we might as well get along, don't you agree?"

I nodded and exhaled; relieved that everyone had agreed and that no one had gotten smart because I didn't want to fight either.

One day, as I walked home after hanging out with the guys at the park, I heard someone yell out, "*Oralé*, Draggy."

I looked across the street and there, standing next to his shiny car was Richard Torres, a tall 28 year old guy from the *barrio*. It looked as though he had just finished washing his car. Richard Torres was one of five brothers who lived on the corner of Pomegranate and Antelope; the main cross streets that lead into the neighborhood. Everyone in the *barrio* feared these brothers because they would fight at the drop of a hat. Richard was the second to the eldest brother and for whatever reason, he decided to mock the way my foot dragged.

At first I was too scared to say anything. After all, he was much older than me and I'd heard about his reputation as a violent guy. But I hated when anyone made fun of the way I walked. Glaring at him as I continued on, I threw caution to the wind and yelled at him to quit calling me names. He didn't stop. In fact, he laughed even more and seemed to be getting real pleasure out of making me mad. His laughter infuriated me, so I started throwing rocks at his car as I kept walking backwards towards my house.

"You better quit throwing rocks at my car, you little bastard!" he screamed.

"Stop making fun of the way I walk and I'll stop throwing rocks at your stupid car!" I yelled back as I continued heading toward my house.

"I'm going to get you!" he roared.

I flipped him off and ran inside my house. The next day, as I walked to the park, I had to pass by the Torres house. I was scared Richard was going to come out and beat me up, but he never did.

Later, when I got to the park, Poppers, Claw, Chris, and Jr. told me they had heard about what I had done. They said I was crazy to mess with the older guys, especially with one of the Torres.

"Hey, I wasn't messing with him. He was making fun of me. I meant it when I said wasn't going to let anyone make fun of the way I walk."

None of the guys responded, but I could tell by the way they nodded their heads that they were impressed with what I had done.

From that moment on we got tighter and hung out every chance we got. Nobody in the group thought they were better than anyone else. Everyone except Anthony and Claw had come from different states and each of our families was just as poor as the other.

Anthony, whom everyone called Sach, was from Los Angeles. He was eleven years old, and knew a lot about gangs. He was always ditching school, so his parents would call the cops on him and he would get arrested for "being out of control." As a result of his behavior, Sach was constantly in and out of Juvenile Hall. When he wasn't locked up, he would hang out with us. When Sach had first moved into the *barrio*, he told us that he had gotten jumped into a gang called, "*El Hoyo Maravilla*," one of the oldest gangs in Los Angeles. He said that guys were jumped into the gang by three or four members to determine if the new recruit could take a beating without giving up or crying out. The whipping usually lasted two or three minutes.

"You don't want weaklings in your *barrio*, do you?" he asked me one day.

He went on to say that we should start jumping guys into our neighborhood like they did in L.A. But the fact was we never jumped anyone into our group. In our neighborhood, if you lived in the *barrio* you were one of us. It was that simple. Unlike many of the groups in the big cities of Los Angeles, San Jose, and San Diego, we didn't consider ourselves a gang. But the police did, and they kept a constant eye on us because Poppers and Jr. had been caught breaking windows out of cars owned by people who lived on the "good side" of Woodlake. The "good side" was where White people lived. Whenever we ventured into that part of town, the cops were quick to make sure we went back to our side.

No one in our group liked the police and we stayed as far away from them as we could. They were considered the enemy and they seldom came into our *barrio*. But when they did, it was usually to arrest one of the *Vato Locos*, the crazy ones— the name given to the older guys who were always getting into trouble with the police—these guys were the true gang members in our neighborhood. Once in a while, someone from the neighborhood would call the cops, but that didn't happen very often because anyone caught having anything to do with the police was considered a "Rat." So if you wanted to stay healthy and not get beaten up all the time, cooperation with the police was out, no matter what!

Most of the time things were pretty peaceful in the neighborhood. We kids played on the streets under the watchful eyes of any adult who happened to be close by. There was an unspoken agreement among adults in the neighborhood that any kid caught misbehaving would get his butt whacked on the spot. Afterwards, when our parents got home from work, they were told what we had done and we would get a second round of punishment. So we kids had to be cunning when we got out of line because getting caught always resulted in a double whammy.

About two months after I had been living in the barrio, Jackie and another kid, very appropriately nicknamed Palio because he was as thin as a stick, were introduced to me by Poppers. I had seen them around, but we had never spoken to each other. For some reason none of the guys in our group liked them and whenever they came around, everyone ignored them. Jackie and *Palio* never said anything when they were shunned by the others, and kept coming around anyway. They weren't quitters. I liked that about them and we became good friends. Maybe I also warmed up to them because their lives seemed worse than mine and to a certain extent I felt sorry for them. Neither Jackie nor *Palio* had a father living at home and their mothers were constantly shacking up with different men.

Palio didn't even know who his father was because his mother, Big Nellie, one of the local barflies, had had sex with so many men she didn't have a clue who the father was for any of her children—*Palio*, or his two brothers and two sisters. The first time I met Big Nellie, I was intimidated by her masculinity. I had never met a woman who looked and behaved so much like a man. She sported a man's crew-cut, and wore manly clothes. She even lived with a woman named Florentina who, it was rumored, was her lover.

On most nights Big Nellie could be found at the *El Rancho Cantina* drinking until the bar closed. Then she would go home and beat the crap out of *Palio* leaving him with large purple bruises on his body. *Palio* didn't talk about the beatings, but I could tell it was hard on him. So whenever he came around with an angry scowl on his face, I knew that it was because he had gotten beaten by his mother.

"Hey, let's go find the rest of the guys and play a game of hide and seek," I said to him one day trying to make him forget about the ass whipping his mom had given him the night before. "Or better yet, let's go check out Maria," I said, smiling mischievously.

"*Oralé*," he answered with a hint of excitement.

Maria was the prettiest woman in the *barrio*. She had come from a small town in Fresno County after marrying one of the *Veteranos* from our neighborhood. She had thick, black, wavy hair and dazzling hazel eyes. She had full lips that she covered impeccably with bright red lipstick, and when she smiled her perfect white teeth made her lips look even more succulent. She had a small waist, wide hips, a nice round ass, and a great pair of legs. Many of the women in the *barrio* didn't like Maria because she always wore blouses that exposed her flat stomach and tight shorts that showed off her body. I think the women were just plain jealous of her because many of the men from the *barrio* would stare at Maria with open admiration whenever she sashayed down the street.

Watching Maria through her bedroom window was a favorite pastime of ours. I personally had never seen her completely nude, but I had caught glimpses of her wearing nothing but her underwear. It was so easy to see her semi-naked that sometimes I wondered if Maria didn't leave her curtains opened just enough to allow us kids to peek inside and view her loveliness every night. And to be sure, many of us took advantage of the opportunity she so generously provided.

When we arrived at Maria's house, I nudged *Palio*.

"We're in luck," I whispered.

He looked at me with eyes wide open and we both turned to Maria's window. The curtain in her bedroom was open just enough to give us a clear view inside. We waited and a few moments later, Maria walked into the room. As always she was a vision of loveliness. She was dressed in a pair of black lace panties and matching bra. Her hair cascaded loosely down to her prominent ass, which stood out like two perfect spheres. She was wearing black nylons and black garter belt that enhanced her smooth caramel-colored legs. I stared in complete awe, breathing heavily, unable to get enough of that spectacular image. I felt a slight tingling between my legs, but I didn't know what I was feeling. All I know was that it felt good. Maria reached to turn off the lights in her bedroom, as she called out to her husband in a sensual tone that seemed to indicate she was ready for him. Just before she shut the lights, Maria turned in our direction and smiled seductively as if she knew we were watching. *Palio* and I quickly ducked and scurried off like two scared rats afraid that we'd been caught.

"Did you see how sexy she looked?" *Palio* asked.

My mouth was so dry I could only nod my head.

Just like *Palio*, Jackie didn't have a father living at home either. He had a father figure in his uncle Big *Indio*, who, unfortunately, was serving time in Folsom State Prison for selling drugs. Jackie said Big *Indio* had been in prison for many years, but that he would be getting out soon. Big *Indio* was a regular topic in the neighborhood and whenever the older guys from the *barrio* discussed him, I would see absolute admiration on their faces. They spoke about him as though he was Godlike, and I couldn't wait for him to get out so I could meet him.

Jackie told me he hadn't been born when Big *Indio* was sent to prison, but that he had gone to visit him every month for the past three years with his mother. Big *Indio* had promised Jackie that when he got out he would take care of the punks his mom brought home.

"They're not going to have it so easy once Big *Indio* is home," Jackie told me on a number of occasions.

Jackie lived with his mom, Ofelia, an attractive woman with brown eyes and long straight bleached blond hair that hung down to her lower back. It looked like Ofelia could get any man she wanted and she often did. Every time I went to visit Jackie, there would invariably be a different man at her house. What annoyed Jackie the most was that the men his mom brought home tried to tell him what to do. Often, he would argue with them, and tell them they weren't his father, and that they didn't have any right to tell him anything. More often than not, his mother would beat him for being disrespectful to his elders.

Sometimes he even got whipped by his mother's lover as well.

Once, as I sat in Jackie's living room, I saw Ofelia's lover beat her while they were in the bedroom. She tried to fight back, but the man was too strong for her. He struck her over and over as he yelled at Ofelia not to ever raise her hands to him again. I guess he was mad because she had put up a fight. Watching the man punch Ofelia scared me, but I also felt ashamed because I had done nothing to help her. I felt like such a coward.

When Jackie heard his mother screaming, he rushed into the bedroom and jumped on top of him. But despite Jackie's valiant efforts to save his mom from getting hurt, the man was just too strong for him and he clobbered Jackie real bad. I thought the man was going to hit me as well, but I was invisible to him. I was relieved.

A few days later, I went to Jackie's house again because we were going to the park to meet *Palio* and hang out. As I waited for Jackie to come out of his room, I saw Ofelia and the man who had beat her hugging each other. She was kissing the man passionately as the man fondled her butt. I didn't understand why she was letting him touch her after what he had done to her. Watching them embarrassed me, but I couldn't turn away as the man continued to grope her ass while she massaged the front of his pants. When Jackie walked into the living room where I was waiting, he saw them too and his face turned into a disgusting scowl. We walked out of his house with neither one of us saying anything about what we had seen. Later that day, Jackie told me that when he got older he was never going to let those punks his mother lived with hit her.

Seven years later, when Jackie was sixteen, he came home to find his mother's latest lover beating her. Jackie lost his temper. He grabbed a baseball bat. Bashed the guy on the head and knocked him out. Jackie then splashed gas on the guy as he lay unconscious, lit a match to him, and watched as he burned to death. Jackie was arrested later that evening and prosecuted as an adult. He was convicted of homicide nine months later and sentenced to life in prison. His mother drank herself to death soon after. I never saw Jackie again. Years later he was found hanging in his cell by a prison guard during count time.

AT THE AGE OF SEVEN AND A HALF, I finally started school. I had never attended school before for a number of reasons. For one, our family was always moving from one town to another following the crops. But mostly, it was because I played on Mama's sympathy about my polio. I would tell her my leg hurt too much for me to be in school all day. She would feel sorry for me and let me stay home. This time my ploy didn't work. She said I had to go; that I couldn't hide forever. I sure wished I could though.

On the morning I was to start, Chris showed up to my house all excited that I was going to school with him. I wasn't quite ready to leave when he got there because I had to wait for my older brother Freddy to get out of the bathroom so I could wash up. I poked my head out of the house and told Chris I would be ready in a few minutes.

Waiting for Freddy to come out of the restroom, I tried to convince myself school wasn't such a big deal, but inside I was as scared as a kid alone on a dark street in the middle of night. I knew some of the guys who hung out with me were already in school, but Chris, JR, Jackie, Poppers, and Palio were in fourth and fifth grades so I wouldn't be able to hang out with them. I would be on my own just like when I was in the hospital. What's more, knowing there would be Caucasian kids at school added to my unease.

"Come on, Jesse, let's go or we're going to be late," Chris yelled, from outside the house.

"Okay, don't get excited. I'm almost ready."

I checked myself in the mirror one last time to make sure my hair was combed and walked outdoors to meet Chris.

"Climb on my back," he said. "I'll give you a piggyback ride to school."

Even though school wasn't very far, Chris got into the habit of carrying me there. I don't know why he did it, but every morning he was at my house like clockwork ready to do the deed. I know I was heavy, especially since I had to wear the brace. Chris wasn't built big either. In fact, he was thin, but he was all sinewy and very strong.

Chris would chase kids who weren't from our group when they made fun of the way I walked and roughed them up. I used to tell him to hold them for me so I could kick their butts, but he always let them go before I could get to them. He said I was too crazy and didn't know how to control my anger. I told him that if they made fun of him he would be mad too.

My sisters Dee and Lydia went to school with us that first day. I felt my insides tighten with apprehension when I saw the size of it, but I hid my panic. Chris and Lydia said goodbye and left to their class. Dee walked me to the office where I picked up my nametag and room number, then walked me to my classroom.

"Don't be afraid, okay? Everything's going to be all right." Dee knew me well and I guess she could see I was scared.

"I'm not worried," I replied, with false bravado.

Dee smiled at me reassuringly and left.

When I opened the door, the entire class turned their attention toward me. Every student scrutinized me as though I was a biology specimen being examined under a microscope. Their looks made me uncomfortable. I wanted to disappear. But there was nowhere to hide. Mrs. Freeman, my homeroom teacher, motioned me over to her desk. She asked for my nametag, introduced me to the class, then pointed to an empty desk and told me it would be my assigned seat. I walked over and sat down. Soon after, everyone seemed to forget about me and the day passed without a hitch.

School wasn't so bad and as days turned into weeks and weeks into months, I got used to it. But I didn't like the White kids at our school. Some of them tried to make friends with me, but I shunned them. I didn't trust them. I remembered how Kathy had hurt me and I wasn't about to let that happen again.

There were two groups of Whites at school. The wealthy and the poor. The ones whose parents had money walked around with smug expressions looking down on anyone who wasn't well-off like them. In the cafeteria they sat in areas they had designated for themselves. I would watch them bring out their baloney or tuna fish sandwiches stuffed with lettuce, slices of tomato, and mayonnaise in-between two slices of white Rainbow bread. Their lunches always included some type of treat like an oatmeal cookie or a piece of chocolate cake.

The poverty-stricken Whites were treated with as much disdain by the rich Whites as the Mexican kids were, but I didn't trust the poor ones either. As far as I was concerned they were all the same.

Most Mexican kids got their lunch through a government program or brought bean burritos from home. Sometimes, I would have to bring bean burritos for lunch, but I always threw them in the garbage before I got to school. I was ashamed and didn't want anyone who lived outside the *barrio* to learn my family was so destitute we couldn't afford to buy bread and baloney to make sandwiches for lunch.

In August 1959 my brother Felipe was born during our potato picking time in Hemet. Felipe was the last child Mama had. I really don't know how Mama managed to have all of us and still work in the fields.

After the potato season, we traveled to Fresno to pick grapes, and in October we returned to Woodlake. I went back to school the Monday after we arrived and was promoted to third grade. I was bumped up because I was eight and half and too old to be in second grade. I was also smart. Of course my teachers never complimented me on my intelligence. In fact, I never heard any teacher encourage any Mexican student to stay in school. On the other hand, I often heard teachers tell White students they could attend any college they wanted. They were also provided with extra help to ensure they passed their math, history, or English assignments.

It seemed to me that school was oriented to ensure that White children had every opportunity to succeed, but that it put restrictions on us Mexican kids. For example, instead of encouraging Mexican students not to forget their native tongue, or otherwise encouraging us to be bilingual, school administrators implemented policies that punished anyone caught speaking Spanish. Whenever a teacher caught us they would angrily say, "Don't talk Spanish. You're in America now." It was confusing because at home our parents would tell us not to forget where we came from. What I didn't understand was that I was born an American, but was treated as if I were a foreigner.

In fifth grade, I was constantly in trouble for fighting with White kids, or for speaking Spanish. Sometimes I would speak Spanish just to get the teachers mad. They'd make me sit at the back of the room, separated from everyone else by a short divider, which made me feel even more like I didn't belong. I'd get mad and begin to make noise. Of course, the teacher would increase my dosage of discipline and tell me to stand and face the back corner of the class. After a few minutes of that I would get angrier and refuse to do as the teacher instructed. Ultimately I'd land in the principal's office. That's how I was labeled a problem student by faculty and so I started to live up to my reputation by getting into trouble every chance I got.

Once, when I went out to the playground during lunch recess, I overheard a couple of teachers talking about Mexican students. They didn't know I was close enough to hear them, or maybe they did and just didn't care.

"I don't understand why Mexican students are so lazy," Mrs. Jones said to Mrs. Lloyd. "They're always falling asleep during class. I wish their parents would take an interest in their children's education, but I suppose it's too much to ask of them."

"I know exactly what you mean. They're always falling asleep in my class too. It's sad the way they take advantage of our educational system."

These teachers didn't know most Mexican kids worked in the fields during the months of March, April, and May when the navel orange was in season. Everyone in my family woke up at 3:30 in the morning to pick oranges before going to school. It was always pitch dark when arrived to the orchard. Father would park our pickup with its headlights facing the trees so we could see the oranges. We usually worked until 7:30 and then were driven home by Mama so we could get dressed for school. It was always pandemonium at our house as we tried to wash the pesticides off our bodies and get ready. There was never any time to eat, so by third period, my stomach would begin to growl. It wasn't until after lunch that it would stop grumbling. Afterward, I would nod off in class because I hadn't gotten enough sleep.

During those months, Mama, like many other Mexican mothers, would wait in front of the school to drive us back to the orchard, where we would work until dusk. It was mentally exhausting to learn while having to work in the fields before and after school. There was very little time to finish homework. Naturally many Mexican kids got behind as a result of their inability to get school assignments completed. But teachers never bothered to ask why we were falling behind, and we Mexican kids never talked about our hard outside of the classroom routine. We had all been taught to keep silent about what was happening at home. Besides, we didn't want to get our parents into trouble with school officials.

Listening to those teachers talk about us in such a bad way made me angry. I stormed off with an all-consuming need to unleash my hostility on someone. I decided to take my anger out on Billy, one of the rich White kids. I didn't like him. Billy had been bragging the day before about going to Disneyland and what a great time he had there. On my way to find Billy, I bumped into *Palio* hanging out in the main hallway.

"Hey *Palio*, let's go show Billy he's no better than us just because he went to Disneyland."

I could see by *Palio*'s facial expression that he didn't want any part of what I had in mind, but didn't object. I guess he realized I was very agitated and that not going with me would create problems between us. He followed me to the classroom where Billy was telling his friends about his adventure to Disneyland again.

"Hey, Billy," I said, "I'm tired of hearing you brag about that stupid place Disneyland."

"What! Who do you think you are talking about Disneyland that way?" Billy asked in disbelief.

Billy's response caught me off guard. I couldn't believe he'd had the nerve to stand up to me. My temper, which was already inflamed, flashed. Instinctively, I punched him square on his nose. I must have hit him on the weakest point because I felt the cartilage bend as my fist connected with it. In an instant, blood was pouring out of his nostrils. I grabbed him by his shirt and continued to hammer him. Howling like a scared dog, Billy struggled to get away as I repeatedly struck him. The beating didn't last very long. Someone jerked me off him and began to shake me like a San Francisco earthquake. The shaking was so intense I could hear my teeth rattle. At first I couldn't see who had snatched me with such force. Five seconds later I saw it was Mrs. Harvey, my homeroom teacher. I felt the skin on my shoulder break as she dug her long fingernails into me while she screamed in my face.

"Look what you've done, you animal!"

I tried to see what she was talking about, but I couldn't because she wouldn't stop shaking me. Suddenly, just as unexpectedly as she had started, she stopped. It looked as though she had worn herself out. Leaning against the chalkboard, still clutching my shoulder tightly, she took deep gulps of air trying to catch her breath. I bent my head slightly and saw Billy cowering in a corner of the classroom. He grabbed his nose, whimpering like a wounded puppy. I felt good when I saw the front of his shirt covered with blood. At this point, the shaking, the screaming in my face by my teacher, the names she had called me, and getting into trouble didn't matter. What was important was that Billy would think twice before he got smart with me again. I didn't bother to think that it was me who started this mess in the first place. As far as I was concerned, he had gotten out of line by responding the way he had which had given me the right to punch his nose.

A few seconds later Mrs. Harvey regained her composure and led me roughly into the hall toward the principal's office.

"If you want to act like a wild animal, you should be put in a cage and kept there until you learn how to behave like a human being!" she exclaimed.

Shoving me onto a chair, she told me to sit, not to move, and not to make a sound. The principal's secretary shot me a hostile look. I stared back at her defiantly. I wanted to tell them both to go to hell, but I never talked back to my elders no matter what.

As I sat in the principal's office, I began to think about the way White folks did things as a family. Like Billy going to Disneyland with his family. On occasion, I had heard White families openly express love toward each other as they were exiting the downtown Chaparral Restaurant. I had seen White mothers hug their children when they picked them up after school. Unlike in my family where love was an unspoken word and we were just supposed to know that our parents loved us even though they never told us. I couldn't remember ever being hugged by Mama, and sometimes I yearned for her embrace. I wanted to have the type of relationship with Mama as many White kids had with their mothers, but Mama was always too tired from working in the fields and taking care of household chores. It saddened me to see her so exhausted and in such poor health all the time.

Four months earlier, Mama had been diagnosed with a kidney disease that had damaged one of her kidneys. She had been hospitalized and a team of doctors had operated on her to remove the infected kidney. The surgery had gone well, but Mama had stayed in the hospital for a month recuperating. During the time she was there, Father would take me with him when he went to visit her, but I was never allowed to go inside because I was too young. I would sit outside her second floor hospital room window and wave at her from the ground below. She would look down at me and wave back. I wanted to cry because I missed her so much, but I never did. I knew she would be disappointed if I cried. She had told me many times when I had been in the hospital that men didn't snivel, so I held my hurt inside. A few weeks after she was released from the hospital, she went back to work in the fields. I saw her grimace as we all worked, but she never complained.

I thought about how beautiful Mama had been before the hardships of working in the fields, and raising nine kids had slowly begun to strip her of the good looks she had once possessed.

I wondered why life was so unfair toward good people like Mama. Yet, it seemed to treat some guys with high regard. Guys like *Pato* and Puppet were all well known, feared, and respected in the barrio. It was known throughout our district that if upset, these bad guys would bust your head open and think nothing of it. And it seemed to me, that the meaner they were, the more people went out of their way to treat them nicely. I had seen people from the neighborhood buy them beer, give them money, and move out of their way whenever they walked down the sidewalk acknowledging them with a slight nod as they passed by.

I was so absorbed with my thoughts that I didn't notice the principal walk into the reception area. Mr. White's booming voice startled me. I could see by the scarlet color of his complexion that he was fuming mad. He reminded me of an enraged bull ready to charge the matador right before the bullfighter rammed his sword down the bull's neck. But in this case, I was the Matador and he was the bull. My defiance was my sword, and I would ram it down his neck, I thought as I stared boldly at him.

"What's your problem, young man? Do you realize you broke Billy's nose and he had to be taken to a doctor? You're in a lot of trouble here. We're not going to tolerate this type of conduct in this school. I'll be contacting your parents this evening to inform them about what you did today. You can count on it. Now get out of my office and go home!"

I wanted to tell him I didn't care what he did, but I didn't say anything. I just stared at him with intense antagonism before I walked out his office boiling mad. I left the school and went to the park until school was out. I didn't tell my parents anything about getting kicked out of school for the day. I figured that was Mr. White's job, not mine.

Mr. White went to my house just like he threatened. My parents understood basic English, but they didn't speak the language well, so they called Dee into the room to translate for them. I was in another room eavesdropping as the Principal recounted the sequence of events to mother and father. I heard him tell them I had attacked Billy for no apparent reason, and that Billy had been sent to the doctor because I broke his nose.

My parents listened politely to everything Mr. White said. After he was finished, they told Dee to tell him they would speak to me about my behavior. I was ready with my story when the principal left.

"Come here, Jésus," Mama said. "What's this I hear that you hit a kid at school today?"

"Well, Mama," I replied. "The kid I socked got smart with me for no reason, so I had to hit him."

"Oh my, what am I going to do with you?" Mama said lovingly.

I shrugged my shoulders, hung my head, and looked down sadly giving her my "I'm sorry" look. It worked too, because Mama said:

"It's alright son, but you have to be good from now on. You can't hit kids just because they get you mad. It's not right."

I smiled sheepishly and promised her I would do my best not to get into any more trouble at school.

That night, I dreamed I was hiding in the closet of my classroom. I'd hid in there because I had socked another kid in his face. But I needed to piss badly. I kept grabbing my crotch and squeezing it, trying to hold back the urine, but the need to take a leak was too strong. Finally, I relieved myself in the corner of the closet hoping the teacher wouldn't see the piss seeping under the door. Then I felt the warmth of the urine and woke up. Dang, I had pissed in bed. Mama would be furious with me for not waking up on time to use the bathroom.

I quickly changed underwear, put on my pants, gathered up the sheet and mixed it in with the dirty laundry next to the washing machine on the back porch. I hoped Mama wouldn't notice the huge wet spot on the mattress. As I headed out the door, Mama stormed out of the bedroom.

"*Cabrón mión,*" she said angrily. "You're going to sleep on the cot in the porch tonight."

"No Mama," I replied terrified at the prospect of having to sleep outside of the house where *La Llorrona* could get me.

Mama didn't respond so I quickly left to play outside before she said anything more about having to sleep in the porch. I stayed away from the house until early afternoon and then decided to take a nap on the cot located in the front porch. I don't know what woke me, but when my eyes snapped open, I realized I was still in the porch and that it was nighttime. I immediately went into panic mode. I was so scared that my entire body literally shook and I seemed to be glued to the cot because I couldn't get up to go inside the house. Then I heard the shriek. It was the sound of a woman crying and I started to pray. I knew right then it was *La Llorona.*

"Please God," I whispered. "Don't let her take me away. You know I'm not her child."

Again, I heard the scream. Closer this time, but still I couldn't move. I heard it again, but this time my fear pressed me to take action. I threw the covers off me and darted for the front door as fast as my legs would carry me, but the door was locked. I banged on it loudly, yelling for Mama to open up. Standing there pounding on the door terrified, I didn't look back. I felt as though I could feel *La Llorona* breathing down my neck. I don't know how long I stood at the door before Father unlocked it, but when he did, I shot past him and jumped into bed between my brothers Johnny and *Neto.*

"What's wrong with you?" Father asked.

"It's *La Llorrona*," I replied. "She's outside."

"You're crazy," Father laughed. "Go on, go to sleep."

A few days later I learned that the screams had come from a peacock owned by the Hernandez family who lived down the block. I never liked peacocks after that.

The following Monday I went back to school. Nobody said anything to me about Billy. I saw him in class. He had a bandage on his nose and two black eyes. When he saw me, he lowered his head and went straight to his seat without saying a word. When the recess bell rang I went out onto the schoolyard and hung out with the other kids. At noon, I went to lunch in the cafeteria and the rest of the day went by smoothly. After the last bell sounded, I rushed into the boys' bathroom. I climbed on top of the radiator heater and peeked out the window. Sure enough, standing out front of the school was a group of Catholic nuns waiting to escort us kids to Catechism. They did this every Monday after school.

A lot of kids liked to go to Catechism, but I hated it. The Nuns carried oak rulers and often used them to smack anyone who misbehaved on the back of their hands. I was constantly getting whacked for pulling some girl's hair or talking when I was supposed to be listening. Every week I told Mama I didn't like going to catechism, but she would always say that it was good for me to go. She said being in catechism kept me off the streets and out of trouble while they were at work at least on Mondays.

Two weeks before I had found that I could hide in the boy's restroom and not have to go. I would stand on top of the radiator heater and peer out the window until the Nuns left to the Catholic Church where the classes were held. Then I would leave to the park and head home when Catechism was excused. Mama never knew I wasn't attending.

"Hey Jesse, what are you doing?" Jackie asked.

Jackie and *Palio* had walked into the bathroom and caught me on top of the radiator heater peeking out of the bathroom window.

"I'm hiding from the Sisters. I don't want to go to Catechism."

"We don't want to go either. Can we hide out with you, too?" *Palio* asked.

"Okay, but you guys have to promise not to tell anyone about this hiding place."

They agreed and for the next three Mondays we hid in the bathroom until the Nuns left. Then we made our way to the park. We hung out on the playground and rode the merry-go-round, slid down the huge slide, or swung on the swings. It was fantastic. I was hoping we could hide every Monday for the rest of the school year.

Unfortunately, one of the guys blabbed to a girl about our hideout, and she told Mr. Lee that we were not attending Catechism. I'm not sure if it was

Palio or Jackie who told the girl about our secret hiding spot, but I stayed angry at both of them for a long time afterwards for not keeping their word. To me it was a serious issue if you broke an oath. My father often drilled into my head that if you gave your word you should always stick by what you said.

"Your word is all you really have," he would say.

In the summer of 1961, on one particularly hot day, Poppers, Claw, Jr., *Palio*, Chris, and I were on our way to the Indian cemetery located just over the peak of the mountain range that surrounded the *barrio*. Of course no one remembered to bring water so as the sun beat down on us with a vengeance we found ourselves thirstier than usual.

To get our minds off of being hot and thirsty, Poppers began to tell us stories about the Indians who had lived in the small mountain community we were going to visit. Poppers was a few years older than everyone in our group, so he thought he knew more than us. I was already somewhat pissed at him because he'd been getting smart with me for a while and his "I'm-smarter-than-you" attitude was beginning to get on my nerves.

"Some of the older folks from the *barrio* say the Indians used to kill the cows that roam over these mountains. That's one of the reasons people don't like Indians," Poppers said.

"That's a bunch of crap," I replied. "The only people that don't like Indians around here are White people. Heck, they don't like anyone who isn't like them. Look at how they treat us. We can't even walk on their side of town without the cops getting on our butts. The only reason the Indians left these mountains was because they were forced to do so by *gabachos*."

"Hey Jesse, I'm only telling you what I heard," Poppers replied. "It's up to you if you want to believe it."

"I've heard the stories, too and I don't believe any of them."

Poppers dropped the subject and a short time later we reached the remnants of the Indian village. The shacks they had lived in were small. They were made of logs and mud. None of the huts had bathrooms or running water. Instead, there were outhouses next to each cabin and a communal well in the center of the small township. A bucket tied to a rope sat on the rim of the well. I dropped the pail down, but it came up empty. The water supply had dried up just like the settlement. It looked as though no one had lived here for a long time. The huts were covered with leaves and I had to use my shoulder in order to pry the door to one of the shacks open. Peeking inside I saw it was completely bare with nothing more than a thick coat of fine dust.

Afterward, we sat under the canopy of the huge oak trees surrounding the area to get relief from the blistering sun. No one said anything while we sat enjoying the tranquility of the place. A little later we walked down a narrow trail on the side of a small ravine that led to the actual cemetery. The graveyard wasn't expansive, but there were many burial plots crammed next to each other. I read the markers on a few graves and noted that some dated back to the mid-eighteen hundreds. It gave me an uncanny feeling to be there. I felt like an intruder.

"Let's get out of here," I said abruptly to the guys.

"What? You scared or something?" Poppers asked sarcastically. "I thought you weren't scared of anything."

"Listen, *pendejo*," I answered glaring at him. "I'm not afraid, and if you don't watch what you say, I'm going to kick your ass."

"You know what, Jesse. I don't know who you think you are, but I'm not scared of you."

He was about to say something else, but before he did, I punched him right on his mouth. The unexpected blow sent him reeling back, knocking him on his butt. Without giving him a chance to react, I pounced on him like a prizefighter, striking and pummeling him with blows, trying to hurt him. I felt the guys pulling me off him, but I fought to get away from them so I could keep hitting him.

When they finally pulled me off, I screamed, "Don't ever talk to me that way again. The next time you might not be so lucky to have someone save you!"

I was breathing heavily and my heart was pounding rapidly as bursts of adrenalin shot through my bloodstream. I felt an immense sense of power when I saw the fear in the guys' eyes after they witnessed how I had reacted to Popper's insolence.

"Does anybody else have anything to say?" I demanded, balling my fists ready to fight again.

No one said a thing.

Poppers got up off the ground, brushed the dust from his pants, lowered his head and didn't say a word as we made our way down the mountain. When we got back to the *barrio*, everyone went their separate way except *Palio* and me. We walked home together. On the way *Palio* mentioned that maybe I had been a little too hard on Poppers.

"Look man, Poppers has been getting smart with me for a long time and if I hadn't punched him on his mouth, he would have kept being a smartass. Now he knows he can't do that with me."

"Well, I'm just saying that you might have been a little too tough on him, that's all."

"What do you mean, *Ese*, you have a problem with what I did?" I asked, giving him a piercing look.

"Naw, I was just saying –ah, forget it. What do I care anyway? If he doesn't stand up for himself why should I?"

"You've heard what the older guys say: If you talk crazy to someone it's because you know you can beat their butt, or you're ready to take a beating," I replied.

"Yeah, I guess you're right."

Arriving at my house *Palio* and I went our separate ways. I quickly forgot about the day's events as the delightful aroma of Mama's homemade food hit my senses. Mama was truly a Mexican woman when she got in the kitchen with her pots and pans and the *palote* that she used to make flour tortillas. I loved to eat Mama's tortillas as they came off the hot *cómal*. Sometimes I would ask her to toast one for me. Then I would spread butter all over one side of it and roll the tortilla into a burrito before stuffing it into my mouth. They were delicious.

"Hey, Elisa, your long lost son is home from the streets," my brother Freddy said sarcastically. I flipped him a bird and gave him a dirty look.

"Come here, *Chuy*."

"*Hola*, Mama, what's the matter?"

"Where were you? Getting into trouble?" she asked looking at me sternly.

"I wasn't doing anything wrong, Mama. Some of the guys and me were just hanging out. We went to the Indian graveyard up in the mountains. I didn't like it. I'm not going up there again. The place gave me the creeps."

"Well, you better be careful. You don't want God to punish you for molesting the dead, do you?"

There she goes with that religious stuff again. I didn't like hearing about God. He was a subject that scared me and I always had trouble falling asleep whenever Mama told me God was going to punish me for misbehaving. I had already learned that if I didn't reply to what Mama said, she would usually drop the subject. When I didn't answer, Mama told me to throw out the trash and wash my hands before sitting down to have dinner. When I got back, she served me a steaming plate of rice and beans. After I finished eating I went into the living room and stayed glued to the TV, fighting the urge to fall asleep. When Mama told me to shut off the tube and go to bed, I did so grudgingly. That night I tossed and turned as I worried about God punishing me for trespassing on the Indian gravesite. Oddly enough, I wasn't worried that God might punish me for punching Poppers in the mouth.

When I finally fell asleep, I dreamt that I was falling rapidly into a dark hole. When I woke up, right before I hit the bottom, I was terrified and gasping for breath. Looking around I realized I was still in bed. Then the aroma of fresh baked Mexican sweet bread struck my senses and I remembered it was Saturday.

Every Saturday morning, *Chavo's* father baked Mexican Sweet Bread and its delightful scent would settle on the entire *barrio* like a sweet-scented blanket. I jumped out of bed, got dressed, washed my face, brushed my teeth, and rushed next door to *Chavo's* house to talk him out of a few pieces of his father's yummy bread. It was the same routine every week. I would be nice to him and he would use the bread as bait to try and bribe me into getting what he wanted. I never gave in, but he always broke down and gave me two pieces of bread.

Chavo wanted to be the leader of our group real bad, but none of the guys respected him because whenever a new kid moved into the *barrio*, he always tried to take advantage of the kid. It wasn't until the new kid stood up to him that he would stop being a bully. He attempted to get tough with me when I first moved in, but I let him know the very first time I met him I wasn't someone he could push around and get away with it. He had let up on his bullying, but he didn't stop completely. One day, a few months after I moved into *La Rana*, I convinced Poppers, Claw, Chris, and Jr., that we should kick *Chavo's* ass for being a bully.

"We need to teach *Chavo* a lesson so he'll stop throwing his weight around" I told the guys.

It seemed everyone in our group felt the same as me. So one evening, when Chavo stood up in front of us and said that from then on he was going to be the new leader of our group. I looked over at the others and without saying a word we all stood up and knocked him to the ground. We kicked him in the ribs, head, and legs, until he shouted, "I give! I give!"

Afterwards, he seldom tried to intimidate anyone, and every time he did, someone would remind him of the ass whipping we had given him. *Chavo* never did anything about the beating either. Had the guys beat me like we whipped him, I would have gotten revenge on each and every one of them one by one no matter how long it took. Walking over to *Chavo's* house, I got ready for his line of crap.

"Hey *Chavo*, what's happening?" I asked when I arrived to his house.

"I know what you want man," *Chavo* said, with a knowing look. "But I can't give you any bread. My father will beat the heck out of me if he catches me giving it away for free."

"Oh, cut it out. You know you can give me some and your father will never know."

"Oh, he'll know. He knows everything. But maybe I can give you a few pieces of this yummy bread if you convince the guys to let me lead the group?" he asked, timidly.

When I didn't answer, he went on.

"Well, what's it going to be? You going to back me up with the guys and tell them I'm the new leader?"

"Sorry, man. You know I can't do that. Besides, they won't go for it."

"They will if you tell them."

I shook my head.

"Ah, all right," he replied as he handed me two pieces of bread.

I took a big bite of one. I closed my eyes and let the bread dissolve in my mouth and savored every morsel.

Chavo and his father were complete opposites. *Chavo's* father looked as though he could take care of himself. I had never seen him take any back talk from anyone either. He had a weathered face, a red bulbous nose from too much tequila, and a sour disposition. He seldom spoke and he never smiled. Many of the older folks from the *barrio* called him a *"Brujo"* because he performed strange rituals during certain times of the year.

One full moonlit night, *Palio* and I hid behind some wooden crates and watched him do a bizarre ceremony. He had built a large fire in his backyard and wore nothing more than leather pants and moccasins. Sweat ran off his shirtless body as he moved wildly around the fire. During the unusual ritual he lifted his arms toward the sky as he danced and sang in a language I had never heard. *Palio* and I were mesmerized by what we were witnessing. Finally, after working himself into a complete frenzy, he abruptly came to an absolute stop and turned slowly to look toward *Palio* and me. It was as though he knew we had been spying on him. It scared us and we quickly scampered off. We never snuck around *Chavo's* house again after that.

Other folks in the *barrio* called him a *"Currandero,"* because he sold them herbs that healed their ailments. Many of the mothers living in the neighborhood took their children to *Chavo's* father when they misbehaved. They would ask him to exorcise evil spirits that made their children drink alcohol and get into trouble. Since many of our parents had recently arrived from Mexico, they still believed in a lot of superstitious crap. They often tried to pass their beliefs onto us. Some of the more traditional customs like loyalty, keeping our mouth shut about what happened at home, and helping each other in time of need were easily adopted by most of us first generation Mexican Americans. But other traditions, like believing in witchdoctors and healers were simply too incredible to accept.

Mama never took me to him when I misbehaved, but she did take me to him once to get my ankle massaged when I sprained it after jumping off the roof of our house. I tried to talk her out of taking me, but she said I didn't have a choice. Since my ankle hurt so bad and looked as though it was ready to burst from the swelling, I didn't resist very much.

When Mama knocked on the door to *Chavo's* house, it was *Chavo's* sister Thelma who let us in. I hobbled inside holding onto Mama's shoulder tightly so as not to put much weight on my ankle and avoid the jolts of pain shooting to my brain every time I stepped on it.

As we walked in, the smell of incense was overpowering. Thelma signaled us to follow her and she led us to where *Chavo's* father was waiting. She opened a beaded curtain and motioned us to step into a room lit by many candles. I stepped into the room and I looked around worried that something bad was going to happen. I glanced at Mama and noticed she wasn't concerned, so I gripped her shoulder tighter. The place gave me the creeps.

Soon my eyes adjusted to the dimness and I saw *Chavo's* father sitting with his legs crossed in the middle of the room. He nodded at Mama and she began to tell him what had happened. *Chavo's* father never said anything as Mama talked. Even after she finished he simply gestured for me to lie on a mat located on one side of the room. I did so tentatively, still worried that he was going to hurt me, or something. Once I lay down, he took hold of my swollen ankle and began to massage it. He did it gently at first, but then he began to apply more pressure to the affected part of my ankle. I wanted to yell out in pain, but I held back hearing my mother's voice in the back of my head telling me in Spanish, "Men don't cry." But tears snuck their way out of my eyes and ran down the side of my face as I fought the urge to scream from the pain. After *Chavo's* dad worked his magic on my ankle, I was able to walk out with very little pain and minimal swelling. Nevertheless, I still didn't believe all that jive about healers and witchdoctors. But I had to admit he was good at giving massages.

DURING THE SPRING and summer evenings, when the weather was nice, many of us kids from La Rana met on the corner of Antelope and Manzanillo streets. There, we would hold competition on a knoll next to the Hallelujah Church. We called it "The Hallelujah Church" because whenever they held services its members' could be heard hollering out Hallelujah over and over again.

"King of the Mountain" was the game we most often played. The objec - tive of the game was to see who was left standing on the hill after everyone had tried to knock each other down. All of us wanted to be King so we fought to the finish. Pushing, shoving, and socking each other until only one stood on top of the hill. And although it was rare that we came to blows with each other seriously, we argued about everything.

Arguing was a *barrio* past time.

One of the main subjects everyone quarreled about was who had the toughest and meanest dog. Almost every family in the *barrio* had at least one dog. Dogs were everywhere. You had to be careful when walking on the streets at night in the neighborhood because sometimes dogs would jump out of their yard and attack you. I always carried a stick to beat down any dog that tried to bite me as I walked home late at night.

I didn't own a dog personally, but Mama did. The dog's name was Smokey. He was half Cocker Spaniel and half Mutt. I never got involved in any of the dog arguments because Smokey wasn't tough, but he was obedient and protec - tive of our family. I did, however, believe "King," an Alaskan Husky that be - longed to Larry, a kid who hung out with our group once in a while, was the toughest dog in the *barrio*. King walked around with his head held high and his chest puffed out as if he knew he was number one. He never growled and seldom barked at anyone until they crossed an imaginary line he had made marking his property. Whenever anyone crossed that line, they were in deep trouble. King had bitten a couple of the kids who had made the mistake of stepping onto his property. Chris was one of the kids King had bitten. He showed me the gash where King had ripped the flesh off his leg.

"Man," I told Chris when he showed me his ugly scar. "If that dog ever bites me, I'll shoot him."

One evening, after the heat of the day had subsided; a big argument between *Chavo* and Larry ensued after a game of "King of the Mountain" concerning their dogs.

Chavo was screaming that his dog Tuffy was tougher than King.

"Come on man," Larry countered sarcastically. "Your dog is nothing compared to mine. He's nothing but a Mutt."

I silently agreed with Larry. There was no doubt Tuffy was tough, but I didn't think he could beat King. I had seen Tuffy win a lot of fights with a lot of other dogs, and once, I saw him chase a cat through our yard. During the pursuit, the cat had sprinted up a ladder that was leaning up against our neighbor's house. Tuffy, without breaking stride climbed the ladder too and almost caught the cat. Luckily for the cat, there was a tree next to the house and it was able to spring onto the tree and get away. For a second, I thought Tuffy was going to jump onto the tree too, but he seemed to know that he would hurt himself if he tried to jump. It was an incredible sight. I had never seen any dog do what Tuffy did that day and I had never known any dog that hated cats as much as Tuffy did either. Tuffy had been taught to hate cats by *Chavo*.

Chavo loathed cats. Sometimes, he would capture a cat and throw it into a rattlesnake pit he had built in his back yard. He liked to watch the rattlesnakes bite the cat over and over as the cat tried to claw its way out of the pit. He let me watch this deathly spectacle once. It was a gruesome sight. One I never cared to witness after that day.

Another method *Chavo* used to eliminate cats was to shoot them with an arrow. I caught him crouched under a tree one day with his bow and arrows, peering up into the branches.

"What are you looking for?" I asked, glancing up at the tree.

"It's a damn cat," he whispered vehemently.

I saw the cat perched high on a branch staring down at us wide eyed. He seemed to know he was trapped.

Chavo then placed an arrow on the bow, aimed it at the cat, and shot it. The cat landed at our feet with the arrow stuck half way through its body. It tried to crawl away, but *Chavo* stomped on it until the cat was dead.

"How come you hate cats so much?" I asked *Chavo* afterwards.

"They're Devil creatures," he said. "Haven't you ever seen how their eyes shine evilly at night?"

I had heard the stories about black cats and their association to witches. It was also rumored in the *barrio* that a cat had sucked the breath out of Chris's baby brother while he had been asleep in his crib causing the baby to suffocate to death. I had never really liked cats either so when *Chavo* told me they were Devil creatures, I hated them after that, too. But I didn't loathe them to the point that I would go out of my way to kill them like *Chavo* did. As long as they stayed away from me, I didn't bother them. But killing cats and climbing ladders didn't have anything to do with which dog was the toughest in the *barrio*. That issue had to be determined by a fight between Tuffy and King.

"What do you mean your dog is tougher than mine?" *Chavo* demanded, as he held Tuffy back by a thick chain that was wrapped around his neck. "My dog will kick your dog's ass without ever losing his breath."

King and Tuffy choked on their chains as they lunged at each other growling and baring their long sharp teeth. Both dogs were so wound up that saliva foamed and ran down their jaws. Their ears were pointed and the hair on the nape of their necks stood straight up and their tails were as stiff as a board too. It looked as though the dogs were ready to rip each other apart if *Chavo* and Larry let them go.

"You're full of crap!" Larry exclaimed. "Anytime you're ready, all you have to do is cut your dog loose and watch King tear him apart."

Suddenly, they let the dogs go! The dogs leapt on each other, growling, and biting one another as they rolled over and over on the ground. The clash between King and Tuffy didn't last very long. It was over within a minute or so. But in that time, King had pinned Tuffy to the ground and had his jaw clamped around Tuffy's throat. Tuffy was incapacitated and King shook him to and fro like a rag doll.

Larry grabbed King's chain and pulled him off. King let go of Tuffy's throat and left him on the ground whimpering. Blood was everywhere. I could see Tuffy's throat ripped open where King had torn away the flesh. There was nothing anyone could do to help Tuffy. *Chavo* fell to his knees, sorrow clearly carved on his face. He lifted Tuffy in his arms as if he were his child and carried him home with tears streaming down his face. I felt sad for *Chavo* so I walked with him to his house. When we got there, he gently laid Tuffy on the grass and walked into his house. He returned with a 22caliber rifle and without hesitating, placed the barrel on Tuffy's forehead and pumped a bullet into his head ending his misery.

The shot rang out across the neighborhood and reverberated through my mind, reminding me to stay strong, fit, and ready to fight.

I was eleven years old.

CHAPTER FOUR

"**C**ome here Jesús," Father commanded. "I'm going to teach you how to play the guitar."

Father played the guitar well and sometimes talked about playing music professionally, but because he had to work in the field to provide for us he had never gotten the opportunity to fulfill his goal.

"But I don't want to learn," I complained. By now, both Mama and Father understood English well enough although they never spoke it.

"I'm not asking you!" Father exclaimed in Spanish in a tone of voice that clearly indicated I didn't have any choice in the matter.

I was only eleven when Father set out to teach me. He bought a secondhand guitar that was bigger than me so I could practice on. Every afternoon when I got home from school, Father made me rehearse what he had taught me the day before for at least an hour.

At first, playing the instrument was painful on my fingertips, but after I developed calluses there was no more pain whenever I played. Once I understood the rhythm of the instrument, I spent hours practicing and daydreaming about becoming a great musician, getting rich, and eventually buying Mama a big house on a hill that would allow us to look down on White people the way they looked down on us.

"Hey," Father said, as he cuffed me gently upside my head after he caught me daydreaming. "Pay attention to what you're doing, *Menso*"

One Saturday evening, after I had been rehearsing for about a year, I decided to venture over to *El Venadito*, the local pool hall where the older men hung out after they got off work. By then, I had learned the lyrics and chords of three Mexican songs written by Jose Alfredo Jimenez, one of the great songwriters from Mexico.

The first, *"El Caballo Blanco,"* was about a White Horse that sets off from southern Mexico to Tijuana trying to get home to his master. The next, *"Las Rejas No Matan,"* was a love ballad about a man in prison who pointedly states that being confined wasn't so difficult, but being deprived of his woman was pure agony. *"Ella,"* the third song, was a heartbreaking love song about a man begging his lady not to leave him, but no matter how much he pleads she walks out on him anyway.

It was a cool 1963 spring Saturday evening when I went to the pool hall to test my musical skills. When I got there, I stood petrified at the door with my guitar slung over my shoulder afraid to step inside. I was scared the men would laugh at me. It seemed as though I hesitated for a long time, but it was actually just about a minute or so before I mustered the courage to go indoors. The first thing that struck me as I walked in was the strong mixture of cigarette smoke, body odor, and alcohol. The smell was nauseating and it made my nose cringe. I wondered how these men could tolerate the stench. A blanket of cigarette smoke, illuminated by the florescent lights hanging over each pool table, covered the entire hall. I could see men scattered throughout the establishment playing pool, drinking beer, and talking loud. Their clamor pulsated off the walls and every time a Q-ball was shot at the racked balls at the end of a pool table, it made an earsplitting clapping sound that added to the noise. I wondered if the men would even be able to hear me sing and play over all the commotion. I tentatively walked over to the bar and sat on an empty stool with my oversized guitar on my lap and began to strum it.

"Hola, Chuy," the owner said. "Are you going to play something for us?"

I nodded.

"Listen up," the owner yelled loudly. "Pay attention. We have a treat tonight. *Chuy's* going to entertain us."

I closed my eyes and began to play. The chatter lightened up a little as I strummed my guitar and began to sing. The noise calmed down even more as I continued my performance. When I finished, the men clapped and hollered, *Otra! Otra!* I played the three songs I knew for them and was surprised to find out how much the men enjoyed my musical talents. I earned nine dollars that night.

Afterward, I raced home reeling with excitement at the prospect of showing my Father how much money I made. I thought he would be proud of me for doing so well. To be fair, I think he was proud of me. Nevertheless, he still took my hard-earned cash. He said nine dollars was too much money for a twelve-year old. I didn't say anything, but inside, I was livid. I thought he had taken advantage of my trust and silently promised never to tell him how much money I made the next time I performed. I never forgave him for taking my money either.

A few months later, while rummaging through my mother's private dresser drawers looking for coins, I came across my birth certificate that appeared to be mine. It listed my first name, birth date, and Mama as the woman who gave birth to me. The problem was that the last name said LIMON, not DE LA CRUZ. And it named someone by the name of Onesimo Mungina as my father—not Juan.

Did this mean Father wasn't my real father?

I was devastated by what I found that day and walked around in a state of bewilderment for weeks desperately wanting to ask someone what it all meant, but I didn't dare for fear of what my parents would do to me. How could I explain snooping around in mother's private dresser drawers without getting into trouble? So I kept the finding to myself and stuffed it like I did when the teachers humiliated me, or White people acted like they were better than me, or when I would see White parents hug their children and I couldn't get a hug from my parents even though I believed in my heart that they loved me.

About six months later, Raquel, one of Mamas' younger sisters, told me she had overheard Grandma say my real father had left to work as a *"Bracéro"* during the time Mama was pregnant with me. Raquel said that was all she knew about him and he remained pretty much a mystery to me.

"HEY, JESSE, where you going man?" Frank asked as he pulled up to the curb in his bullet-riddled 1939 Chevy. "It looks like you're pretty pissed off. Is someone giving you a hard time?"

I was walking home with thoughts about my real father flowing through my mind, but I didn't want to tell Frank about my dilemma.

"Naw, I'm not mad. I'm just tired," I lied.

Frank was one of the *Vetéranos* from the *barrio*, but everybody called him "Vek." He was interested in my older sister Dee, but my Father didn't like him. According to Father, Vek would never amount to anything. As far as Father was concerned, Vek was nothing more than a lazy bum who would rather steal than work. But the truth was that Vek wasn't a thief. He was one of the hardest workers in the *barrio*. Vek's trouble wasn't being lazy; his problem was that he spent most of his money on booze. Father had made it clear to Dee she was not to have anything to do with Vek, but Dee disobeyed Father, and would often sneak out of the house to meet Vek.

"You want a ride?" Vek asked. "Jump in."

I climbed in. Vek was one of the few guys in the neighborhood who had a car. His car was full of bullet holes because some guys from Visalia had shot at him but hit the car instead. Even though it wasn't in the best condition, I was still impressed with his car, bullet holes and all. To me, anyone who could survive after being shot at as many time as he'd been, was someone to be admired.

As I got in, I spotted an open beer can of Coors stuck between his legs. Before he drove off, Vek grabbed the beer and took a big drink. I could see his Adams apple bob up and down as he guzzled the beer. He didn't seem worried about getting arrested for driving drunk even though he was plastered. I could tell he was drunk by the way he mumbled his words when he talked, and how his eyes drooped as though he couldn't keep them open. But he acted like he had life under control and no one could tell him what to do.

Vek drove into the parking lot of Diamonds Market, slammed on the brakes to keep from running into the store wall. He pulled a fistful of money from his pant pocket and handed me a couple of one-dollar bills.

"Go get whatever you want," he slurred, after which he took another swig from his beer.

I wondered where Vek had gotten the wad of money he had pulled out of his pocket. I was sure he worked in the fields picking fruit like everyone else in the *barrio* did and I couldn't believe anyone could make so much money picking fruit and spend it so carelessly as Vek was doing now. Of course, I didn't ask him what he did to earn his money. I just accepted the cash and shot inside the store and bought a small carton of chocolate milk, a cupcake with cream filling, chocolate icing, and white swirl on top.

Getting back into the car, Vek drove to my house and began to ask me all sorts of questions about my sister Dee, but I wasn't paying much attention. I was more concerned with the chocolate milk and cupcake. It wasn't every day I got to eat these treats. I simply nodded my head or said yeah as he continued to quiz me about Dee.

I was glad when he pulled up to our front yard and dropped me off. He was beginning to bug me with all his questions about my sister. I said goodbye and sat down on the front steps of our house to finish the chocolate milk and cupcake. Once done, I brooded over what I was going to do once I got older. I didn't want to work in a warehouse or as a ranch hand and live from paycheck to paycheck like many of the men in the *barrio* did.

The heck with that!

I wasn't lazy and when I worked, I would put all my effort into my labor, but I wasn't going to toil like an ox in the fields for the rest of my life. What kind of future was that? I hated going to work every weekend and during summer vacation so someone else could get rich off my sweat, but it wasn't going to be easy to stand up to my Father. I wasn't afraid of him, but I respected him and challenging his commands went against everything I had been taught.

"Wake up, *Chuy*, it's time to go to work," Father said as he shook me awake.

"I'm not working in the fields anymore," I replied.

"What did you say?"

I saw Father's complexion turn dark red and his nostrils flare even though the room was dimly lit. He walked rapidly into his bedroom muttering that he was going to beat me within an inch of my life for disobeying him. I saw him grab the thick brown leather belt he kept hung on a wall in his bedroom. I braced myself for the beating as Father rushed back to whip me. I took the flogging without complaint and used my anger to keep from crying out in pain.

My Father rarely hit me, but he wanted to let me know disrespect would not be tolerated in his home and that I was going to work whether I liked it or not. After a week of daily thrashings, however, he realized that no matter what he did, I would never give in. So he quit whipping me.

Later that week, after winning what I considered a victory with my refusal to work, I walked over to the street corner where the older guys from the *barrio* hung out. When I arrived, I saw *Pato, Pancho,* and Blue hanging out there. *Pato,* who was about 20 years old, carried himself as though he was much older and was considered the leader of the guys in the 'hood.' He was tall, and wide-shouldered from working out with weights. His jet-black hair was slicked straight back and shone brightly in the sun because of all the pomade he was wearing. *Pancho* was a little younger than *Pato,* and not as tall. He also didn't seem to have the confidence that *Pato* had, but I heard he seldom lost whenever he got into a scrap. Blue was a short, dark-skinned guy with wavy hair and a perpetual smile. He liked to clown around and make others laugh.

I watched how these guys seemed to enjoy life, joking and laughing with each other without seemingly a care in the world. I felt envious. It looked like these guys had life figured out. They wore nice clothes, had pretty girls hang out with them, drank alcohol, and did whatever they wanted. They listened to "Oldies but Goodies" on their car radios until late into the night and if someone didn't like it, too bad.

I checked out *Pato,* dressed *Cholo* style, in his spit-shined French-toed shoes, razor-sharp creased black Frisco Jean pants, and matching Pendleton shirt. I noted how he only buttoned the top two buttons on his shirt, and how he let the shirttails hang out of his pants as though making a statement that he was different. I was impressed with the way he strutted, with a dip in his hip, happy and carefree, carrying himself as if he owned the world. *Pato* saw me and strolled over to where I was standing.

"*Oralé Carnálito.* What you doing, *Dragón?*"

"Just taking it easy."

"I've been checking you out *Ese,* and I like the way you carry yourself. I hear you're the leader of the younger guys from the *barrio.* That true?

"*Simón Ese.*"

"Maybe it's time for you to start hanging out with us older *vatos* so you can learn what this crazy life of ours is all about. You interested?"

"Hell yeah, man!"

Pato smiled at my response. "Here, take a drink of this," he said, handing me a bottle of cheap rotgut Red Mountain wine.

I wanted to say no, that I didn't want any. I had tasted alcohol before when my parents had taken us kids with them to a Christmas party at one of their friend's house. *Palio* had been there too. We had snuck a half empty bottle of Coors beer to the back yard and tried to drink its contents. It had tasted nasty and I had spit the alcohol out. But I couldn't say no to *Pato*. It would make me look weak, so I grabbed the bottle, took a few deep breaths, put the bottle to my mouth, and gulped the wine down. *Pato* watched me and sang a short rhyme as I guzzled the wine:

"This is to the Bee that stung the Bull that got it to start bucking. This is to Adam and Eve, who started the whole world fucking. Over the lips, down the gums, lookout stomach, cuz here it comes."

I had never drunk wine before and it tasted even worse than beer did. I almost puked it up, but after a few minutes a warm sensation came over me. And I noticed that the alcohol seemed to temporarily extinguish the anger that always simmered deep in the pit of my gut. *Pato* smiled, seemingly impressed that I had been able to keep the booze down.

After a while, I asked *Pato* for another drink and before too long I was drunk.

It was late when I stumbled home that night and lay on the bed I shared with my two younger brothers, Johnny and *Néto*. Lying down, the room spun and I could feel the rumbling in my stomach as the alcohol tried to force its way out. I had to hold my breath to keep from throwing up. When my stomach finally settled, images of the guys hanging out on the street corner rushed through my mind. In my drunken state I visualized becoming someone everyone would fear and respect. I faintly heard the music from Blue's car radio and the homeboys' laughter as it filtered through my bedroom window while they partied down the street from my house. One day, I'll be one of them, I thought.

Then I passed out.

AFTER THAT NIGHT, I began hanging out with the *Vato Locos* every chance I got. I started drinking and smoking marijuana with them on weekends even though I didn't like to smoke weed very much. It made me feel self-conscious about the way I walked, but I did it anyway. I had to be cool.

After school, instead of going directly home, I would stop off at the park and hang out with *Pato*. It was always late when I got home, but I never got into trouble because my parents were too busy working to pay much attention to what was I was doing. One night, Mama stayed awake and waited for me to get home. By now she had found out I was associating with the older guys from the neighborhood. When I walked in she asked me why I was hanging out with guys like *Pato*? I told her he was my friend and that there was nothing wrong with him.

"He's nothing but a hoodlum!" Mama screamed. "If you don't stop hanging out with him, I'm going to have you locked up. At least I'll know where you are, and I won't have to worry about something happening to you."

I told her not to lose sleep over me.

I wasn't worried about getting hurt or dying. I was young, full of energy, and to me, nothing was more significant than becoming one of the *Vato Locos* at whatever price necessary.

Pato spent hours instructing me on how to represent the neighborhood and on the aspects of living "*La Vida Loca*." He would often tell me that I would have to stand up for the *barrio* no matter what. He said I was never to leave my homeboys in the face of danger. He drilled into me that I was to respect my elders and never to steal from the people who lived in the neighborhood. They have it hard enough without getting ripped off by us. Besides, there are plenty of ranchers who have way more than they deserve living on the outskirts of town. Rip them off, he would say.

About a year after, I started hanging out with *Pato*, Manuel and Rudy, two guys who lived in the 'Hood' but who didn't hang out with us, went to Visalia to visit their girlfriends. There, they were confronted by some guys from Visalia who asked them where they were from. Not realizing they were being asked what gang they represented, they innocently responded by saying they lived in Woodlake. As a result of their response, the guys from Visalia beat them down badly. Manuel and Rudy were not gang members. They were normal guys who went to school, and probably on their way to becoming insurance salesmen, store managers, or maybe even owners of their own businesses. The day following the ass whipping, Manuel bumped into *Pato* and told him what had happened. That evening *Pato* approached me.

"*Sabes que, Dragón*? We've got a serious problem with those punks from Visalia. They jumped Manuel last night and beat him pretty bad so we have to go into their neighborhood and hurt them. Let them know we won't tolerate anyone messing with anybody from our *barrio*. Blue has a .22 rifle and since you're the youngest, you have to prove you're down for the Hood, *tu sabes?*"

"*Simón, Ese*. Whatever needs to be done, you can count me in." I was game for anything because I wanted to be a *vato loco*.

But even though *Pato* had been preparing me for the last three months to be a tough guy, inside I was terrified. Shooting someone was a huge undertaking that would require a callousness I wasn't sure I had. Hitting someone on the mouth was nothing compared to this.

Later that night, all the guys who wanted to go to Visalia met at Mickey's Drive-In. Many guys didn't fit into Blue's car and were left behind, but I was allowed to go and I felt like I was one of the lucky ones. As we drove to Visalia in Blue's 1941 Chevy, *Pato* handed me the 22 semiautomatic rifle.

"It's that time, little brother," he said.

"*Simón, Ese*," I answered looking at him seriously.

It was cold that night when we pulled up to the stop sign on the corner of Court and Vine streets, the main hub of their *barrio*. A dense Tule fog clung on the ground obscuring the area and I could scarcely make out the shadows of some guys from Visalia standing around a fifty-gallon drum. They had built a huge fire to keep warm from the wintry temperature. They didn't even notice we were watching them until Puppet yelled out.

"*Puro* Woodlake *Putos!*"

I was scared as I stuck the rifle out the car window, aimed it at the guys positioned around the fire, and began to squeeze the trigger. I had my eyes closed tightly when I started pumping bullets at the small group of guys from Visalia. But, a second or so later, when I opened them, I saw guys drop to the ground to avoid getting shot. It was then that a feeling of complete poise came over me. It made me feel good to see the guys crawl, so I continued to blast away as fast as I could.

In a matter of seconds I emptied the rifle and just as quick as it had begun, the shooting was over. I was left tingling with excitement, and felt immensely powerful. As we drove back to the neighborhood, *Pato* praised me for shooting without hesitation. Of course, he didn't know that I had been scared, and I never told him.

The following day, one of *Pato's* girlfriends from Visalia called to let him know two guys had been shot. She told *Pato* the guys hadn't died, but that they were critically hurt. *Pato* informed me about what his girlfriend had said when I ran into him at the park later that day.

"You did a good job, Homeboy," he said as he slapped me on my back. "Those punks will think twice before getting out of line with us again."

I simply nodded.

After that incident, all the guys from the *barrio* seemed to respect me more. Whenever I showed up at our hangout, they always acknowledged my presence by nodding and including me in whatever conversation they were having at the time of my arrival. Prior to the shooting, I had always felt as though I was invisible to everyone except *Pato*. But now everyone knew who I was. It felt great to be recognized.

A few weeks following the shooting, *Pato* and I were at Mickey's Drive-In hanging out. *Pato*'s girlfriend had called him earlier in the day to warn him about an impending attack on our neighborhood by the guys from Visalia. She told *Pato* she had seen them preparing to get even with us for hurting some of their guys. She said there were a lot of them and that they were really pissed.

"What do you think, *Pato*? Are they coming?" I asked.

"Of course they're coming. What do you think? Some of those guys are just as crazy as we are. So why wouldn't they come? Look at what we did to them when we found out they jumped Manuel. And he's not even from our clique."

"Yeah, I guess you're right."

I had wanted him to answer differently, but in my gut, I knew he was right. It was always about respect and pride. And pride was a powerful emotion that many of us were pathetically full of. I must admit it drove me too. Pride motivated us into doing things with total disregard for the consequences. Since we had disrespected their *barrio* it was only fitting that they get even with us. After all, the neighborhood was all any of us had and most of us would do whatever it took to uphold its honor.

The cold night air was rife with anticipation as *Pato*, Manuel, me, and some of the guys who hung out with Manuel waited for the imminent attack by the guys from Visalia. Everyone at the drive-in was walking in place trying to stay warm. No one was talking. I don't think Manuel and his friends really expected the guys from Visalia to come into our *barrio*, but I knew they would come because *Pato* had said they would.

Suddenly, the sound of screeching tires skidding around the corner of Main and Antelope Street broke the night silence. I looked at *Pato* to get instructions on what to do, and he told me it was time to get down. Manuel and the guys from his group began to break the legs off one of the picnic tables at the drive-in to use as weapons.

In the meantime, car after car came barreling around the corner. The first car was a black 1951 Ford. Even before it came to a complete stop, a guy jumped out of the car and immediately gunfire exploded. After that it was complete pandemonium as everyone tried to get away from the area.

I saw *Pato* hit a guy who had sprung out of the same black Ford upside his head with a leg from one of the drive-in tables. Then *Pato* shot off like a bullet into the darkness. That's when I figured it was time to make my exit too. I couldn't run fast because of my bad leg, but I scooted towards the downtown apartments as fast as I could, trying to get out of harm's way. As I fled, I glanced back and caught a glimpse of a tall guy pointing a weapon at me. I saw the streetlight reflect off the gun barrel, making it look even more menacing. This spurred me to run faster. All the while, I expected to get blasted. Luckily, I reached the safety of the downtown apartments and hid behind a tree breathing hard from the exertion and panic. A few seconds later, I peeked around the tree and saw a guy standing over someone lying on the parking lot pavement. I watched him pump five bullets into the guy on the ground in rapid succession as though the guy were a sack of grain. Pop! Pop! Pop! Pop! Pop! And within a matter of three minutes tops, the melee was over. Everyone from Visalia jumped into their cars and fled the scene.

As soon as the guys from Visalia drove off, I cautiously walked back to find out who had been gunned down. At first I thought it was *Pato* wheezing on the asphalt, but was relieved to discover it was Manuel instead. As Manuel lay on his back, he stared at me with blank eyes in a clear state of shock. He kept trying to tell me something, but only a hissing sound came out of his mouth. I stood next to where he lay unable to help him and saw his eyes lose their light as his life drained onto the pavement. For a fleeting moment I thought it should have been me on the ground and deep inside I was thankful I had cheated death that night.

The police arrived on the spot within a few minutes after the shooting, and as soon as they did, they began asking if there were any witnesses to the killing. I already knew to keep my mouth shut and never cooperate with the police, so when Chief Mayfield asked me if I had seen anything, I told him no. Nobody who had been at the site of the shooting told the officers anything about what had happened.

The following evening around 6: 00 p.m., I was picked up by two Tulare County Sheriff's homicide detectives conducting the murder investigation of Manuel. They put me into an unmarked police car and took me to headquarters. At the station, they offered me a soda, but I declined. I knew they were just trying to get me to talk. They showed me pictures of Manuel's bullet-riddled body as it lay on a gurney covered by a white sheet soaked with his blood. One of the cops told me Manuel had been shot twice in one lung, once in his chest, and that one bullet had grazed his head, and another slug had entered his shoulder.

"You know," one of the Detectives said. "This could've been you."

At first, the detectives were nice to me, but once they realized I wasn't going to cooperate, they got angry. They raised their voices, and told me that if I didn't help put the shooter in jail they were going to arrest me. I stuck to my story so they put me in a cell, but after a few hours they let me go. They didn't take me home afterwards either.

"Walk home," one of them said.

Two days after the murder, a couple of guys from Visalia ratted on the guy who committed the homicide. The informants told the cops it was a guy named George who had shot Manuel. An article in the Visalia Times Newspaper portrayed George as young, full of hate, and constantly in trouble with the law.

There was a picture in the piece that showed George in handcuffs as he was being escorted by police into Juvenile Hall. He didn't appear angry to me. He looked like many of us from the *barrio*.

The "rats" told the cops it had been George who had convinced the guys from Visalia to get revenge on us for driving into the heart of their neighborhood and shooting at them a few days before. I always thought the *Veteranos* from Visalia hadn't done a very good job of schooling their younger homeboys because if they had, no one would have snitched on George.

Where was the loyalty?

After the slaying of Manuel, *Pato* got more serious about educating me concerning the *barrio* lifestyle. He spent hours every week talking to me about crime and serving time. He drilled into my mind that I was never to let anyone disrespect me and that — no matter what — I was to hold my mud (not snitch). I was like a sponge, absorbing everything.

Not long after, I began to shoplift and break into houses. At first, I stole only candy from the Payless Grocery store. Then I started to pinch bigger stuff like radios and cameras from the Western Auto store located on Main Street. I usually sold the stolen goods to people I trusted. It seemed as though lots of people in the *barrio* had larceny in their hearts. There were always folks lined up to buy the goods I offered. They knew the merchandise I was peddling was stolen, but they didn't seem to care. Everyone who bought stolen stuff from me was looking for a deal and as long as they didn't get into trouble with the police, they were game.

The first time I got caught stealing I was at Payless. I was wearing a black imitation leather jacket I had stolen from Michael's Clothing Store. I loved that jacket. It had lots of pockets that allowed me to stuff bags of candy into them. The owner snatched me as I walked out with a couple of large bags of M&M's Peanuts stuffed into one of the many pockets.

"Come here, you little bastard," the owner hissed through clenched teeth as he took hold of my arm tightly. "I've been watching you come in and out of my store without ever buying anything. Something told me you were stealing," he said as he pulled the bags of candy out from my pocket. "All you wetbacks are the same, always taking things that don't belong to you. You should get a job and work like decent folks," he said, a snide look on his face. "But I have you now you little bastard. You're not going to steal from my store anymore, I guarantee you that. I'm going to make sure they put you in jail where you belong. You hear me?"

Yeah, yeah, I hear you, I thought.

Half an hour or so later, when the policeman arrived, the storeowner went on to tell the cop what he thought should be done to punish me. Of course, he didn't say anything about calling me a wetback.

"There's no telling how long this little thief has been pocketing stuff from my store. I think you should lock him up so he can learn a lesson."

He talked about me like I was a deranged monster that needed to be caged, just like my fifth grade teacher Mrs. Harvey had said when I broke Billy's nose.

During the storeowner's tirade, the cop nodded and promised to handle the situation. Afterward, the officer led me to his police car, roughly shoved me onto the backseat and slammed the door. He climbed into the car and drove to my house. On the short ride, I kept thinking this was how it was supposed to be. I felt good because even though I had been caught, I hadn't squealed on Jackie, who'd been waiting for me outside the store.

During our many sessions, *Pato* had trained me on the aspects of honor and loyalty.

"Never snitch on your friends. If you can't handle being locked up, you shouldn't get involved into this crazy life of ours because going to jail is part of the job description."

I also remembered how the guys from the *barrio* had talked about the guys from Visalia who had snitched on George. They had called them sissies and said that informants were considered the lowest of the low. I didn't want anyone looking at me as if I was infected with some sort of contagious disease because I had ratted on my partner. I wanted to be part of the neighborhood *Vato Locos* real bad, so I made sure to follow all the rules. I didn't tell the cop anything when he asked me if anyone else had been with me when I stole the candy.

When we arrived to my house, all my brothers and sisters came outside. They looked scared that a police officer had come to our house, and I'm sure they must have been curious to find out why I was in the back seat of the police car like some common criminal.

"Who's in charge here," the cop asked?

"Me," Dee replied apprehensively.

"Well, look here. Your brother was arrested for shoplifting at the Payless."

I could tell Dee was embarrassed and scared because her complexion turned crimson and she kept fidgeting when the officer told her I was headed down the wrong road.

"I'm not surprised we caught Jesse breaking the law. He's been messing around on the other side of town with some other kids on a number of occasions, and some of those kids have been caught breaking car windows over there. I've also seen him running around with some of the older guys from the neighborhood, guys who are real criminals. I suggest you tell your folks to keep a tight leash on Jesse before he finds himself in Juvenile Hall."

The cop made it sound like I was a dog. I wanted to tell him to go straight to hell, but I kept my mouth shut.

As soon as the officer left, Dee started in on me.

"You just wait until your mom gets home, *Chuy*. I'm going to tell her the police brought you home because you got caught stealing."

"Well, Dee," I replied angrily, "you go ahead and tell her. I guess I'll just have to tell Dad how you've been sneaking around meeting with Vek. I'm sure he'll be glad to hear about that."

Dee didn't know that I knew how she'd sneak out of the house and meet Vek at Jacob and Eva's house where they'd hang out late into the night. They couldn't go out in public because the town was small. They'd be seen by people who could tell my father.

Needless to say Dee decided to keep quiet about this incident. She had no way of knowing that I would never have snitched.

A few months later, Vek convinced Dee to run away with him. One night, when everyone was asleep, Dee slipped out of the house through her bedroom window and ran off to Los Angeles and married him.

In April of '65, just after I turned fourteen, I decided I wanted to take a trip to Los Angeles to visit Dee and Vek. I missed her, but I knew my parents wouldn't let me go. So I decided to go anyway. Sach had moved back to East L.A., and I wanted to visit him too. I remembered the stories Sach told us guys about Whittier Boulevard and the vitality surrounding the Golden Gate Theater on the corner of Whittier Boulevard and Atlantic Boulevard. He often described the excitement of going downtown L.A. to the Olympic Auditorium to watch professional boxing. During the short time Sach had lived in Woodlake, he often told us he had seen Armando *"Mando"* Ramos, an up-and-coming lightweight Chicano boxer, fight at the Olympic Auditorium before he became the WBC Lightweight Champion of the world.

I used to sit captivated, listening to Sach describing how there were always people out even at night in Los Angeles. He said he often went to Whittier Boulevard just to look at the displays in storefronts and that even at night the bright street lights made you feel as though it was still daytime. He said that on Sunday evenings hundreds of people would cruise the Boulevard to show off their customized cars with newly installed hydraulics which the owner would manipulate to make their cars bounce up and down as they drove slowly down the Boulevard. His vivid narratives about Los Angeles always sounded exciting. It gave me goose bumps whenever I heard him talk about L.A., and it made me want to leave to the big city immediately. The problem was I couldn't just get up and go and I didn't have any money. But, a friend of mine did. So I decided to convince him to go with me.

Gibby was a pudgy, light skinned, curly haired boy who always complained about how bad he had it at home. But as far as I was concerned, Gibby had it made in the shade compared to everyone else in the *barrio*. I'd seen his mom give him $10.00 every week like clockwork and Gibby did nothing with the money but save it. He definitely had enough for an L.A. trip. I just had to convince him to take the risky trip with me.

Gibby lived on the corner of Pomegranate and Cypress Streets in a big white house with red trim. He had his own bedroom and a bed bigger than the one I slept in with my two younger brothers, Johnny and Ernesto. He had a television, a record player, stacks of record albums, and 45's galore. He also had more clothes and shoes than anyone I had ever known. And last but not least, he had his own bathroom. What a luxury that must have been.

Maybe the reason why he felt so discontented was because he didn't have a father. He told me his dad had been killed in an automobile accident when he was just a baby and that he had never known him. I understood his unhappiness because I didn't know my father either.

Gibby's mother was real strict with him. She rarely, if ever, let him to go anywhere except to school and back. She did let *Palio*, Jackie, and me visit him. We spent hours listening to music and watching TV in Gibby's room after school. One day, I decided to broach the subject about taking off to Los Angeles.

"Pancho Lopez and *Cerrillo* are going to Tijuana next Friday night to get Pancho's car interior tuck-n-rolled. We can catch a ride with them."

"I don't know," Gibby replied. I could tell he was afraid and since he had never been exposed to the street life like me, I understood his apprehension.

"Don't be scared Gibby. I'll look out for you, I give you my word."

"You sure they'll give us a ride?"

"Yeah, man. I talked to Pancho yesterday. He said he would drop us off downtown L.A. Can you imagine all the fun we'll have without anyone telling us what to do?"

Gibby hesitated. "Well, okay."

When Friday night came, Gibby and I met up with Pancho and Cerrillo in the alley behind Mickey's Drive-In. Gibby had brought three hundred dollars with him. I didn't have a cent.

We headed out of town around 9 PM in Pancho's '59 Chevy El Camino. Pancho had recently painted his car a glistening root beer brown. He had also mounted a set of new tires on shiny chrome rims that were capped off with Baby Moon hubcaps. The white walls had been scrubbed to a sparkling white and stood out brightly in the moonlight.

"We're going to the city in style," I told Gibby.

Pancho said we were crazy for taking off without permission.

"You don't even know where Vek and Dee live," Pancho said.

"Don't worry about it," I replied.

He just laughed and said we were nuts.

He drove south on highway 99 until we reached Bakersfield. Then we began to climb the Grapevine. It took about an hour to drive through the winding mountains. When we finally came around the last bend and the panorama of Los Angeles came into view, "Land of a Thousand Dances," a song by a group named Cannibal & the Headhunters, was playing on the radio. The beat of the song added to the thrill of the moment.

"Look at that, Gibby!" I exclaimed.

Gibby just stared, openmouthed. The view was truly a spectacular sight with the lights of the city seemingly never ending.

Pancho dropped us off on the corner of Sixth and Los Angeles Streets and reminded us not to tell anyone he had given us a ride.

"Hey *Ese*, who do you think we are, a couple of rats?"

"No, man, I just want to make sure you understand the seriousness of what I just did. I can get into a lot of trouble if the police find out."

"I already told you not to worry about it. We're not going to say anything."

With that, Pancho and *Cerrillo* drove off, leaving Gibby and me on our own. I looked up at the tall downtown buildings with awe. I wondered how anyone could have constructed these huge structures in this enormous city.

"Come on Gibby. Let's go get something to eat."

We entered an eatery where a sign read, "Fried chicken, all you can eat: $1.25." The chicken was almost as good as Mama's.

"How are we going to find your sister's house?" Gibby asked.

"Don't worry. All we have to do is find Whittier Boulevard in East Los Angeles."

I didn't have the slightest clue as to where Whittier Boulevard was, but I was going to find the street one way or another.

After we ate, we walked over to a bus stop and asked a bus driver where we could catch the bus that would take us to Whittier Boulevard. The driver told us that the number 47 on Sixth and Broadway would take us there. Following the bus driver's instructions, Gibby and I headed toward the bus stop. We waited until the 47 arrived, then we climbed on board and I asked the driver to let me know when we got to the corner of Whittier and Ford. When we got to the "Boulevard," the driver told us we were there. I thanked him and we got off the bus. I couldn't believe we were actually on the famous cruising spot in East L.A., known throughout every southwestern Mexican community. There was even a song named after it sung by "Thee Mid-Nighters," a local group from East L.A.

It was Friday night, and Whittier Boulevard vibrated with energy. I had never seen so many magnificently painted lowered cars as they cruised bumper to bumper. There were crowds of people hanging out on the sidewalks and "Oldies but Goodies" blared out of cars as they moved slowly down the boulevard.

I was fascinated by the way the guys and girls were dressed. The girls wore miniskirts that were so short you could almost see their underwear. They wore lots of makeup and their hair bouffant style. The guys were dressed in two different styles. Some wore the *Cholo* uniform of Khakis, Pendleton, and French-toed shoes, while others wore the uniform of the Ivy Leaguer, which consisted of slacks, plaid shirt, and Florsheim shoes.

Suddenly I heard someone yell out my name. I looked around trying to see who was calling me and spotted my brother-in-law Vek coming toward us.

"What are you guys doing here?" Vek asked, stunned to see us.

"We decided to visit you guys," I replied smiling broadly.

"But how did you end up here," he asked pointing to the spot we were standing on.

"Well, you know how it is," I said pointing to the side of my head. "When you got it, you got it."

He shook his head.

"Come on. Your sister's going to be even more shocked than me to see you when we get to the house."

We followed him into a liquor store where he bought himself a "Short-Dog" (a small bottle of Thunderbird Wine) and two sodas for us. We then headed to the apartment where Vek and Dee lived.

"What are you doing here, Jesse?" she asked, completely bowled over to see me.

"I decided to leave home and find out what it's like to live in the big city," I said, smiling brightly trying to lighten the tension.

"You know I have to call your mom. She'll be worried about you."

"Come on, Dee. Don't do that. Let me stay for a few days before I have to go back to Woodlake. Okay?"

Dee didn't call my mom that night. But the next morning she told them I was at her house. My folks and Gibby's Mom drove to L.A. to retrieve us. As Father drove back to Woodlake, Gibby's mom told him I wasn't welcome at their house anymore.

As soon as we got back, Mama turned me over to the cops, and I was placed in Juvenile Hall for three days. I didn't mind. I figured it was all part of what was supposed to happen. The Hall was a little dull, but I met guys who were doing the same things I was. They were looking for a reputation and wanted to become *Vato Locos*. I was impressed with how these guys seemed to know their purpose in life. In a strange way, going to the Hall and meeting these guys validated that I was on the right path and let me know that if I wanted to become a true gangster I would need to continue the course I was on.

I met guys from other *barrios* who were just like me, and walked around with their chest out, their shoulders back, head held high, believing that the world took them seriously. The guys at the Hall treated each other with respect, saying "excuse me" quickly whenever they crossed each other's path, or bumped into one another accidentally. They paid one another recognition by nodding whenever they encountered each other in the dayroom. It was an unspoken rule that to get respect, you gave respect, unless you were ready to fight.

When I was released, I returned to school. *Palio* told me *Pato* had been arrested for armed robbery. It was upsetting to hear *Pato* was in jail, but I knew going to jail was part of our lifestyle. *Pato* getting arrested gave me the opportunity to meet Big *Indio,* the number one *Vato Loco* of the *barrio.*

Big *Indio* had just finished serving twelve years in Folsom State Prison. He had been out about two weeks when I convinced Jackie into taking me to his house so I could see Big *Indio* up close and maybe even meet him.

"Come on Jackie; let's go to your house. You know I've wanted to meet your uncle ever since I was a little kid."

"Okay, but you have to promise to keep quiet. My uncle doesn't like anyone bothering him, and I don't want him mad at me."

I readily agreed and we sped off to his house. I was thrilled at the prospect of meeting the guy everyone talked so much about. The kind of man I wanted to emulate.

Big *Indio* was all I expected him to be. He was tall. Had big arms with wide shoulders and a huge chest from working out with weights while he had been in Folsom. His complexion was bronze colored and he had the darkest, most intense brown eyes I had ever seen. He sported a bushy mustache, with thick, shiny, black hair combed straight back. Big *Indio* was shirtless, and I could see that his entire upper body was covered with the most magnificent and elaborate tattoos I had ever seen. He reminded me of an Aztec Warrior I had seen in a picture book in the school library.

As I studied him, I took note of how he stood with his shoulders squared and his chin out as if he was ready for battle. His whole persona conveyed strength, courage, and self-assurance. I clearly saw why everyone from the *barrio* feared and listened to him when he spoke. He was an imposing figure.

Checking out Big *Indio* iron his pants was an educational experience too. I had never seen anyone take so much time to make sure every crease was razor sharp. I saw how he subtly glanced my way without looking directly at me.

Suddenly, Big *Indio* called me, "Come here, little *vato.*"

"Who me?"

"*Simón, Ese.*"

I strolled over to Big *Indio* with my ego as big as a house.

"What's your name?"

"My name is Jesse, but everyone calls me *Dragón,*" I said, flexing my chest. Big *Indio* smiled at my gesture.

"You know who I am?"

"Of course I know who you are. Everybody knows who you are," I said with open admiration.

"Well, pay close attention to what I'm about to tell you little *vato*. Don't ever trust the White or Black Man," he barked harshly. "Always stick with your *Raza*. In the penitentiary we are at war against those people. You gotta watch your back because *Gabachos* and *Mayates* usually come smiling in your face trying to get close to you so they can take you out. You hear me, *Dragón*?" he said forcefully.

I simply nodded.

I didn't really understand what he was talking about, but since I already knew White people, especially those with money, were treated better than Mexicans, what Big *Indio* told me that day simply gave me confirmation that they were the enemy. I'd never had any type of interaction with Black people up to this point. There were no Blacks in Woodlake and the only time I had actually seen them was during the Watts riots on TV and when I had run off to L.A. with Gibby. Nevertheless, Big *Indio* said they couldn't be trusted either so as far as I was concerned they were on the bad people list just like Whites.

Not long after I met him, Big *Indio* began to educate me about the penitentiary. He trained me on the aspects of doing time. He told me about what I should expect once I got to prison. Everything he said fascinated me and I couldn't wait to find out if I would be just as cunning and fierce as he seemed to be. I spent hours with Big *Indio*. Most of the time no one in my family knew what I was up to or that I was being taught about life on the inside by Big *Indio*. If anyone knew they never said anything. I valued Big *Indio*'s teachings to the fullest and trusted his opinion without question. I considered him a much better instructor than the boring old fools at school. Besides, the information Big *Indio* taught me was much more relevant to the type of life I intended to live than the dull material I was being taught in school. What did I care about some guy sailing across the Atlantic Ocean and discovering America? None of that stuff meant anything to me. I wouldn't be able to use that information once I got to prison.

Besides, I didn't like school for a number of reasons. Teachers often told me I was nothing more than a dumb troublemaker and whenever I misbehaved, they would make me sit at the back of the room facing the wall. I would get angry because it made me feel as though they were trying to break me down so the more they punished me the more I rebelled. A couple of times I got whacked on my butt with a hard wood paddle, but I put a stop to that practice once I got to the eighth grade.

Mr. King, my eighth grade teacher, was a fat, bald, bushy-browed man with a perpetual scowl on his face. He was constantly on my case, always trying to humiliate me in front of my classmates. On a couple of occasions he swatted me with a paddle that had been made for him by the students in woodshop class. The paddle had holes in it so that his swing wouldn't be impeded by the air as he brought the paddle down. This allowed him to smack the recipient of his swats harder. On the third time he tried to wallop me, I told him I wasn't going to let him hit me anymore.

"I'm not your kid," I said defiantly. "My parents don't even beat me."

"Well maybe they should. And if you're not going to follow my instructions, go report to the principal's office."

The principal sent me home for the day and told me I had to bring a note from Mama indicating she was aware about my conduct before I could come back to school. I wanted to tell the principal that I didn't care what I had to do, but I was not ever going to let Mr. King or any other teacher hit me again, but I didn't say anything and left his office mad as could be.

When Mama got home from work late that evening, I told her that I had been sent home because I had refused to let the teacher spank me.

"You can get mad at me for not obeying the teacher Mama, but I'm not going to let anyone hit me," I said angrily.

I could tell that Mama got angry because her complexion turned red, but she held back her anger. She just said I had done the right thing by not letting them hit me and told Dee to write a note to the Principal that let him know she would make sure I wouldn't misbehave in school anymore. I went back to school with the note the following day. After my defiance, Mr. King never tried to put his hands on me again.

A few weeks later my entire class went on a field trip.

"Okay, class, listen up," Mr. King said. "As all of you know, we're taking a field trip into Visalia today. We're going to visit the Tulare County Jail so you kids can get a better understanding about how our judicial system works."

All the while Mr. King was giving me a piercing look. It was clear he was directing his comments toward me. I didn't care. I wasn't afraid. And to show him that I was not intimidated, I stared back boldly.

Everyone climbed on board the school buses parked out in front of the school. I sat next to the window. As we traveled down Freeway 198 toward Visalia, I saw a crew of people on ladders propped up against orange trees harvesting the fruit just like my parents did. I knew picking oranges was hard work. I had done it myself and it always wore me out. I could only imagine how tired those people were having to pick fruit day in and day out. It always depressed me to think about how hard my parents and people like them had to work just to survive so I turned my thoughts to other things.

I wondered why grownups were always trying to deceive us youngsters about what was going on. They never meant what they said and never said what they meant. Mr. King's crap about this trip being set up to teach us about our judicial system was a prime example. This wasn't a civics lesson at all. I believed this outing had been set up to scare kids like me into obeying the law because I was already getting into trouble.

I had already appeared before a Juvenile Judge who had deemed me out of parental control and placed me on probation for taking off to Los Angeles without permission. As a result, I was being monitored by my probation officer, Mr. Jessup, who checked on me on a weekly basis.

Being on probation was no big deal to me. In fact, I enjoyed all the attention I received from my classmates when I returned to school after my release from Juvenile Hall. Most guys in my class had looked at me with awe when I swaggered into class with my hair freshly cut butch style, a practice used by Juvenile Staff to prevent the spread of head lice. The guys who hung out with me asked how it had been in the Hall. I told them it was cool because I had met guys just like me who didn't like school and didn't let old geezers like Mr. King tell them what to do. Most of my classmates had responded with wonder. There were a few kids who rolled their eyes and made exaggerated faces when I told them it had been all right in the Hall, but none of them expressed disapproval. They knew I would beat them up if they said anything to get me mad. I didn't care what they thought anyway, and as far as I was concerned, they were just a bunch of sissies who thought education was the way out of the neighborhood. But I knew different. The only employment opportunity for anyone like me was working in the fields like my parents and I wasn't going for that.

No way!

When we arrived at the jailhouse, my classmates looked around with eyes and mouths wide open as they listened closely to the police guide explain the daily routine of an inmate confined in the jail. I, on the other hand, felt a sense of excitement. My blood felt as though it rushed through my veins faster, and my chest swelled as we walked along the passageways of the cement tomb. My eyes were wide open with enthusiasm. For some unknown reason, I felt I belonged there. Looking down the dimly lit hallway I saw hands sticking out through the steel bars of the cells. The hands held fragments of mirror. I found out later this was how inmates looked out for the Man so they wouldn't get caught breaking the jailhouse rules.

During the tour, the officer in charge informed us about an inmate's daily routine.

"The only time inmates are released out of their cells is to shower three times a week, to see an occasional visitor on Saturday afternoons, or to appear in court. Otherwise they are in their assigned cells all the time. As you can see, there's a toilet, a sink, and three tables with sixteen stools to accommodate the inmates inside every cell. These cells are self-sufficient. No need to go anywhere."

Just then, someone in one of the cells called out my name. "*Órale Dragon. What's happening, Carnálito?*"

I recognized the voice. It belonged to my homie *Pato* who had been in jail for about a year and was on his way to the penitentiary after being convicted of armed robbery.

"Are these people trying to scare you into going straight, *Carnálito?*"

"*Simón, Ese,*" I replied smoothly. "They're trying."

Some of my classmates gawked at me when they saw that one of the guys in the cells actually knew me.

When we left, some of my classmates said they knew they couldn't handle being confined in a cell like a caged animal day in and day out. But I felt different. I was the only one acknowledged by someone in the jail, and this accolade by my homeboy, in its own twisted way, solidified my belief that I was supposed to end up here and eventually in prison. And I was all right with that prospect.

CHAPTER FIVE

B Y THE TIME I was fifteen, I was already deeply immersed in the criminal lifestyle. I had shot a couple of guys and carried a knife most of the time. I would practice pulling it out and flicking my wrist so the blade would snap open quickly. I had a dummy hung in our backyard and would stick, bob, and weave at it until I learned to use the knife with proficiency. Up to this point I had never stabbed anyone, but I knew I wouldn't hesitate to do so.

One Saturday evening after I had practiced stabbing the dummy, I went inside to get ready for a party being thrown by Carmen and Christina, two sisters from the neighborhood. After taking a shower, I pressed my black slacks, my white long-sleeved shirt, and laid everything out on my bed, including my thin black belt that matched my black French-tipped shoes.

Afterward, I got dressed, slipped on my shoes, put my trusted knife in my pant pocket, and left to meet the guys at Mickey's Drive-In.

Walking downtown to meet the guys I felt excited. I knew they would see I was dressed to impress. As I walked by a large storefront window on the way to Mickey's, I stopped to examine myself and make sure everything was in its proper place. Looking at my reflection I noticed that my body appeared lopsided. It was as though I was looking at myself through one of those distorted mirrors at a circus. I also saw that every time I lifted my foot to take a step; it hung like a wet noodle just like that kid had said when I lived in Lineal Camp. I also noted that I stepped on the side of my foot. I had never really paid attention to how I walked or looked before and staring at my image made me cringe with shame that was immediately transformed into anger.

I picked up a big rock lying on the side of the road, and I threw it hard at the window. The rock smashed into the window, shattering it into small pieces, but the picture of my crooked body remained imprinted in my psyche. I limped home as rapidly as I could with an aching sense of humiliation. Mama was surprised to see me return so quickly. "What happened son?"

"*Sabes qué*, Mama," I replied angrily, "I want you to make an appointment with the doctor first thing Monday morning so he can fix how I walk the way he said he could."

"Okay," Mama replied smiling brightly.

Ever since I had been released from the hospital in Texas back in '57, Mama had taken me to a doctor at least twice a year so my physical condition resulting from the polio could be monitored. When we moved to California, I had been assigned a bone specialist by the name of Dr. David Whalen. He was a tall, lanky man, with thick, bushy eyebrows and a deep, booming voice. He resembled the Frankenstein monster, except that he had a ready smile and was always nice to me. He had told me on several occasions that he could fix my foot.

"Hi, Jesse," Doctor Whalen said when he entered the examination room one morning. "How are, *Señora* De La Cruz?"

I nodded my head, and Mama answered she was fine.

"You know, Jesse," Dr. Whalen continued, "I've been looking at the X-rays of your foot I had you take a few months ago and I think I can fix it so you don't have to wear the brace or walk with such a pronounced limp. I also know I can fix it so you don't step on the side of your foot anymore."

He then turned to Mama and began explaining what needed to be done to "fix it" as he put it. He was talking about surgery. That didn't sound like something I wanted done any time soon. After he finished, Dr. Whalen turned back to me and asked me what I thought.

I thought he was crazy, but I didn't say so.

"Hey, Dr. Whalen, there's nothing wrong with me. I've been this way since I was a kid and I'm used to walking the way I do."

The thought of letting someone cut on me scared the crap out of me. Besides, I still remembered the isolation I had gone through when I had been in the hospital in Texas and I never wanted to feel that loneliness again.

Doctor Whalen smiled.

"Well, whenever you change your mind, I'll make the necessary arrangements to have the surgery done, but the sooner the better."

Not long after, Mama and I left his office.

"You should think about what the doctor said. It'll probably make you walk better," Mama stated.

"But, there's nothing wrong with me Mama," I replied adamantly.

"Okay son. Just think about it."

The Monday after the window incident, Mama called Doctor Whalen and within a week, I was admitted into the hospital. I felt sick to my stomach with fear, but I didn't dare tell anyone I was terrified about the impending operation. Mama always told me that "*Los hombres no llorran.*" And Big *Indio* and *Pato* had drilled into my head that real men never displayed fear. So I couldn't show weakness.

After Mama and Father went home, and I was left alone in my hospital room, I literally shook with apprehension. I tossed and turned until I finally passed out from sheer exhaustion. That night, I dreamt about masked men dressed in green outfits. They had bulging eyes, carried big knives with grotesque sharp blades. In the dream, I ran and ran as the men chased me down the hallway trying to catch me so they could cut my leg off. Finally, with my lungs screaming for air and my legs hurting from the exertion I stopped to catch my second wind. I could see the green men approach me and in a panic I realized I was trapped. Just as they were about to chop my leg off, I was startled into consciousness with a fear so severe it brought tears to my eyes. Not wanting anyone to see me cry, I quickly brushed the tears away and took deep breaths to regain my composure.

Just as I began to regain self-control, a male nurse came into my room to shave my legs. I told the nurse I didn't want my legs shaved, but he said it needed to be done.

I felt like a sissy and dreaded the thought of anyone from the *barrio* finding out I had shed tears and let a man shave my legs. When the nurse finished, he gave me a shot on my butt.

"This will relax you," he said knowingly.

Within a few minutes, the drug took effect and my fear disappeared completely. By the time Mama and Father arrived to visit an hour or so later, I was in a drug-induced euphoria. I lay on my bed with a lopsided smile. Mama reassured me everything would turn out all right.

"I'm not worried, Mama," I bragged. "You know I'm not afraid of anything."

Time sped by, and before too long, it was time to get the show on the road. Two hospital attendants came to transport me to the operating room. They lifted me onto a gurney and wheeled me down the hall into an elevator. When we got to the operating room, they lifted and laid me on a surgical bed. There were tubes and machines everywhere. The huge round light above the surgical bed blinded me and made it difficult for me to see how many people were actually in the room. The people I could see were dressed in green uniforms and had masks covering their faces with only their eyes visible, just like in the dream I'd had the night before. I'm sure I would have shot out of there like a chicken to a corn field if it weren't for the shot I had been given earlier and the courage it had provided me.

"Are you ready, Jesse?" Doctor Whalen asked.

I recognized his deep voice and smiling eyes.

"Hey, Doc. Sure, I'm ready."

An anesthesiologist fit an oxygen mask over my mouth and nose and told me to inhale. He instructed me to take deep breaths and count from one hundred backwards. I counted silently.

One hundred, ninety-nine, ninety eight and then everything went dark.

The next time I opened my eyes I was in excruciating pain. I couldn't remember where I was until I saw Mama and Father. They seemed to be standing far off in the distance. I wanted to tell them to come closer, but my mouth was so dry I couldn't talk. I wanted a drink of water badly. Mama seemed to read my mind and wet my lips with a damp washcloth. She said I couldn't have any water because it would make me sick.

A nurse administered another injection on my hip to ease my pain. I felt the needle prick my skin and instantly fell asleep again. The entire day was spent in and out of consciousness and filled with physical anguish, and narcotic induced nightmares.

On the second day after the operation I felt a lot better. Dr. Whalen explained what he had done to my left ankle and right leg. He said he had fused my bad ankle with two stainless steel rods. He went on to say that once the rods were removed, my left foot would not hang anymore and I would step normal again. I looked down at the stainless steel contraption hooked to the cast on my left ankle. Doctor Whalen went on to explain that he had also made an incision on both sides of my right knee and clipped the nerve that made my leg grow. This was done so my good leg would quit growing and give my bad leg a chance to catch up. He said it wouldn't eliminate my limp completely, but my limp wouldn't be so noticeable within a few years. His explanation sounded a little confusing to me, but Doctor Whalen was excited and seemed sure that I would be able to walk much better as I got older.

A week later, I was released from the hospital. I had casts on both legs and was stuck in a wheelchair for the next sixty days. Being confined to a wheelchair was frustrating, but my friends tried to make life on the chair easier for me. Sometimes Chris or one of the other guys would push the wheel chair as fast as they could down the steep hill on Antelope Street and release me. I would go flying past the growling dogs, the junked cars, and often wind up in the canal next to my house. It was always an exhilarating ride. Luckily for me there wasn't any water in the canal at that time. Chris always came to my rescue and helped me back onto the chair.

I was on the wheelchair until the cast on my right leg was removed. The steel rods were removed from my left ankle at that time too. When Dr. Whalen took the rods out, he used an electric saw to cut the cast. Once it was off, he sprayed a red solution around the entry areas where the rods were implanted and with a smile on his face asked me if I was ready.

I was scared to death!

But I didn't say anything. Instead, I smiled and told him to go ahead. He gave me one of his warm smiles and using a pair of stainless steel pliers quickly pulled one rod out and then the other. The rods came out smoothly and didn't hurt at all. He put a new cast on my ankle. I walked on crutches for six months.

Two weeks after he removed the cast off my left ankle, I got involved in a game of "King of the Mountain" with some of the guys from the neighborhood. Carra, a guy who weighed well over three hundred pounds, fell on my left foot and broke it. I heard it crack when he fell on it and the pain was agonizing. I sat on the mat grimacing until Mama came to take me to the hospital emergency room. Dr. Whalen was called to the emergency room so he could put another cast on my ankle. I could tell he was upset with me because I had put myself in harm's way, but he didn't get on me about it. He just said I would to have to wear a cast for another six months. When the cast was finally taken off a year after the operation, I had to go through physical therapy so I could learn how to walk again. During my therapy session, I noticed that if I dipped my left hip when I took a step my limp wasn't as obvious. From that moment on, I created a new stroll that I thought made me look cool.

When I got home that day, I went straight to the bathroom, took off my pants and took a hard look at my lower body. I saw that my left leg was still thinner than the other, but my left foot no longer hung like it did before the operation and that I could step on my foot regularly and not on its side. I was satisfied with the outcome.

IT HAD BEEN a smoldering day with the temperature rising above 100 degrees. I had stayed inside my house all day, but once the sun set, a slight breeze had kicked in, and the evening turned into a perfect occasion to go hang out with the guys at the river. Big *Indio* picked me up and we went to Rocky Fort River. The river had gotten its name because it was surrounded by huge walls of rock and dirt that gave it a fort like appearance. Everyone from the neighborhood went to Rocky Fort to cool off on hot days. The water that flowed swiftly down from the snowcapped Sierra Nevada Mountains was cold, clean, and clear.

After Big *Indio* picked me up, we swung by Chipmunk's house to gather

"Be still you old bastard or I'll cut your throat," I told the man as I searched his pockets.

In the next instant, he hit me with his elbow solidly on my mouth. The blow jarred me. I instinctively stuck him. I heard him groan as the blade penetrated his neck and blood immediately poured out of the wound. He grabbed his throat in an attempt to stop the bleeding. I had never heard anything like the gurgling sound that came out of the victim after I stuck him. I saw his lips move as he tried to say something, but nothing came out except a hissing sound from the puncture in his neck. He dropped to his knees and for a brief moment looked at me panic-stricken. Displaying no mercy, I shoved him into the swiftly moving water of the river. The last thing I saw were his arms flailing about as the current carried him rapidly downstream.

The other man lay on the ground unconscious from the blow Big *Indio* had delivered to his jaw. I saw Big *Indio* relieve the man of his wallet. I had forgotten all about Chipmunk, but then I saw him standing in the background. He was next to the car with his mouth gaped open as though he was terrified about what had just happened. He hadn't done anything to help. Big *Indio* shot him a cold stare.

"Get in the car and don't say a damn thing. I'll talk to you about this tomorrow."

Chipmunk nodded and slunk into the backseat. He didn't say a word as we drove back to the *barrio*.

"Damn, *Dragón*," Big *Indio* said. "I sure hope you didn't kill that old buzzard. I mean, if he doesn't die from the hole in his neck, he'll probably drown."

"Hey, *Ese*. That punk hit me on my mouth. I had to stab him."

"That's bullshit," Big *Indio* laughed. "You know you were waiting to hurt those two fools all night long."

"Yeah," I replied, sheepishly. "But they had it coming for driving into our party uninvited."

Generally speaking, guys involved in the criminal lifestyle didn't hurt civilians, but these two men had infringed on our party. I convinced myself that I had done the right thing; that I hadn't gone looking for them; they had come on their own free will. By my way of thinking, they deserved what they had gotten for being stupid.

We drove into town using the back streets so as not to arouse suspicion. I wasn't worried about the guy dying. I had accepted violence as part of my lifestyle and going to Juvenile Hall wasn't anything I found frightening. Of course, we weren't just going to let the police arrest us either. It was all part of the game. The police tried to catch us, and we tried to get away.

As we drove into town I thought about what had just happened. I understood this was only the beginning of my serious criminal career and that in order to become a real gangster, I would have to do much more than what I had done tonight. I didn't have any doubt I would end up in prison and by now I also understood that going to prison wouldn't give me real recognition as a gangster; it was coming back to the neighborhood that would elevate me to true mobster status. I remembered how everyone showered Big Indio with respect after he had returned to the 'hood' after serving time in Folsom State Prison. I had seen people move out of his way when he walked down the sidewalk and had heard about the big welcome home party that had been thrown in his honor by the guys in the barrio. Someone told me he had shown up to the party with Thelma, a stunning, statuesque lady who had been waiting for Big Indio ever since he went away twelve years before. I had seen Thelma a few times during the time Big Indio was gone, but those times had been rare. She seldom went anywhere. It was like Thelma was serving time with Big Indio.

We pulled up to Chipmunk's house and dropped him off. Big Indio told him he would talk to him later about not doing anything to help out at the river. Chipmunk hung his head and walked inside his house. Big Indio drove off and told me Chipmunk was weak.

"He will never become one of us," he said.

Suddenly, as Big Indio maneuvered his car around a sharp curve, we were cut off by two police cars blocking our path. Big Indio slammed the brakes. The red lights on top of the police cars flashed round and round, and before we had a chance to react, the cops had us completely surrounded. Every headlight and spotlight on each police car was aimed in our direction, blinding us like deer on a dark road. I made out the silhouettes of policemen crouched behind their cars with guns pointed toward us. I couldn't tell how many policemen were on the spot, but they seemed to be everywhere. A cop yelled for us to slide out of the car with our hands raised high over our heads. We did exactly as instructed. Before long I felt the cold steel of handcuffs on my wrists as an officer snapped them on tightly, cutting off the circulation in my hands. Big Indio whispered for me to keep my mouth shut about what had happened at the river. I looked at him with complete disbelief and wondered why he thought I couldn't keep quiet about what had just happened. Besides, I was the one who had stuck the man and I surely wasn't going to snitch on myself.

As Big Indio and I were placed into separate police cars, I wondered how the police had found out so quickly about what had occurred at the river. I never did find out how they learned it was us.

Once we got to the police station, the interrogation started. Almost immediately Chief Mayfield leaned in on me with his persuasion tactics trying to trick me into telling on myself. He found out soon enough he couldn't fool me into talking. I simply didn't say anything.

"You know, Jess," Chief Mayfield said, "I knew you would hurt someone someday. Lucky for you, the man didn't die. But if you don't quit hanging out with these guys, you're going to get into serious trouble and wind up in prison some day."

I didn't respond. I knew he was trying to engage me in conversation so he could get evidence to use against me in court. I wasn't going for the okey-doke. Mayfield was going to have to look elsewhere for a statement. He surely wasn't getting anything from me.

"So what do you have to say for yourself?"

"I don't have anything to say. It's really very simple, either you let me go, or lock me up."

"Okay," he replied angrily. "If that's the way you want it, that's the way it's going to be. I'll have Curtis take you into Visalia and book you into Juvenile Hall."

I shrugged.

"Curtis, take Jess here to Visalia and book him."

Curtis nodded and motioned me to stand up. Curtis was a tall, lumbering cop with a peanut for brains. Everyone from the *barrio* called him Muldoon after a police character from a popular sitcom of the time called "Car 54 Where Are You." The show chronicled two dimwitted cops who blundered through every episode, but somehow their slipups always turned out for the good. Curtis wasn't slipping on this day. He efficiently frisked me for any contraband, escorted me to a waiting police car, and shoved me inside. Within a matter of seconds we were on our way to Visalia so I could be deposited into the hands of Juvenile Authorities. I didn't see Big *Indio*, but I found out later he was taken to the county jail and booked on suspicion of assault and robbery. Three days later, he was released because the man from the river identified me as the person who had assaulted and robbed him.

Driving down the highway, I worried a little about the reception I would receive from the guys at the Hall because the majority of them were from Visalia and our neighborhoods had been at war with each other for a long time. I had heard through the *barrio* grapevine that the guys from Visalia wanted to hurt me bad. They were still mad because I had shot a couple of guys from their *barrio* a few years before. I was nervous because I wouldn't have a weapon at my disposal and realized this would be the perfect place for them to get me. I made up my mind that I would make them earn whatever they got from me. Nothing was free. I would represent my *barrio* no matter what the odds.

One day, during one of our many sessions, Big *Indio* had told me that anyone could act tough when they were in a group, but that the test of a man was how he handled himself when he was alone.

"That's what separates real gangsters from the phonies," he said. "It's okay to be afraid, but don't let fear paralyze you. Use it to keep you on your toes."

It was a little confusing, but in the end, Big *Indio* had done his job. He had drilled into my consciousness what needed to be done when I got arrested. I had a hunch Juvenile Hall was going to change me in a big way.

Before long, we were at the double-gated entrance of the Hall. It was an old red brick building set in the middle of a large grassy area surrounded by a tall fence with barbed wire wrapped around the top. Curtis identified himself to someone at the other end of a speaker located at the entrance of the main gate. I heard a series of clicks and hums as the gate automatically opened. Curtis drove the car into the sally port. Once inside the gated area, he let me out of the car and talked into another speaker by a large steel door. There was a loud buzz and Curtis pulled the steel handle on the door and motioned me to step inside. I walked in and he slammed the door shut. I had been here once before briefly, but I hadn't noticed the clanging of the door shutting with such finality.

Curtis and I walked through another two doors before reaching the booking area. When we got there, Curtis and a guy behind the counter with flaming red hair and freckles covering his entire face and arms exchanged greetings. Curtis signed some documents, un-cuffed me, and turned me over to the custody of Juvenile Authorities and left.

"When was the last time you were here, De La Cruz?" Riptoe, the guy behind the counter, asked.

"About two years ago."

He pulled a thin file from a huge row of cabinets located against the wall.

"You weren't here very long then. It looks like you're going to be with us for a while longer this time."

I didn't respond.

He then began the arduous booking process. He asked me where I was born, my age, next of kin, etc.

Afterward, Riptoe escorted me to a shower room with five spigots and told me to jump in. I was embarrassed to let another man see me naked, but it was part of the routine, so I got undressed and got into the shower without complaint. Riptoe gathered my personal clothing and put them in a large plastic bag. My clothes were then placed inside the property room for safekeeping until I was released.

"I'll be back to spray you with head lice medicine and bring you some clothes and bedding. What size of pants you wear?"

"Hey, man. I don't have any bugs."

"I'm not saying you do, but I have to spray you anyway. So let's get it done and don't give me any lip. What size pants do you wear?"

"2626."

I had just finished showering when Riptoe returned with a strange looking apparatus resembling a paint hose. The kind used to paint cars.

"Close your eyes," Riptoe instructed.

He then sprayed me with a nauseous smelling liquid. No wonder this stuff killed bugs. The stench was awful.

"Make sure you wipe the liquid off your face. It burns really bad if it gets into your eyes," he said after spraying me. "Here are your clothes."

I scrubbed my hair with a towel trying to get rid of the dreadful odor, but the smell clung to me like a bad habit. After getting dressed, Riptoe escorted me down a dimly lit hall to my cell. He stuck a brass key in the lock mechanism, turned it, and unlocked the heavy steel door. It squeaked as it opened.

The cell was designed to hold four guys and although it was semi-dark, I could see the outline of bodies on three of the beds. One of the guys was awake. It looked as though he had been waiting for us.

"Hey, Dreamy," Riptoe said. "This is the guy I told you about. He'll be staying with us until the courts determine what they're going to do with him. You know the routine. Give him the head-sup, and explain the rules so he doesn't get into any more trouble, okay?"

"Yeah, all right Riptoe," Dreamy answered.

With that, Riptoe turned, slammed the door shut, and locked it in one swift motion. I walked over to the empty upper bunk and climbed up.

"Where you from, *Ese?*" Dreamy asked.

"I'm from Woodlake. Everybody calls me *Dragón.*"

"*Órale.* I've heard of you. That's Spunky on the bottom bunk," he said pointing to a kid sleeping on the lower bunk next to his. "*Lóngo* is next to you. You'll meet them tomorrow. It's late now so we better get some sleep."

I laid my head on the pillow and immediately fell into an effortless sleep. The following morning I awoke to the sound of loud music coming from somewhere down the corridor. At first I didn't remember where I was, but then it came to me. I was in the Hall. The guys in my cell were jumping out of bed and getting dressed. I climbed off my bed and followed suit. No one said anything to me, so I didn't talk either.

I heard doors being unlocked and soon our door was opened too. Everyone stepped out and I followed my cellmates into a big recreation room. I copped a spot against a wall in order to keep an eye on everyone in the dayroom. As I surveyed my surroundings, I noticed two guys staring in my direction giving me dirty looks. They looked like twins and were ugly to the point of being repulsive. Their complexion was dark, dull, ashy, and they had a bad case of acne. But what made them so unattractive were their eyes. They held no light, no humor, and they were sunk deep into their sockets with huge black rings around them. Something told me these two would be giving me a mess of trouble. The thought of having to fight them both worried me for a brief moment, but I pushed my anxiety deep inside. I knew I could handle myself in a scrap and up to this point I had never lost a fight. If these guys wanted to brawl, I would not disappoint them. I would use them to establish my reputation as someone not to be messed with.

Aretha Franklin's latest hit "Respect" was playing loudly in the background as the two guys approached me. I stood up and felt my blood begin to pump faster as they got closer.

"Where you from, *Ese?*" the uglier of the two asked.

"I'm *Dragón, Ese.* I'm from Woodlake. Who wants to know?" I asked, puffing up my chest and balling up my fists ready to fight.

"You talk like a big shot, *Ese,*" he replied.

I didn't respond with words. Instead, I socked him in the mouth, catching him completely by surprise and knocking him flat on his back. Rapidly, I turned to the other guy and began punching him before he had a chance to react. I pinned him against the wall and kept swinging until I was tackled to the ground by a couple of staff members. I heard someone say, "That guy's crazy."

As I lay on the floor, I scrutinized the room and saw that everyone had gotten the message I was someone they didn't want any trouble with. I didn't struggle with the two workers as they carried me to the far end of the Hall like a twisted pretzel. Once there, another staff member opened a cell door and I was carried inside. They placed me on the cement floor and slammed the door shut leaving me in complete darkness. I lay still with my heart pounding wildly, waiting for my eyes to get accustomed to the darkness. After a few seconds my eyes adjusted and I distinguished the outline of a bed in front of me. I reached for it like a blind man. I stood up and sat on the steel bed. I noted that the only light in the cell came from a window that had been covered by steel plates to keep the cell pitch black, but small slivers of light snuck their way in through cracks that hadn't been completely covered. I vaguely made the outline of a toilet and sink against another wall. And then I heard a rustling noise come from underneath the bed. Hastily, I lifted my feet off the floor and placed them on the bed.

Damn, there's a fucking rat in here!

I wanted to beg the staff to let me out of that dark cell, but I knew I couldn't whine or show fear, especially of a small rat. Everyone in the hall would clown me for sure if I did that. I sat on the bed with my legs pressed against my chest, taking deep gasps of air as I tried to calm myself. It took a few minutes before I regained my composure, but I finally controlled my panic. Afterward, I decided to lie on the steel plate bed even though there was no mattress, blankets, or sheets. As I lay, I thought about the events that had just taken place. I believed I had done the right thing by beating those two guys. I hadn't been the one to start the fight. I had only finished it. It wasn't me who had tried to push his weight around.

A couple of hours later, the door to my cell swung open and the light streaming in temporarily blinded me.

"What the hell you doing, De La Cruz?" Riptoe asked. "You haven't been here twenty-four hours and already you're in isolation."

I didn't respond.

"Well, you might as well know from the start, this type of behavior will cost you ten days in the Dark Room," he said.

I shrugged my shoulders and he slammed the door shut, leaving me in darkness again.

I don't give a shit my mind screamed! I'll stay here as long as I have to, but I won't let anyone disrespect me.

The only time I was allowed out of my cell during my entire ten-day stay in the Dark Room was to shower on three different occasions. Apart from that, I ate, slept, defecated, and pissed in my cell. At breakfast, lunch, and dinner, someone would open the slot on the steel door and slip me a tray of food. When I finished eating, I would slide the tray under the door, and the hand would pick it up. I gave the person that name because all I could see was his hand.

Throughout the ten days I spent in the Dark Room, I was kept incommunicado and the silence drove me crazy. There was nothing to do but sit in darkness and think all day. I would get incensed when I thought about Ugly Face and his brother and used my anger to maintain my sanity. Rage kept me from crying out in desperation and pleading to be released into the main population.

I stayed in darkness day in and day out, and as I did, I got angrier and angrier. I let my vehemence consume me to the point that it didn't matter how long they kept me in the Dark Room. By the tenth day I was fuming at those two ugly punks for pushing me into jumping them. I decided to make them pay even if I had to stay in the Dark Room the whole time I was in the Hall.

When they finally let me out, it took a few seconds for my eyes to adjust to the bright lights in the hallway. I strolled into the recreation room as everyone was lining up for the short walk into the dining hall. All heads turned to catch my entry as I strutted into the room. I was the talk of the Hall that morning, but my reputation was about to balloon even more with what I was about to do next.

"There's that crazy guy from Woodlake," someone in the crowd said.

"Did you see how he socked homeboy?" said another.

I felt uneasy about what I had planned, but I didn't let my nervousness show. I examined the area briefly, searching for Ugly Face and his brother. I spotted them standing in a corner like two scared rats. As nonchalantly as I possibly could, I followed everyone's lead. I got in line making sure I didn't get too close or too far from Ugly Face and his brother. Walking through the breakfast line, I got a steel tray, heaped some scrambled powdered eggs, hash browns, a couple of pieces of white toast on it, and sat down. The seating arrangement worked out fine. Ugly face and his brother were seated across from me, which would make it easier to make my move on them when the time came.

Every table had two heavy stainless steel pitchers that contained cold milk and fresh squeezed orange juice. After all, we were living in the orange capital of the nation. I hurriedly wolfed down my food, knowing I would be back in the Dark Room within a matter of minutes. Ugly Face made eye contact with me for a split second and I saw fear in his eyes. I turned away quickly, not wanting to give him any sign about my next move.

As soon as he took his eyes off of me, I grabbed one of the stainless steel pitchers and hit him on the head with it as hard as I could. The thumping sound of the pitcher connecting with his head caught everyone off guard. He didn't have a chance to react and I hit him again before he hit the floor unconscious. Without hesitation, I rushed his brother and beat him with the pitcher like I owned him. He tried to get away, but there wasn't any place for him to go. He lifted his arms to defend himself and screamed as I continued to hit him with the pitcher. His shrieks spurred me on. I felt bursts of adrenalin rush through my body as I continued to strike him over and over. In a matter of seconds I finished the job and both brothers were laid out on the floor. One was out cold with blood oozing from a wound on his head, while the other writhed in pain against a wall. I scanned the mess hall with a crazed look and knew nobody would challenge me any time soon. In the meantime, I had to pay the price.

"Put that pitcher down, De La Cruz," Riptoe commanded.

The pitcher clanged loudly when it hit the cement floor. Riptoe and another staff member had been at a table located at the farthest corner of the dining hall when I jumped the two guys. This had given me plenty of time to beat those two bullies. None of the staff jumped on me this time, and without further instructions, I began walking toward the Dark Room. I didn't care. Beating Ugly Face and his brother made me feel good. They were nothing more than a couple of wannabe tough guys without any courage trying to take advantage of anyone who would let them. They had made a mistake when they chose to pick on me.

For the next few days in isolation, I replayed what I had done to those two guys in my mind. I found comfort in remembering how the guys had looked at me when I had made my entrance into the center complex after being released from the Dark Room. It felt even better when I remembered the look of utter admiration the guys had on their faces after I beat Ugly Face and his brother with the pitcher.

During the next few days, I did a lot of thinking regarding the things Big *Indio* taught me about serving time. It was reassuring to know I would eventually have a reputation as solid as Big *Indio's*. I would fall asleep dreaming of the day when I would get back to the *barrio*. I thought about the reception I would receive from my homeboys and believed the Homies would think highly of me for standing up for the neighborhood even though I didn't have any back up.

On the fourteenth day of isolation, Riptoe came to see me. He offered me a deal that took me by surprise.

"Listen, De La Cruz," he said. "If you promise to behave and not jump on anyone else while you're here, I will let you out of isolation today and house you in the Big Tank."

The Big Tank housed fourteen guys and was the best place to do time in the Hall. The guys housed there could watch TV until eleven o'clock every night or play chess, dominos, cards, or other games to pass time.

"Well," I replied cautiously. "It sounds good, but why are you being so nice? I mean, what do you expect from me?" I asked suspiciously.

"I don't expect anything except that you don't cause any more trouble."

"Okay, but if someone gets out of line with me, I'm not going to back down."

"That sounds reasonable. So, we have a deal?" he asked, extending his hand so we could shake.

"Okay," I answered, as I clasped his hand.

I moved into the Big Tank later that day, and everything went well for the rest of my stay at the Hall. Ugly Face had been shipped off to the California Youth Authority, and his brother had been released onto the streets. My reputation as a tough guy was rock solid, and before long I was sentenced to Boys Camp, a microcosm of the penitentiary. I was there for a year. During my incarceration, I developed relationships with guys from other *barrios*. Many of the guys serving time at Boys Camp would end up in prison just like me. I would run into them occasionally as we traveled down our individual journeys of confinement. Boys Camp was the beginning of the criminal justice system taking control of my life and moving me like a pawn from one institution to another for the next thirty years.

Boys Camp was situated on the outskirts of Visalia in the middle of no-man's land with open space for as far as the eye could see. The dorm we lived in held eighty-two wards from different *barrios* in Tulare and Kings County. It was located in the heart of the complex, which consisted of educational classrooms, vocational shops, a Laundromat, counseling offices, and a huge dining room.

As soon as I arrived at the Camp, I was approached by a guy who thought he was a big shot. I knew the guy because he had lived in my *barrio* before he was arrested.

At the camp everyone called Tomas "Chicken Man." He got the nickname because he was suspected of having sex with chickens while working on the farm detail. Suspicion had been cast on him when staff had found a number of dead chickens with their anuses ruptured as if someone had stuck something into them. Although it was never proven that Chicken Man was the culprit, he was never allowed to go near the farm animals without staff supervision again and Staff never found any more dead chickens after he was relieved of his post, either.

"Where you from, *Ese?*" he asked, in his best tough guy voice.

I tensed up, clenched my teeth, and stared at him with my eyes fixed, focused, and unblinking.

"Don't act stupid, *Ese.* You know who I am, man."

Chicken Man was about to reply when a tall, lanky guy cut him off. The guy must have been six feet four inches tall. He had a large hooked nose and the biggest hands I had ever seen. He was shirtless, and every muscle on his upper body was clearly defined. It looked as though he had been lifting weights for some time.

"Hey, punk," he told Chicken Man. "I already warned you about trying to get tough with the guys coming in. You want me to kick your ass in front of everybody?"

"No, *Poncho,*" Chicken Man sputtered meekly.

"Then get your stupid ass out my sight before I embarrass you some more," *Poncho* commanded.

"*Oralé, Ese,*" the tall guy said to me as he stuck his hand out so we could shake. "I'm *Poncho.* Don't pay any attention to that *pendejo.* He's always trying to impress someone with his tough guy crap. He's nothing but a candy ass."

"I heard that," I replied. "I'm *Dragón.*"

Chicken Man had to be a coward. Had anyone talked to me in the manner *Poncho* had talked to him, I would have tried to kick his ass no matter how big they were. Chicken Man didn't do anything but cower down. He was pathetic. Afterward, he stayed away from me, and I settled in to serve my time.

Life at the Camp wasn't so bad. Every morning we were awakened to the sound of the Temptations Greatest Hits. My favorite song was "The Way You Do the Things You Do." I loved it. That song always put me in good spirits and made me want to dance.

During the week every ward went to school half a day and worked the other half. On Saturdays we were given the day off and Sundays was visiting day. Every Sunday Mama, Father, my younger brothers, Ramiro, Johnny, Ernesto, Tingo, and my sister Gracie would come visit me. Mama always brought fried chicken, rice, cold sodas, and plenty of her homemade flour tortillas for me to eat. I missed her tortillas and always grubbed on as many of them as I could when my family came to visit. I never had so much time devoted to me by my parents as when I was at Boys Camp. All the attention I got from Mama on Sundays made me feel extra special.

Poncho and I became close friends after the incident with Chicken Man and spent lots of time hanging out. He arranged for me to work on the irrigation crew with him. During the spring of '68, when the corn was tall, we spent many nights under the star-filled sky making sure the water didn't overflow. We would sit around talking about what we were going to do once we were released.

"*Sabes que, Dragón,*" *Poncho* said, one evening as we sat keeping watch on the water. "I was going to get out and immediately take care of some dude from the *barrio* who tackled me for the cops when I was trying to get away from them. That's why I'm here. Can you believe it? Sometimes, when I think about what he did, I can't wait to kill his ass."

"You're bullshitting, right?" I asked seriously.

"Naw man, he really did. I had just jumped over the fence surrounding his yard when he comes running out of his house and tackles me to the ground. I couldn't believe it. But it's cool. I'm going let him think everything's forgotten. Let him believe I'm not going to do anything. Then I'm going to get him, but I'm going to wait until after you get out. I want to party with you at least one time before I kill that rat," *Poncho* said.

"*Oralé, Carnál,*" I answered, looking at *Poncho* with total admiration.

A few weeks later *Poncho* was released. I walked him to the release area where we shook hands.

"Remember, *Dragón,* I'll pick you up when you get out so we can party," he said smiling.

"*Simón, Ese.* I'll catch you on the rebound."

I missed my friend, but I stayed busy and the two months I had left flew by. *Poncho* picked me up on the evening of my release just as he had promised. There were two other guys from his neighborhood with him when he drove up to my house in his 1954 Chevy.

"This is *Dragón,*" he told them.

I shook hands with the guys and we cruised in *Poncho's* '54 Chevy drinking beer until the following morning. When it was time to go, *Poncho* shook my hand. "I'll see you when you get to the penitentiary," he said ruefully.

"*Oralé.*" I didn't find his remark strange. It had always been a given that I would get there. It was just a matter of time.

That evening, *Poncho* shot and killed the guy who had tackled and got him sent to Boys Camp. Wow, I thought when I heard about the killing—*Poncho* was a man of his word.

I ran into *Poncho* about twenty years later at the age of forty. He had re-cently been released from Oregon State Prison after serving sixteen years out of a twenty-year prison sentence. I had just gotten out of prison for the third time myself. It became apparent that we no longer had a close connection to each other. Too much had happened in our lives. Both of us were now addicted to heroin and had become suspicious of everything and everyone after being exposed to the deception, treachery, and manipulation which came hand in hand with the criminal lifestyle. We had both learned that friendships and brotherly love didn't exist in the world of drug addiction and crime. Making money by any means necessary to feed the heroin habit we had acquired had become the driving force for everything we did, and nothing else mattered.

CHAPTER SIX

IN THE SUMMER OF '69 America was in complete social chaos. Conflict raged in Vietnam and Americans were disgusted with the country's political leadership. People wanted change. Antiwar demonstrations were being held throughout the nation. In 1965 Americans witnessed violent scenes splashed on their television screens during the Watts riots, which lasted six days and nights and left 34 people dead and over 1,000 people injured. There had been approximately 4,000 people arrested, and 600 buildings had been damaged or destroyed.

Many Mexican Americans no longer called themselves Mexicans; they preferred to call themselves Chicanos. Like their Black counterparts, Chicanos were beginning to raise their voice and fight against discrimination, too. In 1965, I went to a meeting held in my *barrio* by the United Farm Workers Union (UFW). My father took me to hear Cesar Chavez, President of the new UFW, speak about standing up against inequality, better working conditions, and increased wages. Chavez spoke into a bullhorn so everyone could hear him clearly. I remember he spoke well, but at the end of Chavez's speech, my Father decided not to get involved with the UFW. Father said that as far as he was concerned everything was fine just the way things were. He said he didn't trust anyone who talked so much about helping people without getting something in return.

"I can't believe he's going to help people for nothing," Father said.

Rich and poor Whites joined the social revolution as well. It was never quite clear to me why White folk got involved with the social problems of the times. I didn't think they had anything to complain about in the first place. Nevertheless, thousands of White people got involved. They came from all over the U.S. and the world. Many of them moved to San Francisco and became hippies. Turning on, tuning in, and dropping out of mainstream society.

Hippies established communes in the Haight-Ashbury District of San Francisco and shared everything, including each other sexually. From what I heard, it was all about "free love" in those places.

I constantly heard the rhetoric being espoused by social radicals. They talked about unity and raising our consciousness concerning the dire conditions in the hood. I didn't believe any of it. As far as I was concerned, their talk didn't mean anything. Nothing had changed in the *barrio*. My parents still worked in the fields like burros with nothing to show for their hard labor.

One day, I was invited by Alex, one of my homeboys, to a demonstration that was to be held at Fresno State University that summer, but I told Alex I wouldn't be caught dead at one of those things.

"*Oralé, Carnál,*" Alex said excitedly. "Let's go to Fresno and get down for the cause."

"What 'cause,' homeboy?" I asked angrily. "That bullshit going on outside the *barrio* isn't our 'cause.' Those people don't give a fuck about us. Shit, I remember when *César Chavez* came to the *barrio* talking that jive about improving working conditions for the farm worker and the only thing I saw he did was create separation. Before he came, everybody got along. After he left, people had to pick sides. Besides, those people don't live in our *barrio*. We do."

"I hear what you're saying. That's why the organizers want to bring awareness to the *barrio*. Help the people understand what's happening, you know. But we have to get involved," Alex countered.

"What the fuck are you talking about? Those people aren't like us. And at the first sign of violence they'll run and leave you holding the bag. They don't know a damn thing about sticking together. I've never seen any of those people do anything to benefit anyone in the neighborhood. You know damn well people only understand one type of language and it's not peace and love. They only understand brute force," I glared at him for believing in those stupid people.

Alex went to the demonstration that day and just as I suspected, he was the only person at the protest who got arrested and sent to prison. I ran into him a few years later when I got to prison too. He told me he had jumped on a cop after the policeman hit him on his head with his baton. Everyone else had run off.

"I should have listened to you."

"Hey, you live and learn," I replied.

In the meantime, I was injecting heroin on a daily basis. I used heroin the first time on New Year's Eve 1966 when I was fifteen years old, and by now, the summer of '69, I found myself addicted without even knowing I was hooked. No one from the barrio knew much about the psychological or physical dependence of heroin. The drug had only recently been introduced into our area by "Old Man Mike," from East Los Angeles. He had smuggled a large quantity of heroin into Visalia and set up a distribution center at his house. A lot of guys from Visalia, including his sons Juan and Ruben, were already hooked on the drug.

Old Man Mike was one hundred percent *Técato*, with bulging eyes with dark round circles, buckteeth, and sunken cheeks. His hair was long and scraggily and he smelled as though he hadn't showered for days. His clothes were crusty and stained from not being washed too. I would have never been around him had I not wanted to buy drugs.

Old Man Mike had served time in San Quentin for selling drugs and often spent hours educating his sons on the aspects of diluting, bagging, and preparing heroin for street distribution. Sometimes I was at their house during his lectures on heroin.

"Remember, Juan," he would tell his son as he carefully cooked the powdered heroin into liquid form so he could inject himself. "Don't drink alcohol or take pills. Stick to heroin. This stuff will keep you young like me."

The first time I used heroin, it was Old Man Mike who injected me with it. I had gone to his house to buy marijuana for Claw and Poppers and arrived just in time to see him prepare a shot of heroin so he could get fixed. I had seen Old Man Mike inject himself before, and each time I was intrigued by the immediate change on his demeanor.

Old Man Mike always made a big ritual out of preparing the dope. First, he would carefully lay out the kit he used to inject himself. The kit was crudely constructed out of the nipple of a baby's milk bottle wrapped tightly with sewing thread around a small glass tube. At the end of the tube was a 26mm stainless steel hypodermic needle.

I watched Old Man Mike intently from a distance as he emptied the powdered heroin into a Thunderbird Wine bottle cap with a do-it-yourself wire handle. Adding water to the powder, he held the cap over a small flame to dissolve the powder into liquid form. He then drew the brown liquid into the makeshift syringe. Wrapping a handkerchief around his left bicep to make the vein on his arm stand out, he brought the syringe to his vein and plunged the needle in. Almost immediately blood shot up into the glass tube indicating he had hit his vein. He squeezed the nipple slowly and injected the heroin into his bloodstream.

The expression on Old Man Mike's face changed as soon as he finished shooting the dope. The heroin relaxed his facial muscles and relieved him of the pinched look, which had been so evident before he had injected himself. Even the sound of his voice changed. It sounded smoother, and his words spilled out with much more ease.

"Come on, *Dragón*," he said effortlessly. "Stick your arm out, man. Let me shoot you up. I guarantee it will make you feel gooood."

I didn't reply. He had caught me off guard. I had never thought about shooting up before. Besides I was afraid of needles.

"Come on man, don't be a pussy," Old Man Mike said, as he cleaned the syringe and began preparing another shot.

"What are you talking about, old man? I'm not afraid of anything and I ain't a pussy. The next time you talk to me like that, I'm going to run this thing deep into your chest," I said, lifting my shirt to show him the knife tucked into my pants.

He looked up at me with an expression that indicated he was about to get crazy on me. Then he saw the knife and quickly changed his mind realizing that I had the drop on him. Besides, he had just injected dope and any type of physical activity would cause him to lose his high. He surely didn't want that.

"Hey, *Ese*, I was just offering you a fix. But if you don't want any, that's cool."

"I never said I didn't want any," I replied impatiently, as I snatched the tie from his hand and wrapped it tightly around my left bicep so the vein in the crook of my arm would stand out just as he had illustrated.

"Just get it done," I commanded sticking out my arm.

I turned my head to one side so I wouldn't see the needle penetrate my vein. I hated needles and was afraid of them, but I couldn't let anyone see I was scared. I felt a slight prick as the needle pierced my skin and was surprised that it didn't hurt at all. Almost at once, a warm, soothing sensation engulfed me entirely. The warmth began at the tips of my toes and spread rapidly throughout my whole body, giving me a feeling that I had never experienced. It made me feel light on my feet and unconcerned with the ugliness around me. Even Old Man Mike didn't look as hideous as he did before he injected me with the heroin. I felt as though I could challenge the world and remain unscathed by its cruelty. Heroin dissolved the deep-seated hate in my gut. It substituted those emotions with an incredible deadening sensation. I sat down on a chair and nodded in and out of consciousness for hours, oblivious to everything around me. Not feeling, not thinking, not anything. From that moment on, heroin became my companion as I journeyed deeper into the sinister world of criminality.

One morning after I had been using heroin for nearly three months on a consistent basis, I awoke with a nasty taste in my mouth and my bones achy. I heard Mama cooking breakfast in the kitchen. I smelled the aroma of her tortillas and for the first time in my life, I was nauseated by the odor. Staggering into the bathroom, I brushed my teeth trying to wash the foul taste out of my mouth, but I couldn't get rid of it. It felt as though I was coming down with the flu. My body temperature would turn cold then hot, and I had a bad case of the sniffles. Slowly, I got dressed and walked into the kitchen to say good morning to Mama.

"*Hola*, Mama, those tortillas sure smell good," I said dutifully.

"Good morning, *hijo*. You going to look for work today?"

I had gone back to school in the fall of '68 after getting out of Boys Camp, but I had been expelled the day before we were to be excused for Christmas vacation for inciting a riot. I hadn't started the fight, but my reputation as a troublemaker had been the basis for my expulsion. I had been minding my own business simply checking out the girls as they walked by during brunch recess. Everything was fine until a White guy walked by and shot me a look that if looks could kill, I would have dropped dead on the spot.

"What you looking at, punk?" he asked with as much contempt as he could muster.

"I'm looking at you, pretty boy," I replied smoothly.

With that, he walked over to me and put his face right up to mine. "Listen you little punk. I'll break your skinny wetback neck; you hear what I'm saying?" he stated forcefully.

I could smell his bad breath.

"So," I asked, looking at him intently, ready for what I knew was coming next. "Is your wetback-neck-breaker broken?"

Saying that to him had the intended affect; and just as I expected, he swung at me. When he did, I simply moved my head slightly to one side, causing him to miss my mug with the punch he threw at me. I sensed the power of his blow as it shot past my face and in one swift motion I snatched him by his jacket lapels and fell backward using his body weight to sling him over on his back. Some of the guys from my group were standing close by and rushed over to help me when they saw what was happening. The White guy was tough, but in the end, we beat him down. I was kicked out of school on the spot even though I hadn't thrown the first punch. School administration didn't want any explanations and I didn't give them any either. They just wanted me out. I didn't care. I didn't like school anyway.

Since my expulsion, I had been hanging out at the park with the homeboys drinking beer, smoking weed, and using heroin.

"Naw, Mama, what kind of work is anyone going to give me without skills or education?"

"Well you're going to have to do something," she said, shaking her head in frustration.

How could I tell Mama I found life hopeless and that the only time I felt good was when I shot heroin? How could I tell her I wasn't going to work in the fields or in a warehouse like some donkey; that I was destined to end up in prison? Not wanting to get into a heated argument with her, I told her I would be back later. As I left, Mama said, "You're going to have to do something or you're going to end up in jail."

WHEN I GOT to the park, Puppet, Blue, and Shark were already there.

"What's up?" I asked.

"Ain't nothing shaking but the leaves on the trees, homeboy," Shark said. "Just taking it easy, drinking wine, and checking out the baby dolls as they strut their stuff. You want a drink?" he said as he handed me the bottle.

Shark was one of those guys who drank all day and talked all the time. He had thick black hair combed straight back and a pointed face just like a shark.

"*Oralé pues*."

I hated the taste of alcohol, but I thought that maybe the wine would help me feel better. I took a few deep breaths to prepare for its disgusting taste and chugged huge swallows of the nasty stuff. I almost drank the entire bottle.

"*Pinché vato!* You always do that," Shark exclaimed.

Once I was able to breathe again, I asked. "What are you talking about?"

"Every time someone offers you a drink, you drink the whole damn bottle," Shark said with indignation.

"Oh, yeah? Well, since you already knew I would drink the whole thing, why did you offer me a drink in the first place?" I asked, glaring at him. "Here's a couple of dollars so you can buy yourself another bottle," I said as I flung a couple of bucks at him. Shark knew he had pissed me off.

"Hey, *Ese*, I didn't mean it like that."

"Well, how the hell did you mean it then? What do you think, Puppet? Is Shark just talking out of his ass?"

"Hey, forget it *Ese*," Puppet replied. "You know Shark talks a lot of crap. He doesn't mean anything by it."

Shark was one of those guys who spoke without thinking. He was steadily getting his ass kicked or ridiculed by someone because he talked too much.

"You know I was only talking out the side of my neck," Shark said with apprehension.

I continued glaring at him, but decided to let it go. I knew Shark didn't mean anything. Besides, I didn't feel too good and getting into a fight wouldn't help.

"Hey, *Dragón*, what's happening? You look sick," Puppet asked.

"I feel like I'm coming down with the flu. My entire body aches and I have a nasty taste in my mouth that I can't get rid of no matter what I do. Even the roots of the hair on my head hurt."

"Are you having hot and cold flashes, and does your skin feel sticky and sweaty?"

"Yeah man. How did you know?"

"You don't have the flu," Puppet said, shaking his head.

"You're hooked on that garbage you've been sticking in your vein for the last three months, that's all."

"You're crazy!"

"You think so? Well, if you want to find out for sure, go get a fix. I bet everything you're feeling will disappear just like that," he said, snapping his fingers.

A few minutes later Steve showed up. I had known Steve for as long as I had been living in the *barrio*, but we had never hung out together until we started using heroin a few months before.

"Hey, Steve. How you feeling this morning?" I asked.

"I feel like I'm coming down with the flu—all achy and feverish."

"I told you," Puppet said.

"Me, too," I replied. "Puppet says we're hooked and that a fix will make the pain disappear. Maybe we should go find out if he's right. What you think?"

"Hell, yeah!" Steve exclaimed. "What the hell are we waiting for? If that's all it'll take to relieve the pain is a shot of dope, we need to get going with the quickness!"

Steve and I put our money together and left to Visalia to find Juan. Old Man Mike had been arrested for sales of heroin two months before so Juan had taken over the family business. He was raking in the money. Old Man Mike was later convicted and sentenced to fifteen years to life.

"*Oralé* Juan, sell me a twenty-five dollar bag," I said as I handed him our money. I could tell by the way Juan was moving in slow motion that he was flying high. I was about to tell him to hurry when he handed me the junk. I rushed back to the car and told Steve to drive to a secluded area at St. Johns River. During the drive, I hastily unwrapped my hypodermic kit from the handkerchief where I kept it. I wanted to be ready to inject the stuff into my vein as soon as we got to the river.

When we got there, I told Steve I was first to fix. He didn't argue, but I could tell by the sulking look he gave me that he didn't like having to wait.

In the world of the streets, the rank system was a continuous cycle with different levels of recognition. Even when it came to using drugs, the rank system was used. Since I had been to Juvenile Hall and Boys Camp, Steve automatically ranked below me.

I cooked the heroin into liquid and drew it up into the syringe. I wrapped the red handkerchief I kept in my back pocket around my left bicep and stuck the needle into the vein on the crook of my arm. As soon as I did, I saw blood shoot up into the glass eye dropper and knew I had made a hit. I gently squeezed the nipple on the syringe and injected the heroin into my bloodstream. Even before I finished injecting the entire portion of the heroin, all my aches disappeared. I handed the syringe to Steve and sat back with my chin on my chest in a deep nod.

"Wow," Steve said, after he injected his portion of the heroin. I looked over and saw Steve sitting on the driver's seat with his head thrown back, his mouth open slightly, and his eyes halfway shut. "Puppet was right, *Dragón*," Steve slurred. "We are hooked. What are we going to do?"

"What do you mean, what are we going to do? We're going to feed this monster we've created. I don't ever want to feel as bad as I did a little while ago. And if all I have to do is shoot dope to keep from getting sick then I'm going to shoot this stuff all day long."

It sounded easy, but I had a premonition I had begun a journey that would eventually get completely out of control.

Becoming a gangster would have to wait. My priorities had changed. In order to keep from going into heroin withdrawals I would have to make lots of money and that would require a lot of my time and energy. I would still be down for the *barrio*, but it wouldn't be my primary focus anymore.

Damn. How had I let this happen?

I didn't have the answer to that question, and I wasn't about to get philosophical right then. All I knew was that I was going to do whatever needed to be done so I would never have to feel so bad again.

Afterwards, I began shoplifting on a regular basis, but graduated to committing burglaries and robberies. There were plenty of ranches located throughout the countryside and I took full advantage of the opportunity to relieve them of their goods. I committed at least one burglary every day. I knew it would only be a matter of time before I wound up in jail. I had already been labeled by the police as a hardcore criminal, and they kept their eye on me whenever they spotted me on the streets. I didn't hang out in my *barrio* much because there weren't any guys, except Steve, using heroin. I mostly hung out with the guys from Visalia. Many of them were heroin addicts and involved in heavy criminal activity, too.

One day, in the summer of '69, as I sat at the Oval Park, a park where many heroin addicts from Visalia hung out, Bebo and Robert, two guys from Visalia, approached me with a venture they said would make us a substantial amount of money with very little risk.

"Hey, *Dragón*," Bebo said. "Check this out. I have a bag of marijuana that I want to sell. I know there are a lot of potheads in your *barrio*, and Robert and I are willing to cut you in on part of the profit if you help us sell it."

"How much do I get?"

"We'll split the profit three ways."

"Let me see what it looks like."

Bebo handed me a large brown paper shopping bag. Peering inside, I saw the bag was at least half full with weed. This could make enough money to keep me from getting heroin sick for at least three days.

Before I agreed, however, I had to make sure it was real marijuana. After all, my name would be going out on this stuff and I could get seriously hurt for selling bad merchandise to the guys from my barrio, especially when guys from Visalia were involved. I took a deep whiff of the contents and determined it was real.

"Oralé. Let's do it."

"The guys from your barrio aren't going to jump on us, are they?" Bebo asked apprehensively before we began the drive to my neighborhood.

"Don't worry about it, Ese. I'll make sure you guys are safe."

Bebo knew everyone from my barrio respected me, so he quickly agreed.

"Oralé pues. Let's go," he said.

We drove the fourteen miles from Visalia into Woodlake in my '51 Ford. Bebo and Robert smoked weed all the way there. They asked me if I wanted a hit, but I declined their offer.

When we got to Woodlake, I drove straight to the park where the guys from my barrio hung out. There were about ten guys milling around drinking wine and talking loud. As soon as Bebo, Robert, and I walked over, the guys from my barrio got deathly quiet and shot Bebo and Robert fierce looks that let them know they weren't welcomed.

"Hey, Dragón, why did you bring these punks into the neighborhood?" Pancho asked loudly.

"It's cool, man. They're with me. Besides, they have a bag full of marijuana, and I know how much you guys like to smoke that stuff so I brought them here to give you first dibs on the weed."

Pancho and the others looked interested. They wanted to know about the quality of the weed.

"Hey, Ese," I said. "You guys know I don't smoke that stuff, but I'm sure you can smoke some before you buy it."

"Oralé," Pancho said. "Tell one those punks to roll a few joints so we can test it." Bebo rolled a couple marijuana cigarettes and passed them out to the guys from my barrio.

After they smoked a few joints, we sold two hundred and sixty dollars worth of the weed within a matter of minutes. At first I was happy we made so much money, but driving back to Visalia with Bebo and Robert, I had an uneasy feeling that something was terribly wrong. I dropped Bebo and Robert off at the Oval Park, bought a few bags of heroin from Juan, and headed back to Woodlake.

I drove straight to Steve's house to turn him onto a shot of dope. Steve was often in some stage of withdrawal because he wouldn't steal to support his habit, so whenever I had extra dope I would hook him up with a fix.

I found Steve sitting on a lawn chair under the big weeping willow in his front yard. I could see he needed a fix badly. He had a blanket wrapped around him as though he was cold, but he had small beads of sweat on his forehead. As soon as he saw me coming he brightened up like a neon light. He knew he was about to get well.

"You sick?" I asked.

"Hell yeah, man!"

"Well, come on. Let me fix you up."

"*Orale, Ese*," he replied. "I've been sitting here for the past four hours trying to figure a way to make some bread without having to steal, but I'm pretty much burned out with everyone. They're all tired of me asking them for money. I can't steal like you. I get scared. I don't know where you get the courage to break into people's houses."

"I didn't break into anyone's house to get the cash to buy this dope."

I told Steve what I had done and how I had a feeling that something was wrong.

"I don't think the stuff we sold the homeboys was Pot at all. I mean, it looked like weed and it smelled like it too, but there was something about it that didn't seem right, you know."

"Ah man, don't worry about it. I mean, the guys smoked the stuff before they bought it, right?"

"Yeah."

"Well, it's not on you. If they were stupid enough to buy the weed even after they smoked it, it's on them."

A few days later, as Steve and I drove into town after coming back from Fresno, we were cut off by David, one of the guys from the *barrio*. He drove right in front of me as I attempted to make a U-turn on Main Street.

"*Ese, Dragón*. The guys want to talk to you. Everyone's waiting under the big tree. Be there," he said coldly as he flipped a U-turn and was gone before I had a chance to respond. David was nobody in the *barrio*. Yet, he had gotten the nerve to deliver this message to me as though he was a tough guy.

"Damn. The guys must really be mad at you. David would've never talked to you like that unless he had a lot of back up," Steve said.

"I hear you."

Driving toward the park, I noticed everyone who had bought weed from me was waiting under the tree. I knew they would want their money back since the marijuana I sold them had turned out to be bunk. I had spoken to Bebo a few days after we sold the weed and he had told me that some guy had given him the weed as payment for a debt he owed him. As it turned out, the guy had cheated Bebo by giving him bogus weed. Well, what was done was done. I didn't have any of the homeboys' money, and even if I did, I wouldn't have given them back one cent.

"Listen Steve, you don't have to go with me if you don't want to. This is my problem and I'll understand if you don't want to get involved."

"Hey, *Ese*," he replied. "I'm already involved. Drive over to my house and let's pick up a couple of guns. There's too many guys, even for a tough guy like you," he smiled weakly, trying to lighten the seriousness of the situation.

Steve owned lots of guns before he had started using heroin, but he had gotten into the habit of pawning his guns to get money to buy drugs. At first, he had been able to take the guns out of pawn, but as his habit grew, so did his inability to pay the pawnshop. As a result of not being able to get his guns out of the pawnshop, he had lost most of them with the exception of a 22-caliber pistol and a 12 gauge shotgun. We drove to his house and picked up the twelve gauge and his nine shot 22-revolver and went to the park to face the music.

As soon as we arrived, I was confronted by Pat, the designated spokesmen for the *barrio*.

"Hey, *Dragón*," he began. "That stuff you sold us was pure garbage and we want our money back."

"Yeah, *Ese*," Ralph said in the background.

"What are you talking about," I snapped angrily at Ralph. "Didn't you smoke the weed before you bought it? Didn't I tell you guys I hadn't tried the weed myself and that I didn't know if it was any good?"

"Yeah, you did," Pat answered. "But we still want our money back."

"Well, hell," I replied, with as much sarcasm as I could muster. "I'd like to be rich and never have to steal again, but that's not the way it works. You guys might as well know right now, I'm not giving anyone any money back and before any of you decide you want to get crazy, let me show you this," I said as I lifted my shirt to show them the gun tucked into my pants.

"Steve, over there, has a twelve gauge shotgun, so I suggest you guys reconsider your approach to this situation."

With that, I grabbed the butt of the gun.

"So, with all that being said and done, let me further say that if you force me to pull this pistol, I'm going to pump a round into you first Pat. Then I'm going to blast you Ralph for having such a big mouth."

Everyone at the spot that day knew I was dead serious, so they backed-off and let Steve and I leave. It took months before the tension eased up, but eventually everyone forgot about it.

FOR THE NEXT six months I committed burglaries on a daily basis and my drug habit grew bigger and bigger each day. My habit was like a huge dark hole that I couldn't fill. The more I used, the more I needed.

One foggy morning in the winter of 1970, I drove into Visalia to meet up with my crime partner Lil Joe. By this time, Lil Joe and I had been using heroin together and committing burglaries for about three months. That morning, after administering our morning dose of heroin, we decided that the area located just south of Woodlake would be a good place to commit a burglary. The houses in that area were isolated and from each other and would give us plenty of freedom to break in without being detected. We relaxed at Lil Joe's house for about an hour and enjoyed our high. Then we left on our moneymaking venture.

We drove around for about an hour or so before finding the perfect house to break into. It was located off the main highway, hidden amongst large oak trees and completely surrounded by an orange orchard. We drove up to the front of the house through a narrow gravel driveway. I climbed out of the car and walked to the front door. I knocked hard, ready to ask for directions to a fictitious address if anyone answered. As luck would have it, no one was home. I motioned Lil Joe to come on, and he was at the door in no time. Using a pair of channel locks, I snapped the lock off the front door and within a matter of seconds, we were inside the house.

Lil Joe and I worked quickly, unplugging electrical equipment to carry off. We methodically moved from one room to another in search of valuables. I emptied the contents of dresser drawers in the master bedroom onto the floor to make sure I didn't miss anything of value. Looking under every mattress and rummaging through the closets, I came upon a collection of guns and ammunition.

Bingo!

These guns would bring plenty of cash, and we could keep a couple of handguns for ourselves in case we needed them for protection or to commit armed robberies.

"Hey, Lil Joe! I think we hit the jackpot."

Lil Joe was just as excited as I was when he saw what I found. There were twelve handguns and an assortment of rifles and shotguns. We carried the guns, color television, stereo, and other electronic items to our car and left. I felt good about how quickly we had gotten in and out of the house, but I knew we weren't home free. We still had to make it to Lil Joe's house.

As we traveled down the main highway heading back to Visalia, we crossed paths with a sheriff's patrol car that happened to be at a stop sign. The cop eyed us suspiciously as we drove by. As soon as we passed, he turned onto the road and began following us. Soon the red lights on top of his patrol car lit up, and I knew we were busted.

The officer approached our car carefully. He had his hand on his gun and I could see that he had flicked the small leather strap off of the trigger, ready to pull his gun and shoot us if we made a wrong move. Looking inside of our car from the driver's side, he asked Lil Joe for his driver's license. Not long after the initial stop, two other policemen arrived at the scene. After that, "it was all over but the crying" as we used to say when anyone from the *barrio* got caught and put in jail. It didn't take long before we were taken into custody for suspicion of residential burglary.

Lil Joe and I were handcuffed and placed into the police car and transported to the county jail. I had been in jail one other time, but my stay had been brief. This time I figured I would there for at least a year. After we were booked into the County Jail, we were taken upstairs to our cells. As soon as I walked into my housing block, I ran into Shark.

"*Oralé, Dragón*, what kind of case you got?"

"Lil Joe and I got busted for burglary."

"That ain't nothing homeboy. You'll probably get a year county time."

"I can handle whatever they give me," I replied.

The following morning I felt awful. The first stages of heroin withdrawal had begun. I had the familiar nasty taste in my mouth, my bones were beginning to ache, my stomach was in knots, and my nerves were on edge. I had never kicked before, but I had heard that once the withdrawals symptoms intensified, the pain would be excruciating. I braced myself for the inevitable torture of coming off of heroin. I couldn't get weak now. I would have to take the pain like a man, without sniveling.

Remember, I thought. *"Los hombres no lloran."*

Time moved slowly that first day in jail. I paced all day trying to wear myself out so I could fall asleep from sheer exhaustion, but to no avail. For the next thirty days, I didn't sleep a wink. I shivered from cold chills and then suffered from hot flashes. I puked everything I ate or drank. I had diarrhea, defecating and vomiting at the same time. Every muscle in my body ached. I was in so much pain that even the roots of the hair on my head hurt. I tried to smoke, but the smoke made me sick. I wanted to scream as I suffered through the constant anguish of withdrawal, but I couldn't. I had to maintain my tough guy image even under those dire circumstances. So I hung in there, never letting anyone know how bad I felt. Finally, after about a month of sheer torment, I began to slowly recover and the pain disappeared, but I suffered from "Long Gut," a symptom heroin addicts go through after kicking Cold Turkey.

Long Gut is an emptiness of the stomach that can't be filled no matter how much you eat. For the next two months, I ate anything and everything and regained the weight I had lost during the time I had been injecting heroin.

I started exercising to get my strength back and before long, I forgot all about the unbearable pain I experienced during withdrawals and couldn't wait to feel the warmth of heroin again.

But first, I had to serve my time.

I was sentenced to a year in the county jail and placed on three years felony probation. Afterward, I was transferred to the Tulare County Road Camp. The road camp got its name because everyone, except for the guys assigned to maintain the camp, were put on road crews that went out every day to patch potholes on county roads, pick up trash, or cut weeds around stop signs and such. Every inmate was required to work during the week. On Saturday mornings, a volunteer crew went out to work at Mooney's Grove Park in Visalia. Many guys volunteered to go on that crew because lots of girls from different neighborhoods went to the park during the weekend. There were some guys who got lucky and scored a girl's address and started writing her. They often made plans to meet up at the park on Saturday's. If the guy was really good at manipulation, he would convince the girl to make a run to the liquor store and buy alcohol for everyone in the crew.

I never volunteered to work at the park until one Saturday morning, about three months after I got to the road camp. A guy I met from Visalia talked me into going. The guy's name was Donald. I liked him because he was always clowning around and would make me laugh. He knew the funniest jokes I had ever heard and had a talent for telling them.

"One of my home girls is bringing me some LSD later today to Mooney's Grove," he said. "I want you to sign up for the work crew so we can get high together."

"Hey man, I don't like that psychedelic shit. The one time I took it, I almost lost my mind because I couldn't stop laughing even though there was nothing funny going on."

"Come on. What you going to do here all day anyway?"

In the end, I went to Mooney's Grove Park, took a couple of hits of LSD and in the throes of my high, jumped into a car with some people I knew and left the work crew. I didn't even realize I had taken off until I came down from the LSD ten hours or so later. When reality set in, I felt a tinge of regret, but quickly convinced myself that I was headed to the penitentiary anyway so it didn't matter. I surely wasn't going to turn myself into the authorities. Might as well enjoy being on the streets. Besides, I couldn't undo what was already done.

After absconding from the work crew, I couldn't stay in my *barrio*. I was too well known by the cops so I made plans to live in San Jose, California with Porky, one of my older homeboys. As soon as I got there, I began committing burglaries and shoplifting to support myself and the heroin habit I acquired soon after I escaped. I stayed out about six months before an informant told the police I was a fugitive. A few nights later, officers from the San Jose Police Department came to my house, kicked in my door, and arrested me. Tulare County sheriff's picked me up a week later and placed me in the Tulare County Jail.

In October of '72, I was sentenced to the California Rehabilitation Center (CRC), an institution located just outside of Norco, California. At that time, CRC was considered a drug program, but mostly it was a prelude to state prison. My attorney told the judge I was a heroin addict and that I needed drug treatment. The judge agreed and sent me there. Three months after I arrived at CRC, I was excluded from the program for participating in a race riot. I was held in *Chino* State Prison for a few months before I was transferred back to the County Jail for resentencing. I was sentenced to prison two months later.

THE PRISONER holding tank for the Superior Court in and for the County of Tulare was packed with anxious inmates, and the smell of body odor, bad breath, and cigarette smoke permeated the cell. Sitting on hard wood slats bolted to the wall, or on the cement floor, everyone waited nervously to appear before the judge for their freedom or continued incarceration.

The tension was as thick as Texas crude oil. We were all trying to stay cool, working hard at keeping our faces devoid of expression, not wanting to show we were nervous, but the sweat stains under the armpits of our jump suits, the furtive glances we shot toward the steel door, and the anxious chatter revealed our apprehension.

The swooshing sound of the steel cell door opening caught everyone's attention and brought an instant hush to the room as everyone listened closely to hear if their name was being called by the deputy marshal.

"Mendoza, Clark, Jones, and Martinez, it's your time."

"Good luck," *Hueró* said to the guys as they walked out of the holding cell to get sentenced.

As soon as the deputy slammed the door shut, the nervous conversation resumed. *Hueró*, a tall, light complexioned, curly haired guy, who had a knack for telling great stories, had been recounting one of his many sexual escapades before being interrupted by the opening of the door. Most of us knew *Hueró* had never done half the things he talked about, but he was entertaining nonetheless.

I had heard his jive before so I shut him off and began to think about my future and what it would be like once I got to the penitentiary. I couldn't believe I was finally going to the "Big House." Ever since I was a kid I had known I would get there and now it was only a matter of days before I would fulfill my destiny.

Two days before, a probation officer had come to interview me at the county jail. He had told me that I would be going up the river. That was his way of rubbing his recommendation that I should be sent to prison in my face.

"They ought to keep guys like you locked up for good," he had said coldly.

I wasn't surprised to hear his opinion of me. I had been told by many law enforcement people I was natural penitentiary material. I was young, full of hate, and ready to take my hostilities out on anyone who wasn't my friend. Policemen had often told me I was heartless and that I fit the profile of the type of guys the Department of Corrections was looking for.

What's happening?" George asked, as he sat next to me while I waited my turn to appear before the judge.

George was the guy who had shot Manuel during the gang fight between Woodlake and Visalia back in the mid-sixties. He looked a lot more threatening now than he did in the picture I had seen of him in the newspaper after he had been arrested for killing Manuel five years before. The tattoos he had covering both his arms and the fact that he had served time in Youth Authority for murder gave him an even more imposing look. Earlier that morning he had been sentenced to serve six months to fourteen years in state prison for assaulting a cop. "Are you thinking about what it's going to be like when you get to the Joint?"

I nodded.

"It's no big thing, *Ese*. We've been waiting to get to the penitentiary ever since we were kids. You want to know something else? Out of all the guys here today, the only ones going to prison are you and me. You know why?"

I shook my head.

"Because, *Ese*, these guys are just wannabes, *tu sabes?* And you and I already are. You understand what I'm saying?" George said, with a cool smile.

"*Simón.*"

Ever since I started getting arrested, I would visualize what prison was like in order to prepare myself for what lay ahead. Once, when I was placed in segregation for thirty days, I'd stare at the wall and count the thousands of tiny holes. I disciplined myself to keep quiet and not let the stillness of solitary confinement affect my state of mind. I'd been placed in isolation because I threw my food tray at a guard who constantly messed with me. He hated junkies and every time he went by my cell, he would take his keys and run them across the bars of my cell and mockingly ask me if I wanted a fix. The screeching noise of the keys scraping against the bars and his leering face was more than I could handle. I let him get away with it the first time, but the second time he got out of line, I threw my tray at him.

"How you like me now punk?" I screamed.

The Hole was located on the fourth floor of the jail. Each cell had nothing more than a hole in the center of the cell used to defecate and urinate. Every thirty minutes the toilet would automatically flush and make loud gushing noises. I welcomed the noise much more than the quiet stillness. Sometimes the stillness could injure people. There was this guy who broke under the quiet intensity of the hole. One day he was fine, but the next day he could not stop shouting out the logic of a lunatic, spouting conspiracies, blaming everyone for his confinement, cursing both God and the Devil. He was transferred to Atascadero State Hospital, where hardcore psychiatric criminals were sent. I never saw him again.

The sound of the door opening caught everyone's attention.

"De La Cruz, Matthews, Garcia, let's go. You're up," the marshal said.

The marshal fitted me with a stainless steel chain around my waist and then ran a set of handcuffs through the chain and snapped the cuffs securely around my wrists. I felt my heart pound in my chest. Taking a deep breath, I strolled into the courtroom with my head held high. Scanning the audience I spotted Mama as she sat alone in one corner of the spectator's area. She looked small and fragile and concern was written on her face. I smiled at her and nodded my head in an attempt to let her know everything was all right. She cracked a weak smile in return.

"Well, Mr. De La Cruz," the judge began, "today is the day set aside for sentencing in your case. The probation officer, Mr. Little, has recommended that you be sent to State Prison for the term prescribed by law. He doesn't believe local time will benefit you or the community and the report from CRC also indicates that you should be sent to prison. Furthermore, this court doesn't have any information that would sway the court into disagreeing with these recommendations. It appears you have been getting into trouble with the law from a very young age, and that the nature of your crimes has progressively worsened. Do you have anything to say for yourself?"

"What does the court want me to say? That I'm sorry? You've already said there's nothing to show I should be given any other sentence besides what the probation officer and CRC has recommended. Does the court want me to beg for leniency?"

"Listen, Mr. De La Cruz. This court will not tolerate any disrespect from you and if you continue, this court will make an example out of you."

"How are you going to hurt me, by sending me to prison?"

He shook his head.

"I can see you are a young man in need of long term confinement. Therefore, it is the judgment of this court that you be sentenced to State Prison for a term of no less than six months and no more than fifteen years as prescribed by law."

I heard Mama begin to sob as the judge read my sentence. After he slammed his gavel, I turned, arched my eyebrow at her, and shook my head, letting her know I didn't want her to cry. Mama immediately stifled her moans, but the anguish fixed on her face was plain to see. I guess the thought of me going to prison terrified her. My feelings were a mixture of happiness and fear. On the one hand, I was elated that I had finally graduated to the Big House, on the other, I was afraid.

I nodded at Mama as the marshal escorted me out of the courtroom back to the holding cell. I felt a sense of relief that the legalities were over. I had done a good job of letting the judge know I didn't care what he did to me. It had given me pleasure to answer him with such insolence. Most guys would have tried to fake that they were sorry about what they had done, but judges were smart, and they knew when someone was trying to get over on them.

I wasn't going to grovel. As far as I was concerned, he had done me a favor.

When I got back to the holding tank, George asked me what had happened. When I told him, he smiled knowingly.

"I told you, *Ese*. It's you and me going to the penitentiary."

Thirty minutes later, a deputy shouted, "Let's go, fellas. It's time to get back to the County."

"Home sweet home," someone among us answered back.

One by one a deputy called out our names, and one by one we were chained to each other for the short walk to the jailhouse. As we walked out of the courthouse basement and into the bright sunlight, I wondered how long it would be before I would be on the streets again. The average time served for my type of sentence ran approximately two and a half years. Since I wasn't an average type of guy, I figured I would have to serve more time. It didn't matter. I would do the time and return to the streets whenever I was done.

Once we entered the jail, everyone was unchained and went through the routine of undressing and having an officer look in every orifice of our bodies. We were then loaded onto an elevator and whisked up to our respective floors. I was the only one who lived on the second floor and was dropped off there. The floor officer opened the main door and slammed it shut once I stepped inside the main galley.

"Go lock up, De La Cruz," the floor officer commanded.

When I stepped into my cell, I went straight to my bunk without acknowledging anyone and lay down. I felt emotionally drained. I only intended to rest for a short time, but drifted off into a deep sleep and didn't wake until the following morning.

I awoke to the sound of a toilet flushing. *Topo* was taking a leak. He was a short fat guy, with two huge front teeth like a gopher.

"What time is it?"

"It's almost chowtime. You've been sleeping ever since you got back from court."

"I was burned out. But I'm ready to rock and roll now."

I jumped out of bed to take a piss. I quickly washed my face, brushed my teeth, and combed my hair. I heard the loud buzzing sound of the galley door indicating chow was on the line and would be here momentarily. I looked around and saw that everyone in the cell except *Topo* and me was still asleep. It always amazed me how many guys doing time could rise up out of a dead sleep, get their trays, eat, and hit the rack without ever being fully awake.

When the chow cart got in front of my cell, *Flacó* handed me a tray through the slot on the cell door. *Flacó*, a tall, lanky guy from *Barrio Poros* (short for Porterville), was serving a year in jail and had been assigned to work in the jailhouse kitchen.

"I heard they sentenced you to the 'Joint' yesterday?"

"*Simón, Ese.* The judge gave me six months to fifteen years. He said I needed an attitude adjustment."

"*Pinché perros.* They're always sending the good guys to the penitentiary."

"Hey, *Ese*, don't trip potato chip. It's nothing but a walk in the park. Besides, I've been waiting to go to the Pen for a long time, and I suppose now is as good a time as any, *que no?*"

"Yeah, I guess you're right."

"I'll catch you later. Maybe we can kick it before I'm shipped out."

"*Oralé.*"

The next morning George was transferred to state prison. Before he left, he stopped by my cell to let me know he would be waiting for me at Vacaville, the Reception Center for guys sent to prison from Northern California. George had a huge smile on his face as though he was happy to be leaving.

"*Oralé, Carnál*, it's that time. I'd like to stay, you know what I'm saying, but when you gotta go, you gotta go. I'll be waiting for you at Vacaville."

"Yeah, I should be there in a couple of days. We can do this time on the buddy plan."

We laughed.

"Catch you on the rebound," George said as we shook hands through the bars.

The next few days dragged by.

Mama and Father came to visit me before I was transferred. Mama said she felt as though something bad was going to happen to me. Father told me to be careful. I reassured them both that everything was going to be all right. When our visit was over, I said goodbye to them and made my way to the elevator. I took one last look at my parents and wondered how long it would be before I saw them again. I waved at them and noticed Mama had tears streaming down her cheeks, and Father had a sad look on his face, too. For a split second I felt a tinge of grief. I looked around to see if anyone had noticed my moment of weakness. Fortunately, everyone was too caught up with their own sorrow to take notice of my fleeting sadness.

You can't get weak now, I thought as I recomposed myself.

The following morning the floor guard told me I was shipping out after breakfast. I took a leak, brushed my teeth, washed my face, combed my hair, and ate my last meal at the jail. Everyone in my cell seemed impressed with my obvious elevation from the County Jail to the penitentiary. My ego was swollen with pride.

"Come on, De La Cruz, it's time to go," the guard said as he opened my cell door.

"I'll catch you guys later," I told everyone as I strutted down the corridor.

"Keep your head to the sky and don't let anyone get you down," I heard someone shout.

The guard escorted me to the elevator and took me to the booking area located in the basement of the jail. After the proper documents were signed, I was turned over to the custody of two air-transport officers who would deliver me to the California Department of Corrections. I was escorted to a van that held three other guys and then taken to the municipal airport where I was put on a plane. I had never flown before and I was terrified. I felt my body tremble from the fear, but as usual, I didn't say anything.

The pilot navigated the six-passenger plane onto the runway. He made contact with the tower and replied with a curt 104. Suddenly, the plane lurched forward, pinning me to my seat as we traveled swiftly down the airstrip. In a matter of seconds we were in the air and on our way to the Big House.

When we arrived to the Vacaville airport, my stomach was in knots. I had been waiting for this moment all my life, and even though Big *Indio* had coached me on the things I would encounter when I got to prison, I was still anxious. His words in my head made me tense.

"You have to mind your P's and Q's and stay alert all the time. Make sure you keep your back against the wall so no one can sneak up on you from behind. Familiarize yourself with the key players on the yard. If you study them carefully, you'll discover they do the same things day in and day out and you'll notice when their routine changes. It will be during those times that you have to be extra careful because someone is going to get hurt. Don't ever take a shit while you're on the yard. I saw two guys get whacked as they sat on the toilet in the yard; truly a disgraceful way to die. I don't want that happening to you because I didn't warn you," Big *Indio* had told me time and time again.

CHAPTER SEVEN

THE FIRST TIME I laid eyes on Vacaville, it literally took my breath away. A chill ran through my body as I gazed at this massive institution made of cement, steel, and wire located at the foot of a small mountain range. Two twelve foot fences topped with razor wire and the gun towers stood like giant sentinels surrounding the entire prison. The buildings were huge square cement blocks with three levels of steel-barred windows.

The transportation van pulled slowly into the main entrance sally port and was thoroughly searched by a team of correctional officers before we were allowed to continue inside. As the driver navigated the van around the huge prison, I noticed the large amount of garbage scattered between every building. The wind pitched the debris to and fro, but the trash somehow stayed contained between the buildings. For the next three and a half years, I would be confined or moved from one cellblock to another without being able to leave, trapped just like the garbage between the cellblock.

When we arrived to Receiving & Release (R&R), I climbed out the van, raised my head high, took a deep breath, and stepped inside the building where seven R&R inmate clerks were lounging. Four were dressed in green pants and shirts, and three wore "blues" (the standard attire worn in prison). The green uniforms identified guys going through the orientation process and waiting for transfer to other institutions. Blues were considered mainliners, men classified to stay at Vacaville to serve their sentence. Later, I learned Vacaville was a good place to serve time because there weren't many stabbings or killings and there were homosexuals galore. Anyone who longed for sexual gratification was in heaven at Vacaville. Since I wasn't looking for intimacy, especially from another man, I wanted to be sent to San Quentin, where the real convicts went.

As soon as I walked into R&R, a White clerk asked me where I was from.

"I'm from Woodlake," I replied. "Who wants to know?" I asked puffing up my chest to let the guy know I was someone he didn't want to mess with.

"Hey, there's no problem. I just wanted to know that's all," the clerk answered.

I was going to put the White clerk in check for getting into my business, but before I could a guard started to talk.

"Okay, listen up," the R&R officer said, in a forceful baritone voice that vibrated off the walls. "Have you ever been here before?"

"No," I answered.

"Well," he said, harshly. "We're not here to babysit you and I'm not your daddy. The quicker you understand what's expected of you, the easier your stay will be."

He pointed to the group of guys sitting next to some typewriters located against a wall and told me to answer all their questions.

"The faster we finish, the sooner you'll be housed. So let's get this done."

"What's your name? Last name first," a clerk asked.

"De La Cruz, Jesse."

"Middle name?"

"*Sahagun*."

The clerk asked all types of questions about my family, level of education, marriage status, religious background, vocational training, and ethnic origin. I was stunned when the clerk asked me who should be notified in case of death. I don't know why the question surprised me so much. After all, prison is a dangerous place filled with shifty men; some who had already committed murder. I gave the clerk Mama's name, but I planned on staying alert in order to stay safe.

After completing the necessary paper work, I was fingerprinted and photographed for my identification card. I would have to carry my I.D. with me at all times and memorize my prison number: B47659. The R&R officer then escorted me to a large shower room and told me to get naked. By now I knew the routine.

"Lift your arms over your head. Stick your arms out in front of you and wiggle your fingers. Bend over and run your fingers through your hair. Lift your nut sack. Turn around and let me see the bottom of your feet. Wiggle your toes. Bend over and grab your ass cheeks and spread 'em. Give me three hard coughs. Okay, get dressed. Pick up your bed roll and follow me."

When I finished dressing, he led me through a steel door onto the longest corridor I had ever seen. The walls were painted a dull brown and the ceiling was covered by a thin film of soot. I was in awe of its length. But what struck me the most about the corridor was its lifelessness.

"Listen De La Cruz," the R&R officer said as we walked down the corridor. "You'll be living in U-wing for the next three months. Make sure you get familiar with the rules so you don't get into trouble while you're here," the man continued, as he handed the wing officer my housing card.

"You'll be staying in 213 on the second tier," the unit officer said. "Take those stairs and stand in front of your cell. I'll be up on the tier to lock you down in a few minutes."

Walking up the winding staircase, I took note of the danger the stairs presented. They were hidden from the guards' view and provided an ideal location for someone to hurt me if they wanted to. I made a mental reminder to watch myself whenever I had to use the stairs.

When I got to my cell, I peeked inside through a small window on the door, but before I could get a clear picture of my new home, the door automatically opened. I was startled by it and jumped back. The wing officer at the end of the tier yelled for me to step inside. I did, and the door slammed shut with a thunderous bang.

The cell was cramped. It consisted of a small bed with a thin-stripped mattress, a white porcelain toilet that needed cleaning, a sink, and a steel towel rack bolted to the wall. There was a steel desk with a wooden stool bolted to it by a steel tube that could be swiveled under the desk when it wasn't being used. The walls, painted the same dull brown as the corridor, were covered with a thin yellow film caused by cigarette smoke from previous tenants. The floor was smooth cement. I had been issued a towel, two coarse black woolen blankets, and two sheets. I made my bed and lay down to rest. I was exhausted and drifted off to sleep with images of my homeboys kicking back at the park.

Later, I was roused by the loud ringing sound of a bell, the kind used in schools to excuse students from classes. I jumped out of bed and peered out the window of the cell door, but couldn't see any movement on the tier. I figured the bell was some sort of signal indicating it was time to eat. I took a leak, washed my face, combed my hair, and brushed my teeth using the state issued tooth powder I was given at R&R. The powder turned pasty and granular, but it was better than nothing. A few minutes later, my cell door mechanically opened. I cautiously stepped onto the tier and looked carefully at my surroundings. Turning to my left, then to my right, I saw men coming out of their cells. All of them walked towards the staircase. I followed them like a robot. In single file, we quietly shuffled down a stairwell and into a large dining hall.

The first thing I saw when I entered the mess hall was the self-segregation of the inmates. Chicanos sat with Chicanos, Blacks assembled with their people, and Whites sat with their group. There wasn't any interracial interaction whatsoever. I found out later it was the same on the prison yard. Every ethnic group had their own spot where they congregated, and those areas were strictly out of bounds to anyone who wasn't from that particular group. Guys from other races couldn't come around our spot or they would get hurt with the quickness, pure and simple.

No questions asked. I didn't have a problem with not mixing with other groups since I didn't like Whites or Blacks from the get-go.

Out of nowhere I heard someone call my name. I looked around and saw it was George.

"*Oralé, Carnál*," George said, smiling broadly. "It's about time you got here, *Ese*."

"I heard that," I answered, happy to see a familiar face. "I couldn't wait to get out of the county jail either."

"I have a care package for you in my cell. As soon as I get back, I'll send it to you with one of the tier tenders. In the meantime, take this tumbler so you can make a cup of coffee in the morning before you get released for breakfast. The tumbler won't fit under the door of your cell."

It was customary to give a care package to the "Fish" (new arrival). The packet normally included the bare necessities such as coffee, tobacco, toothpaste, and bath soap. Tier tenders were guys who swept and mopped the cellblock after everyone was locked down. They typically delivered messages from one cell to another as well.

"*Órale*, I appreciate it," I answered.

"Don't worry about it. This is Caboobie. He's from Fresno," George said, pointing to a guy standing next to him.

Caboobie was a young tough with the same predatory look as George and me. His arms were covered with the strangest looking tattoos I had ever seen. After I got to know Caboobie, I asked him about his tattoos. He told me he had used his body to practice tattooing so he could improve his craft. Years later, Caboobie became one of the best tattooists in the California Department of Corrections. His work was renowned within the prison system. Whenever Caboobie worked his creative magic, he would transform entire bodies into visions of artistic beauty.

"*Oralé*," Caboobie said, as we shook hands.

"*Qvo*," I answered.

"So what do you think so far?" George asked.

"I haven't had time to think. After being flown here and going through R&R, I got to my cell and passed out from sheer exhaustion."

"Yeah, I was pretty tired when I got here too. But once you go through orientation, it's okay. That shit begins tomorrow."

Before I had a chance to finish eating, we were being rushed back to our cells. I told George and Caboobie I would check 'em out in the morning.

Strolling back to my cell, I heard a deafening hum that vibrated off the cement walls and steel railings. At first I didn't know exactly where the noise was coming from, but then it came to me. The drone was the sound of hundreds of men talking at the same time, each one trying to talk over the other. My cell door opened and I stepped inside. It closed with a clang, shutting off the noisy chatter. Not long after, I slipped between the sheets and passed out for the night.

The following morning I awoke with a start, excited about being in the joint. It was strange to feel thrilled about being locked up, but that's how I felt. I didn't know what time it was when I rolled out of bed, but looking out my cell window, I saw that it was still dark outside. I began to get ready for breakfast. During the night, someone slid George's promised care package under my door. The package contained instant Folgers coffee, Bugler tobacco, and toiletries like Colgate toothpaste, a bar of Irish Spring soap, a bottle of Jergens hand lotion, and Mennen underarm deodorant. George had also thrown in a couple of zoo-zoos and wham-whams, known in the free world as candy bars.

An orientation and medical ducat had been slipped under my door sometime during the night as well. Ducats were appointment slips authorizing convicts to be at a particular place at a specific time. The ducats indicated I had orientation at 9:00 AM and a medical appointment at 10:30. After rolling a cigarette and making a strong cup of coffee, I sat down to think about the day ahead. It looked as though I was in for a busy day.

Not long after finishing my coffee I heard the sound of the wakeup bell. Approximately thirty minutes later, my door slid open. I came out for breakfast and strolled over to the mess hall, where I located George and Caboobie behind the serving line. They waved at me and came to sit at my table a few minutes later. I noticed that everyone in the mess hall was absorbed in conversations except a group of guys who kept glancing our way as if they had a problem with one of us. These guys seemed different from everyone else in the dining hall. They had an air of unconcern as if they knew no one would mess with them.

"Oralé, Carnál," George said. "Did you get the stuff I sent you last night?"

"Simón, Ese, gracias."

"It ain't nothing, homeboy."

"Hey, Ese, how come those guys keep looking over here?" I asked nodding toward the guys. "Do they have a problem with you, or is it with me?"

"Forget it, Ese. Those guys are in the Nuestra Familia. They're just checking you out. Take my word for it. If they had a problem with you, they would've handled it without hesitation. Those guys are some crazy dudes. They'll move on anybody with total disregard of the Man."

"Moving on you" was penitentiary slang describing a brutal attack that sometimes resulted in death for the victim. I found out later that these guys would move on an intended victim without caring about getting more time or shot by the gunner in the gun tower. I never met anyone with such utter loyalty for each other as these guys. They took a vow to put everything, including family and friends, secondary to the gang.

"Okay, let's go," the Man commanded. "Time to lock up."

Damn, I thought. These punks don't even give you a chance to eat your food much less digest it.

Everyone who wasn't assigned to a work detail went back to their cells for lockup. A few hours later everyone was released for yard call and ducats. When my door slid open, I stepped out of my cell and made my way toward X-Corridor where the orientation was to be held. As I walked down the main hallway, one of the guys who had been in the dining hall earlier that morning during breakfast giving George, Caboobie, and me the once over slid next to me.

"*Órale*," he said coolly. "They call me *Chapo*. I'm from Salinas."

They called him *Chapo* because he had Asian looking eyes.

"We were checking you out earlier, and the *Carnáles* asked me to talk to you. We've heard from reliable people you're a stand up dude."

I nodded.

"I just want to let you know everything's cool. No one will bother you while you're here. If you want to get into our "Tip," let me know and I will make the necessary arrangements with our people to get you into our organization. We have people in every penitentiary and on the streets and would like to have you on our side. Think about it."

"*Oralé*."

With that he was gone just as quickly as he had appeared. I was glad to know I wouldn't have to worry about getting stabbed by those crazy guys from the *Nuestra Familia* while I was at the reception center. Of course, I also knew that just because someone said they weren't going to do something didn't necessarily mean they weren't going to do it. I'd been taught by Big *Indio* that the underworld was full of treachery and deception.

I went through orientation, saw a doctor, and by noon I was back in my cell pretty much done for the day. That evening I decided to write a letter to my Mama and let her know I was all right. In the letter I told her not to worry because I could take care of myself, and that in three to four months I would be transferring to the institution where I would be serving the remainder of my sentence. I then placed the letter underneath my cell door so the night officer could pick it up and mail it off. Afterward I crawled into bed and passed out for the night.

The next morning was the same routine. I woke up, took a leak, brushed my teeth, washed my face, combed my hair, made some coffee, and waited for the cell door to open. When it did, I stepped out and walked to the chow hall. Again George and Caboobie sat with me while I ate. George told me I would be starting to work in the kitchen with them the following morning.

"So get ready," George said. "I know you don't like to work, but me and Caboobie want you with us. Besides, it's better than sitting in that hot cell all day.

"I don't know about that. I sort of like kicking back doing nothing."

"Come on Homeboy. You have to kick it with us, *Ese*."

"Easy Tiger, I'm just jiving you man. I'll hang out with you guys," I laughed.

"*Oralé*," George replied, beaming.

I began working in the kitchen next morning. I didn't do much except wipe a few tables and hang out with George and Caboobie. We called ourselves *"Los Tres Caballeros."* We did everything together and watched each other's back. We talked about what we were going to do once we got out, but I don't think any of us really believed half the stuff we said. Deep down we knew it was different for us than it was for guys out on the streets and that we would probably die from a violent act or from a drug overdose. Dying from natural causes didn't seem to be in our futures. In fact, George was murdered about six months later after his case was overturned by the California 5th District Court of Appeals. He was out on appeal bond pending the outcome of his case when he was shot in the head by a guy from my neighborhood.

Live by the gun, die by the gun.

But in the meantime, we were having fun living out what we considered our destiny.

One day, as George, Caboobie, and I were taking our after work shower; a White guy who resembled a pit bull totally disrespected me. I think he chose to mess with me because I was small and walked with a limp. However, messing with me would be the last mistake he ever made.

"Hey, man, how about some of that?" he said, as he playfully grabbed at my ass. He didn't touch me, but the mere fact that he pretended he was going to touch my butt was enough to merit whacking him. His total lack of respect took me completely by surprise. Where did this punk get the nerve to come at me this way? I saw George and Caboobie tense up, ready to beat the White Boy on the spot, but I kept them in check.

"Hey, *Ese*," I told them in Spanish, "I'm going to hurt this punk tomorrow."

They nodded and let his disrespect slide, but I knew I couldn't let the White Guy's insolence go indefinitely without becoming his bitch. I didn't intend to let that happen; my career as a gangster was just beginning and I surely wasn't going to let anyone blemish my reputation, especially not some White punk.

When I didn't respond to his disrespect with immediate violence, he took it as a sign of weakness. I could tell by the way he grinned at me that he thought he was going to take my manhood the first time he got me alone. Smiling at the White Guy, but seething with rage, it took every ounce of self-control to keep from hurting him on the spot.

That night, alone in my cell, I contemplated what needed to be done. I knew that to stab someone eye-to-eye was much different than stabbing them under the cover of darkness or during the frenzy of a gang fight, or while under the influence of drugs or alcohol. What I intended to do would be premeditated, face-to-face, in broad daylight, and without any mind altering substances to numb my feelings. But I was sure I could do it. Besides, I didn't have any choice if I wanted to keep my reputation and manhood intact.

I knew I could get George and Caboobie to help me give the White Guy a thorough ass kicking, but then I would lose respect, which would send my reputation on a downward spiral. There was no telling what might happen to me after that. I spent most of the night thinking about what had to be done, knowing that I had to follow through with my initial decision of stabbing this punk. What else could I do? I hadn't made the rules, I just lived by them. The imaginary codebook we all lived by clearly stated that disrespect was to be dealt with swiftly and brutally.

The following morning, after being released for yard call, I contacted *Chino*, an acquaintance I had made while in the county jail. *Chino* was a Mexican National who had been arrested for transporting heroin as he drove through Tulare County on his way to the state of Washington. I had advised *Chino* on his case as it was being litigated. As a result of the information I had given him, *Chino* had gotten off with a much lighter sentence. *Chino* had been so grateful for my help, that he had told me if I ever needed his help all I had to do was ask. *Chino* was a Vacaville mainliner and worked on the prison yard crew. I was sure he had access to a weapon, and I was on my way to ask him for his help in acquiring one. Our conversation was held in Spanish because *Chino* didn't talk English.

"Órale, *Chino*. How are you?"

"Everything's as good as can be expected."

"I need your help," I said, fuming with silent rage.

"How can I assist you?" he asked respectfully.

"I need a knife so I can put some White punk in his place."

"I have just what you need," he said excitedly. "I just sharpened it yesterday."

Looking around to make sure no one was watching, he reached behind a steel cabinet and brought out a long screwdriver that had been ground to resemble a large ice pick. Looking at the menacing weapon, I knew it would do the job.

"You like it?" He asked.

I nodded. "This is just what I need, thanks."

"It's nothing," he replied smiling, seemingly happy that he had been able to help me with my problem.

The weapon *Chino* gave me was a specialty that had been sharpened on a grinder in the prison metal shop and came ready to use. Most weapons in prison were made out of large pieces of metal and sharpened on the cement floor of a cell. Sometimes you could hear the *shish, shish* sound of metal being ground against the cement floor of a cell. It was an eerie sound. What was more unsettling was that you never knew which cell the noise was coming from or if the knife being manufactured was going to be used to stab you. Anytime I heard that uncanny sound, I always came out of my cell even more prepared for the unexpected.

I walked over to George and Caboobie and told them I would be taking care of the White Boy in the dayroom.

They nodded.

After yard recall, I entered the dayroom alone so as not to arouse suspicion. I leaned against a far wall and waited for the guy. As he came into the dayroom, he looked me straight in my eyes with his head held high and tilted to one side. I could see that his chest was puffed out as if he was sure I would be his bitch soon. His arrogance made me so angry; it took all my self-control to restrain myself from rushing over and stabbing him right then.

Be cool, Jess, I told myself. You'll get this overconfident punk in just a few moments. I looked away not wanting to give him any sign about what I had planned.

I wanted him relaxed.

Big *Indio* had drilled me on the crucial element of surprise when making a hit. He said surprising the intended victim was especially important in close quarters where everybody studied each other's body language trying to get an edge. He explained how some guys talked and smiled a lot, trying to get the target to loosen up.

"You have to learn to be poker faced, always watching, aware of every movement because a split second's hesitation can be a dead giveaway and turn an easy hit into a fight for your life."

This guy made it easy for me to stab him. He sat down in a secluded corner of the dayroom to play dominoes with some of his friends and gave his back to me as if he was sure I wouldn't do anything to him.

Bad move, White Boy.

The area where he sat to play dominos was perfect for the hit. It provided plenty of cover from the Man, minimizing the risk of getting caught. I took a deep breath, pulled the weapon from underneath my shirt, and walked swiftly toward him. The guy was so involved with his domino game, he never noticed me until it was too late. I rammed the screwdriver down the back of his neck to the hilt. The guy fell and hit the floor with the handle of the screwdriver grotesquely sticking out. The guys sitting on his table just sat there with their mouths open, stunned at what I had done. It had taken less than five seconds to do my part. If anyone in the dayroom had any misgivings about my manhood, those uncertainties disappeared quickly after I stabbed the guy. I walked away casually so as not to attract attention and heard the guy cry out.

"I don't want to die!"

You should have thought about that before you tried to put your hands on me, punk, I thought coldly.

One of the guards who rushed into the dayroom when he heard the screams hit the panic button on his belt that sent out a loud hornlike sound throughout the institution. Within a few minutes guards were rushing into the dayroom and ordering everyone to lie down on the floor. I heard the guy tell a guard he couldn't move. The guard told him to shut up. I watched the guards from a prone position on the floor as they searched the area for evidence that would give them a clue as to who had committed the stabbing, but there wasn't any physical evidence pointing toward me. The only mistake I had made was to leave the screwdriver in the victim's neck. This could have turned out all bad for me. If one of his buddies would have had any courage, they could have pulled the weapon out and attacked me with it. I knew without any doubt that if someone would have hurt George or Caboobie the way I did this guy, I would have pulled the weapon out and rushed the assailant to get revenge on the spot. No question about it.

I never left a weapon in any of the guys I assaulted after that.

Meanwhile, medical technicians' arrived with a gurney to take the guy to the hospital. As he was being wheeled out, I made eye contact with him. He didn't say anything, but the knowing look in his eyes let me know that he knew it was me who had stabbed him. I never saw him after that day, but I heard through the prison grapevine that he had been transported to an outside hospital and wound up a quadriplegic.

A few days after the stabbing, a guy from Fresno snitched on me to prison investigators and I was placed in segregation. Attempted murder charges were filed against me, but the charges were dismissed eight months later due to lack of evidence. The informant got cold feet about testifying in court against me. During the investigation, I was kept in the Hole until I was transferred to Deuel Vocational Institution (DVI) in Tracy, California.

AS WE FLEW down the freeway toward DVI, known amongst us convicts as "Gladiator School," a place where young gung-ho's went to learn the skills of becoming real gangsters, I wondered why the bus used by the Department of Corrections to transport prisoners was referred to as the "Gray Goose." After all, it wasn't gray; it was actually a dull green.

I had heard, through the prison grapevine, it had been nicknamed the "Gray Goose" by the old-timers because the sole intent of those buses was to transport men, young and old, to a place where life would be gray for many years, if not for the rest of their lives. I only had a six-month to fifteen-year sentence. Therefore, the life thing didn't apply to me. Of course, I could easily pick up a life stretch or even get killed if I weren't careful. I had heard the stories about guys getting whacked at DVI all the time while I had been at Vacaville, and for a split second, I wondered if I would make it out alive. I quickly pushed that thought out of my consciousness. I didn't want to panic right before entering the final stage of becoming a true gangster. I would do my best not to catch a new case if I had to hit someone and make sure I was not caught slipping and make it easy for anyone to take me out.

When we arrived at DVI, nine of us got off the bus. The rest continued on to their designated penitentiary. The ones who stayed behind were strip-searched, fingerprinted, and photographed all over again. Afterward, an officer escorted us down the main corridor to our individual cellblocks. I wound up in C-wing, cell 319.

Walking down this hallway, I felt different than when I had been at the Guidance Center at Vacaville. The passageway here was absent of any noise except for the sound of our footsteps. I also sensed a formidable undercurrent of uneasiness, one that was so potent, it made my heart beat faster. Everyone we encountered had a deadpan expression and looked us up and down as if they could determine what kind of guys we were by the way we walked. I didn't make eye contact with anyone. That was a sign of disrespect. I kept my focus straight ahead.

As we continued on, I did notice there were a few guys that looked different. They carried themselves with an unyielding toughness and displayed no emotion whatsoever. They were dressed in pants and shirts creased to perfection. Their arms were covered with tattoos and many of them had a gang plaque NF tattooed on their left forearm written in Old English script. I knew these were the guys in the *Nuestra Familia*—the guys who later became my brothers.

A few days after I arrived, *Quate*, (pronounced KWATE) an acquaintance from Tulare County who was already "Tipped Up" told me the NF was looking to recruit me. He went on to explain that in order to qualify for membership I would have to undergo an intense background check to ensure I had never raped a woman, molested a child, or betrayed my street Homies.

"You don't have anything to hide, do you? These guys find out everything."

"Naw man, everything's good with me."

I must have passed the test because a few days later, *Chuco*, a high-ranking member of the NF, approached me about joining the organization. *Chuco* was impeccably dressed in prison blues when he walked up to me that day. His hair was cut short and slicked straight back. He had a thick walrus-like mustache and was built slim and trim like a long distance runner. But, what struck me the most about *Chuco* were his eyes. They were dark and piercing. It seemed as though he could look right into your brain and see what you were thinking.

"*Órale, Ese,*" he said. "They call me *Chuco.* You know who I am?"

I nodded.

He stuck out his hand and we shook.

"We've heard good things about you. *Chapo* sent word about what you did to that punk from the "AB's" (the AB's were the Aryan Brotherhood; another prison gang and sworn enemy of the NF) at Vacaville and we want to offer you the opportunity to get in with us. You interested?"

I shrugged.

Big *Indio* had told me many times that silence was more useful than words and that I could get a great deal of information by listening instead of running off at the mouth.

Chuco nodded and went on to give me a brief history about the NF. He said the main reason the NF had been formed was to combat the iron grip of the Mexican Mafia, or *La EME,* the oldest prison gang in California penitentiaries. He said guys had gotten tired of paying *La EME* a percentage of the money they made from selling drugs or any other illicit enterprise. *Chuco* went on to make clear the NF's goals were different. He told me the NF was an organization designed to help educate our Raza so our people could live better lives.

"Unlike those *vatos* from the *EME,* the NF wants to eventually get out of illegal enterprises and launch legitimate businesses so our children won't have to break the law in order to live comfortable," you dig?

"Everything sounds good, but I'm going to need some time to think about joining."

"Of course, I know it's a big decision," he replied. "That's why we always give our prospective members a month to make up their minds. But in thirty days you have to let me know one way or the other, understand?" He said looking at me intently.

"*Simón.*" And we went our separate ways.

That night, back in my cell, I thought about what it meant to get into the NF. I knew it would be a lifetime pledge, but I was already dedicated to this lifestyle anyway. And even though most guys knew I was someone to be reckoned with, becoming a member of the NF would no doubt enhance my current status; guys would think twice about messing with me knowing I had an army of violent soldiers behind me.

Chuco had said that the NF was not like the *EME,* but in many ways it was. It was common knowledge that guys who weren't involved in our thing had to pay tribute to the NF if they wanted to sell drugs, peddle pornography on the tier, or conduct any other illegal business within the prison. By joining, I could harness my criminal interests to this organization and get something besides a reputation. I clearly understood that if I was going to become a true gangster this was the ultimate move. I realized that I might have to make sacrifices that could easily cost me additional time or possibly even a life sentence, but in the end I decided it was to my benefit to join.

One morning, after about two weeks of seriously considering whether to get in or not, I contacted *Chuco* on the yard.

"*Oralé, Carnál*, I'm ready to "clique up."

Chuco looked at me intently and nodded slowly.

"You made the right decision, *Dragón* and you'll find out soon enough that this thing of ours is the real deal. I'm going to be in charge of schooling you.

Teach you how to make shanks out of pieces of steel, zip guns, how to make *wilas* (pronounced WEE-LAZ) and read code. You have to learn sign language because there might come a time when you're in a place where you can't communicate any other way, you know. There's a lot to learn, but don't worry, *Carnál*, you'll gain the knowledge quickly. There's one more thing you have to do to be made, but that will happen in a few days. I'll let you know what to do when the time comes."

I simply nodded.

A few days later, I was given an order by *Chuco* to move on a guy who had done something wrong by NF standards. He didn't tell me what the guy had done and I didn't ask. I simply followed instructions. *Chuco* ordered me to carry out the assault the following morning during breakfast release.

My reaction to the command was somewhat casual. I didn't feel any emotion. It seemed as though it was getting easier for me to execute violent acts. That evening, one of my soon-to-be *Carnáles* passed me a shiv underneath my door. I placed it under my pillow and went to bed, instantly falling dead to the world. I woke up at daybreak ready to do the deed. I took a leak, brushed my teeth, combed my hair, and made a strong cup of instant Folgers coffee. Not long after, I heard the wakeup bell indicating it was close to breakfast. I pulled the knife from under my pillow and slipped it up the sleeve of my jacket so I could drop it into my hand and carry out the job quickly.

When the doors racked, I stepped out of my cell psyched and ready to take care of business. I walked straight toward the unsuspecting victim and attacked him with the stealth and deadliness of a slithering King Cobra. I stuck the guy five times leaving him seriously wounded on the floor. After the assault, I slid the knife under the cell door of an NF member so he could throw the weapon out of his window so that the shank wouldn't get connected to me. Everything was over in less than ten seconds. The cellblock guard didn't even know anything had happened until everyone cleared the tier. By then, I had made my getaway. No arrest was ever made.

Following the stabbing, *Chuco* met me on the yard.

"Welcome to the *Clica, Carnál*," he said as he embraced me.

After the hit, my reputation with the NF was rock solid. I had proven to everyone in our Tip that I had heart. Things were good for about six months, but as time passed, things subtly began to change. I noticed that I hardly ever smiled and rarely spoke. The world I had gotten myself into was always serious. It consisted of nothing more than plotting ways to eliminate our enemies and controlling those around us. I found myself slipping into a much more sinister abyss, where viciousness was looked upon as a good quality and "only the strong survived."

One Saturday morning, about three months after I got into the TIP, three guys from the NF were simultaneously hit. They were all supposed to die, but only Fat Mike was actually killed. The other two miraculously survived their stabbings. At the time, I didn't know why those guys had been targeted for death. Later, I was given an explanation by Chuco. He told me Fat Mike, *Meñito*, and *Pollo* were stabbed because they had shown cowardice.

He said two NF members had been murdered by the *EME* in Susanville and Fat Mike had never retaliated. *Meñito* had let Lugo get killed at Soledad and had done nothing, and *Pollo* had frozen up when an *EME* member had killed *Hueritó* right here in our own house. He went on to say that those guys were examples of what happens to anyone who showed cowardice.

"No one is forgiven weakness!" *Chuco* said.

I had never met *Pollo* because he had been in the "Hole" when I arrived to DVI, but I had known Fat Mike and *Meñito* and they never seemed weak to me. I didn't agree with what the organization had done, but I decided that voicing my point of view at this particular time would serve no purpose. What was done was done.

After that incident the seeds of suspicion seemed to have been planted in the minds of many of our members. Many of the soldiers didn't trust one another the way they had prior to this hit on our own people. I wasn't so trusting after that either.

VIOLENCE AT DVI was common and often erupted unexpectedly. One unusually dense foggy morning in mid November of 1973, *Chuco* and I were on the second tier drinking our morning tumbler of coffee. We were discussing a shipment of drugs that was to be smuggled into the prison later that day.

Chuco told me the Bikers had snuck a batch of barbiturates into the penitentiary the day before and that the Bikers had paid us our percentage. I thought back to what *Chuco* had told me about *La EME*, how they forced guys to pay a fee if they wanted to do business on their turf and stay healthy. He had told me the NF was different, yet we were doing the same thing to anyone who wasn't in our clique.

As I listened to *Chuco* talk about the shipment of drugs which was to be smuggled into the prison later that day, I noticed three Bikers staggering toward a cell belonging to a White Guy who lived on the first tier directly across from where we were standing. I had seen the guy around, but I had never paid him much attention.

I had a clear view into his cell, and saw he was making his bed minding his own business. It didn't look like he was expecting company. I didn't know what the bikers were going to do, but I had an uneasy feeling the Bikers were going to do something to the White guy. I looked over at *Chuco* to see his reaction.

"That's a White thing," *Chuco* said shrugging. "It's none of our business."

Just as I suspected, the three bikers rushed into the White guy's cell.

"Okay, punk," Crazy Joe, one of the Bikers, slurred, completely under the influence of barbiturates. "It's either shit on my dick or blood on my knife."

Had it not been such a life-threatening situation, I would have laughed when I heard the Biker's threat. This was something guys threw around jokingly, and I never thought anyone would actually use it. But, Crazy Joe and his two partners were dead serious, and they had pulled out "bone crushers" (huge knives) to let the White guy know they meant business. The White Guy looked at them with absolute contempt and punched Crazy Joe smack on his mouth. Crazy Joe stumbled backwards from the blow, but quickly recovered. He and his friends went berserk. I watched as Crazy Joe and his two associates stabbed the guy repeatedly. Poor guy never had a chance. One moment he was alive, the next he was dead.

Afterward, Crazy Joe and his two associates wrapped the victim in a blanket and shoved him underneath the bunk in an attempt to hide the body. They whispered something to each other and then Crazy Joe coolly, as though nothing had happened, exited the cell. A few seconds later the two other guys stumbled out of the dead man's cell one at a time. They tried to get to their cells without being detected, but the wing officer noticed their clothing was drenched in blood. He pushed the panic button on his waist and within seconds officers from throughout the institution were rushing into the cellblock. Crazy Joe and his two accomplices' were slammed against a wall, handcuffed, and escorted into K-wing, the solitary confinement unit. I never saw them again.

Although I didn't agree with what these guys had done, I understood their animalistic behavior. We were living in a horrible place among depraved people. If a man wasn't a beast when he came to prison, he would surely be a monster once he was released.

NOT LONG AFTER witnessing that murder, I was in the TV room of my cell-block listening to a guy recount how he had been brutally attacked by the *EME* while he had been in San Quentin. Cadillac Tony, as he was called, was a drug dealer from Fresno, California. They called him Cadillac Tony because he had driven nothing but Cadillac's when he had been on the streets. He said his assailants had stabbed him thirty-eight times, but he had amazingly survived.

Cadillac Tony told me there were two reasons why he had lived through the violent assault. One was because he had been humongous when he had gotten stabbed.

"Check this picture of me before I got hit," he said as he handed me his San Quentin ID.

I looked at the picture and saw that his head was so huge that it covered the whole frame of the ID. His head looked as though it weighed at least fifty pounds. It made me think of a bull's head. If anyone had asked me if this was Cadillac Tony, I would have sworn that there was no way it was him. His weight loss was that drastic.

"The doctor told me that every time the perpetrators stuck me, my body fat closed the wounds and that's what kept me from bleeding to death. Otherwise I would have been a goner for sure. But, I believe the main reason I lived through the assault was because God spared my life. You know, *Dragón*," he continued with genuine sincerity. "God can help you too if you let him."

I was so offended by his remark that it had been difficult to restrain myself from socking him in the mouth. I couldn't believe this guy. Here we were immersed in a world of violence surrounded by madness, guys getting whacked all the time, and he was talking about God's mercy. His faith went beyond my comprehension. Besides, I had never seen God do anything for anyone I knew. The only reason I didn't punch him out was that I figured his mental state must have been affected by the attempted murder on his life.

"Listen, *Ese*," I said my voice on edge as I stared at him with the coldest look I could invoke. "If you want to stay healthy, don't ever talk to me about God again."

From then on I stayed clear of him and he didn't come around me.

"THE FOLLOWING INMATES have visits, Jones, B-28769, Rodriquez B-34859, and De La Cruz, B-47659. Report to the visiting room immediately," the intercom on the main yard announced.

When I heard my name over the intercom, I was shocked, yet thrilled someone had come to visit me. But I didn't show my excitement. In prison, happiness can never be articulated, so I kept a poker face and walked toward the visiting room at an even pace.

When I arrived to the visiting gate, I gave the CO my visiting pass. He quickly herded me into a room and told me to strip. The officer had me open my mouth as he peered inside. He then had me raise my feet so he could look under them for any contraband. I was then instructed to bend over, spread my ass cheeks, and cough three times while he looked up my butt. When the inspection was complete, I hurriedly dressed and stepped into the visiting room.

As soon as I walked in I spotted Mama. She was sitting in a corner of the room. The first thing I noted was that she seemed much thinner than I remembered. She didn't look to weigh any more than one hundred pounds. I tried not to look so shaken by her appearance, but it was difficult.

"How are you, Mama?" I asked as I hugged her. I felt her body tense when I put my arms around her. I was a little hurt by her reaction, but quickly remembered she wasn't used to demonstrating affection. I sat across from her as she wrung her hands and looked around the room wide eyed.

"Oh my God," she said fearfully. "I'm afraid something terrible is going to happen to you in this horrible place."

"Don't worry, Mama. Everything's fine. Nothing's going to happen to me," I replied trying to reassure her.

We talked about what was happening at home and in the neighborhood, but we both shied away from discussing her health. I didn't want to know just how sick she really was. There was nothing I could do to help her now that I was in prison. I was torn between wanting to care and not being able to do so. The world I had chosen to live in was completely devoid of everyday emotions such as love and caring. I couldn't afford to feel sad or hurt because I was sure to be taken advantage by the piranhas on the inside.

Mama didn't stay very long. Before she left, I told her not to come visit me anymore. I didn't want her running up and down the state on account of me having chosen to live in this manner. It broke my heart to tell her, but I pushed that emotion deep inside my gut the way I used to do when I was a kid in the hospital after I had been afflicted with polio. I didn't see my family very often after that. They came on Christmas and sometimes during the summer.

ON NOVEMBER 27, 1973 things changed dramatically throughout the California prison system. The Black Guerrilla Family (BGF) killed a correctional officer. This violent act against staff was a bad move by the BGF. It brought unwanted attention to anyone remotely connected with any prison gang and was the beginning of the end for prison gangs as they were at this time. Before this murder, the police pretty much left us alone and let us do our thing. Administration didn't care about us slaughtering each other, but stabbing an officer was out of the question.

The day of the killing remains vividly stamped in my brain. I was coming from the prison yard when suddenly sirens went off, and cops started to run toward J-Wing where the murder took place. Prisoners were ordered to hit the nearest wall and not move.

I heard an officer on a walkie-talkie repeatedly say, "Officer down, officer down. I don't think he's going to make it."

Me and the prisoners caught in the main corridor were forced to stand with our faces plastered against the wall for about an hour before we were escorted, five at a time, back to our cells. As we walked to our housing units, correctional officers stood shoulder to shoulder in the middle of the main hallway holding long black batons in their hands; watching us as we walked by waiting for an excuse to beat us down. When I walked into my cellblock there were at least fifty officers scattered throughout the unit. I had never seen so many cops in one place in my entire life.

For the next two weeks we were fed in our cells and the institution remained at a standstill. No one was given any information about what had happened. A day or so after the killing, I overheard the guy living below me on the second tier tell his friend through the vent located above the toilet that an officer by the name of Saunders had been executed by the BGF.

After the murder of Officer Saunders, Black convicts were treated the worst. They were targets of prison guard retaliation. I saw correctional officers, for no apparent reason; severely beat a Black guy who lived across from me. When they carried him out of his cell, he was unconscious and blood dripped from his head. I never saw him again.

About two weeks after the murder, prison administration established a Management Control Unit (MCU) at DVI to keep gang members segregated from the general population. Anyone suspected of gang involvement was brought before an administrative team for housing reassignment. I was taken before the commission for placement in MCU.

"You are being placed in MCU because you have been deemed a threat to the safety and security of the institution," the spokesperson said when my hearing was held.

"What do you mean? I've never been found guilty of threatening or hurting anyone."

"Look, De La Cruz. We don't know for sure if you're involved with the NF, but all of the guys you associate with are affiliated."

They were right of course, but I had to at least put up an argument.

"Come on," I replied sarcastically. "I hang out with Chicanos. Unfortunately, you folks believe every Chicano is a gang member. I know there's nothing I can say to make you change your mind, but don't use this lame excuse about associating with gang members as the reason for my segregation."

In the end, I was permanently housed in West Hall where I stayed for the next three years until my release in 1976. There were some guys placed in West Hall who had no gang ties whatsoever, but who had been labeled gang members by prison administration anyway. Later, I heard some of these guys had problems trying to convince the EME they weren't in the NF when they were transferred to other institutions. I knew one guy who was killed by the EME after being labeled erroneously an NF member by prison authorities. I would've hated to be marked NF without the gang's backup. It was serious stuff, but prison officials didn't care. Their only concern was to curb the violence, which had now escalated into killing correctional officers.

LIFE IN MCU consisted of nothing more than staying in a cell approximately twenty-three hours a day. The only time we were released was for breakfast, one tier at a time, to eat in a small dining hall. At noon, we were given a sack lunch to eat in our cells. The lunch consisted of two slices of stale baloney stuffed between sour white bread, a small packet of mustard and mayonnaise, a dried orange, a small bag of chips, and a small container of milk. At dinner we were released again to eat in the dining hall. Three times a week, we were allowed a fifteen-minute shower. Twice a week we were permitted to go onto a small yard located next to the building for about two hours.

To pass time, I began to read everything I could get my hands on. Some of the guys in MCU read books on philosophy by Mao Tse Tung, and Machiavelli, and poetry by Kahlil Gibran. I liked to read action books like Sidney Sheldon's "Rage of Angels," or Louie L'Amour's "Sackets Series." I always got a kick out of the characters in L'Amour's novels. He always made the protagonist a super cowboy. The hero would get shot, thrown off a fifty-foot cliff, crawl for miles over desert sands, broken and bloodied, without water, of course, and then out of nowhere, the cowboy's faithful horse would miraculously appear. The horse would nudge the cowboy out of unconsciousness, somehow get him to saddle up and get him home where in a matter of days the cowboy would recuperate.

Someone in the cellblock turned me onto Dana Fuller Ross's "Wagons West" series, which introduced me to the story about early American settlers pushing their way across the continental United States. The author's detailed description about the hardships the pioneers encountered helped me escape, however brief, the monotony of prison life. Sometimes I would think about how absurd it was that I had always wanted to end up in prison, yet now that I was here, confined to a cell day in and day out, I wanted nothing more than to get away from it.

Stuck in a cell during summer months was unbearable especially in July when the heat penetrated through the concrete walls and turned it into a sweltering chamber. I spent most of those days in boxer shorts lying on the cement floor staring at the walls, trying to will the heat away. I filled my tumbler with cold water and poured it on me as I lay on the floor. I didn't move or speak because talking seemed to generate more heat. Even reading was difficult when temperatures reached the 100 plus mark. Many prisoners smashed out the glass of their cell windows in a vain attempt to cool down. I never busted mine. I didn't think it helped cool anything. Besides, when winter came and temperatures dropped below freezing, the guys who had broken their windows froze their asses. It always took the maintenance crew at least a month before they replaced all the busted glass in the cellblock.

Nothing violent happened those first few months in MCU, but in January of '74, right after New Years, Bruiser, a high ranking lieutenant in the gang, told me the NF was about to start cleaning house.

"We have to get rid of the garbage in our outfit," Bruiser said. "One of the hits is going to take place within a couple of days."

Bruiser went on to say that *Trampa* was getting hit because someone in the organization had found out he was an informant. I didn't believe it. Not for one second. Nevertheless, I didn't betray any emotion or voice my disbelief. I acted as though I believed what he saying, but my mind raced with troubled thoughts especially since *Trampa*, the guy getting hit, was someone I had known for a number of years. He had been in the "Tip" from it's beginning and had stabbed a number of guys considered enemies of the NF. *Trampa* had recently been reassigned to MCU after being housed in K-Wing, "The Hole," for the past year after stabbing an AB sympathizer. I felt bad for *Trampa*, but there wasn't much I could do except try to let him know about the impending move. And even then I was putting myself in jeopardy. Nevertheless, the day prior to the move, I went out on the limb and told *Trampa* to be careful.

"I got something for them," he responded, smiling slyly.

The following morning when we were released for breakfast, *Trampa* rushed out of his cell grabbed Art the Rock by his shirt as he emerged from his cell. Art the Rock screamed like a hysterical woman as *Trampa* stuck him in quick succession. *Chato*, another NF member, reacted without delay and tried to get *Trampa* off of Art the Rock, but *Trampa* had too much skill for him. Every time *Chato* swung to knife *Trampa*, he'd miss his bobbing and weaving target. Eventually, the C.O. in the gun port blasted them while another officer on the first tier yelled, "Killem! Killem!" The officer's screams coupled with the shotgun blasts resonated off the walls and added to the life and death scene taking place on the second tier.

When it was all said and done, *Trampa*, Art the Rock, and *Chato* had all been shot. None of them died, but we lost another good soldier. It seemed to me that the NF was out of control, moving on guys for no apparent reason. It was as though guys in our organization were getting hit simply because there was no one else to kill. We were like bloodthirsty hyenas. Not long after this incident, many guys in the Tip began to dropout. *Quate*, who had been in the NF for six years, came to my cell door after breakfast about a month or so after the move on *Trampa*.

"I'm gone Homeboy" he said sadly.

"What do you mean, you're gone?"

"I'm dropping out Bro. These motherfuckers are crazy and I don't trust most of them anymore. Shit, not knowing if they're going to move on me next is driving me crazy."

I understood his paranoia. Sitting in a cell day in and day out did have a tendency to work on your psyche. *Quate* and I were tight and he wanted to know if we would still be friends after he left the organization.

"*Hey, Carnál,*" I said when he voiced his concerns about our friendship. "You know you're my boy and as long as you don't give up any information to the administration, we're cool."

"*Oralé*, Homes, I'll catch you later."

"*Simón,*" I replied sadly.

It broke my heart to see *Quate* leave the clique, but he wouldn't be the last member to dropout.

Two months later, while I was on the West Hall Yard catching some sun-rays, *Perico*, a high-ranking member of the NF, squatted next to me.

"Say homeboy," he said. "Why don't you go kick it someplace else?"

I could tell by the intensity of the look he gave me that it would be wise for me to follow his suggestion. Not saying anything, I got up and nonchalantly walked over to the far side of the yard and copped a spot against a wall. At first I didn't see anything out of the ordinary, but I knew *Perico* had told me to move because something was going to happen.

As I crouched examining the yard thoroughly, I saw *Chito* and Pretty Rudy (two members of the NF) walking with *Payaso*, another soldier, between them. I had always paid attention to who hung out with whom, just like Big *Indio* had instructed years before. Therefore, I found the interaction between these guys uncharacteristic because *Chito*, Pretty Rudy, and *Payaso* never hung out. That's when I realized *Payaso* was probably the intended victim since he was the one in the middle.

Sure enough, when *Payaso* turned his attention toward the far side of the yard, Pretty Rudy stuck him in his neck with a homemade knife. Pretty Rudy had tried to sever *Payaso's* jugular, but he had missed. I knew he had failed because I had seen two guys get stabbed on their jugular and blood had shot out of the wound like a geyser, which was not the case now. Before Pretty Rudy could do him anymore harm, *Payaso* dashed across the yard in a vain attempt to escape certain death.

It made me sick to my stomach to see the horrendous scene before me unravel. I had never seen guys act so crazily. For whatever reason, many of the guys on the yard got caught up in the viciousness of what was happening on the yard. They formed a gauntlet and kicked, punched, and threw hot coffee at *Payaso* as he ran past them.

Once *Payaso* reached the far wall of the building, there was nowhere for him to go. He was trapped. I saw absolute terror written on his face coupled with confusion about why this was happening to him. Just then *Chito* and Pretty Rudy ran up to *Payaso* and tackled him to the ground. Pretty Rudy then commenced to stab him over and over while *Chito* stomped on *Payaso* unmercifully.

The guards had been distracted by a pre-arranged fight inside the cellblock and before they had had a chance to respond to the incident on the yard, Payaso had been brutally murdered. I considered myself hardcore, but I was truly shaken by what had just occurred; not only because of the viciousness of the act, but also because Payaso had been one of us.

Later, the NF hierarchy informed us that *Payaso* had been killed because he had disrespected a high-ranking member of the NF. I found the reason for killing *Payaso* absurd. After all, he was called *Payaso* because he was always clowning. I didn't vocalize my disgust with what had been done, but I began to suspect that no one was safe. I started to wonder when my time to get hit would come and the seeds of fear that I, too, would be betrayed became more deeply rooted in my mind.

Before anyone had a chance to recover from the viciousness of *Payaso's* murder, the leadership of the organization came up with a strict rule that put many members in grave danger. They passed a directive stating that any member caught using heroin from that point on would be put to death. I couldn't believe they had actually implemented a zero tolerance on the use of heroin. Many of us were heroin addicts and had been sent to prison because we couldn't stop using. And I for one had no intention of quitting, no matter what the consequences.

It was after this announcement that I decided to leave the NF. I had been an active member for a little over two years and had gone beyond the call of duty whenever something needed to be done. It was a very difficult decision to make and a choice that made me feel as though I had failed at being a gangster. Furthermore, I had love for many of the guys in the Tip and realized that once I left, they would become my enemies. For the next couple of years I was in psychological turmoil knowing I was going to leave the gang once I got out, but I stuck to my guns about defecting if and when I was released.

One day, after I had been in segregation for about three and half years, six months or so before my release, someone called out my name while I was on the West Hall yard. At first I didn't recognize who it was, but then it came to me. It was Chicken Man from Boys Camp, the guy who had tried to bully me back in 1968 when I was a juvenile. I had stood up to him then and exposed him as a coward.

Since I had been locked down for a number of years, I didn't know he had gotten into the NF. Had I heard he was being recruited, I would have voted against his membership because I knew he was nothing but a weak punk. I found out later that he had been placed in West Hall a few days earlier after taking part in a hit on the mainline.

"Órale, Carnál," he said smiling brightly at me as though we were friends. "How you been man?" "Listen, *Ese*," I snapped, my voice showing strains of anger and betraying the cool look on my face. "Just because you got into the NF doesn't mean you're my friend. I didn't like you when we were in Boy's Camp and I don't like you now, understand?"

"Hey, *Ese*, I only—"

"Fuck you!" I exploded furiously losing control. "The only reason I don't move on your punk-ass is because you're in the Tip. But don't for one second think we're cool."

I stomped away, leaving him completely humiliated and knowing I had made an enemy for life, but I didn't care. Afterward, I would see him on the yard, but we never spoke. Every time I saw him I wanted to run steel into him, but I knew that if I stabbed him I would be in deep trouble with the organization. He was in and I couldn't touch him no matter how much I hated him.

CHAPTER EIGHT

IN MARCH OF 1975, the CDC implemented a law that set limits on the amount of time prisoners would serve for specific crimes. With the exception of lifers, every prisoner in California prisons was impacted. This declaration was a prelude to Senate Bill 42 (SB42), which was ratified in 1977. SB42 did away with the indeterminate sentencing system being used in California at this time and forced CDC to release hundreds of prisoners onto the streets. I was set free in the summer of '76.

Law enforcement agencies throughout California weren't prepared for this new breed of violent criminal being dumped onto the streets of their cities by CDC. Most of the guys pouring out into society should have never been cut loose. Most of these guys were extremely violent individuals, filled with false pride who demanded respect. They expected everyone to follow their instructions to the letter and they controlled their neighborhoods with brute force. When anyone slighted them, they viciously murdered the person, which sent a message to others that insolence would not be tolerated.

Between March of 1975 and the time I got out, I watched television news reports on gangland killings occurring throughout California. Looking at all the homicide reports on TV worried me because I knew that once I left the organization I would be a target of gang revenge as well. My only consolation was that I had been trained by the best and knew all their tricks. I was going to stay ready for an unexpected visit from the NF once I got out and I didn't have any doubts they would eventually try to collect payment with my blood when I defected.

On August 25, 1976, the day I got out, Mama was at the main gate waiting to drive me home. I was happy to see her. I hadn't seen her in more than three years. She didn't hug me, but I could tell by her radiant smile that she was happy. Taking a glancing look at DVI, I climbed into Mama's car and we drove off. I hadn't been in a car in years and to be honest, I was afraid. It felt as though Mama was driving too fast down the freeway. I looked at the speedometer and saw we were only traveling 55 miles per hour. Mama noticed my apprehension.

"Don't worry son, everything's fine. I'm not going to get us into an accident."

I wanted to believe her, but in my head I was still apprehensive about being in a car. I asked Mama if she could stop at a store.

"I want to buy a beer."

I hadn't drunk beer in a long time, but I hadn't forgotten how alcohol always relieved me of anxiety. Mama pulled off the highway and stopped at a 711 where I bought a six-pack of Budweiser. Once back in the car, I pulled a beer out of the bag, popped the tab, and took a big drink. The beer burned my throat as I guzzled it, but I didn't stop until I ran out of breath. I still didn't like the taste, but after a few drinks I noticed I wasn't afraid anymore. The alcohol had done its job.

That afternoon, many of the guys from my neighborhood came by to pay their respect. Homeboy *Pato* had been on the streets about a year and dropped by my house to say hello. He told me there was going to be a party in my honor at his house later that evening.

"There's going to be plenty of booze and women to go around," he said. "I'll pick you up around six."

"*Oralé.*"

Pato kept his word and took me to the party that night. Coming back to the *barrio* after serving time in prison was just like I had always envisioned. Everybody who was anybody from the neighborhood was there to pay me tribute. There were many people I didn't recognize, but *Pato* told me who they were.

"That's little Anna," he said pointing to an attractive young lady looking seductively at me. "Fat Joe's sister."

"She's all grown up," I responded.

"You were gone a long time Homeboy."

"Yeah, I guess I was," I replied as I nodded at Anna.

Anna sashayed over and gave me a tight hug as she rubbed her body against mine. The warmth of her breath tickled my ear as she whispered she wanted to make passionate love to me. I didn't know a damn thing about making love, so I simply nodded and told her I would take her up on her offer at a later date. I was too consumed with the attention being showered on me by the guys from the neighborhood to be distracted by a woman.

Throughout the night guys walked over and shook my hand. Many of them told me that if I needed them for anything all I had to do was let them know.

At the end of the night, I took *Pato* to one side and told him I had left the NF.

"Hey, *Dragón*," he replied. "You're my boy. And no matter what, we're going to look out for you. The homies know it's their responsibility to back you up. Besides, you would be there for us if we needed your backup."

"*Oralé*, thanks."

For the next three days I was too high on heroin to get together with Anna, but about a week later I took advantage of the opportunity she had offered me at the party.

I HAD BEEN released from prison during the Thompson grape season, and three days later I went to work for my Father supervising a crew of about twenty-five farm laborers. My job was to make sure the workers picked all the grapes off the vineyards and spread them on paper trays evenly so the sun could bake them into raisins. Unlike the picker's job, my assignment wasn't so back breaking, but it was dirty work. Every evening I would come home covered by a thin layer of dust which made me look as though I had been in a dust storm. I hated the job, but I took the post to give my parents the impression I was going straight. Even after serving all those years in prison, I never thought about going legit. My plan was to start selling drugs as soon as I found a good connection. I surely wasn't going to work in the fields like a common laborer for the rest of my life. As far as I was concerned, crime was the name of the game.

During the short time I managed the crew; a woman by the name of *Doña* Olivia worked for me. She reminded me of the Wicked Witch of the West in the "Wizard of Oz." She had a mole on her nose and thick frizzy black hair that stuck out from under the old black stovetop hat she wore. All she needed was a cape and a bike with a basket. She was always dressed in the same grimy oversized plaid shirt and Levi pants.

Many of the older folks who lived in the *barrio* called her *La Bruja* (the witch), but never to her face. Most people were afraid of her. They were scared she would cast a spell on them if they got her angry. She also had a reputation of being a murderer. Years before, she had been accused of drowning her husband in the bathtub. She was also suspected of the brutal murder of her previous lover who had been found slumped over the steering wheel of his car with his head bashed in a few years before. *Doña* Olivia's lover had been beaten so badly that dental charts had been used to make a positive identification. Someone had pushed the car into a canal on the outskirts of town. *Doña* Olivia had been interrogated by homicide detectives concerning the killing, but she had adamantly denied any involvement. I personally wasn't afraid of her and didn't care if she was a *Bruja* or if she had killed those men. My only interest was in meeting her daughter, Maria.

I had been attracted to Maria since I was a youngster. Her allure for me had been purely psychical, but I'd never had the chance to meet her in person. Now that Doña Olivia was working for me, I intended to use my position and manipulation skills to have her introduce me to Maria. During the first couple of days she worked for me, I told her the penitentiary had given me an opportunity to look at my life and that as a result I had been able to recognize my wrongs and learn from my mistakes.

"I don't want to be a criminal anymore," I told her one morning. "I just want to do the right thing."

Of course, I was lying. I was already using dope, but *Doña* Olivia didn't know this and she went for my bullshit hook, line, and sinker.

"You know what?" She said a few days later. "I want you to come over to my house and speak to Maria. Maybe she'll listen to your advice and quit getting involved with losers and stop having babies."

I knew Maria had a son and that she was pregnant again, but I didn't care. I was thrilled by *Doña* Olivia's invitation and told her I would come by her house the following Friday.

When Friday evening came, I took extra time to get dressed and made sure my Levi jeans and denim shirt were pressed to perfection. I polished my Florsheim shoes to a glossy shine and shot some heroin for courage. By now I was hooked again, but I had plenty of money because working as a crew boss paid well so I didn't have to revert to crime to support my habit yet.

I approached Maria's house cautiously, and even though I was high on heroin, I was still apprehensive as I knocked on the front door and waited for someone to answer. I could hear my heart pounding, and I pulled a handkerchief from my back pant pocket to wipe the sweat off my hands. My nervousness made me feel like a kid on his first day of school. I pulled a Camel non-filter cigarette from my pack and lit it. Taking a deep puff, I knocked again. Still, no one answered. Just as I was about to leave, *Doña* Olivia opened the door.

"Come in, come in," she said, smiling. "Sorry for taking so long to answer the door. Have a seat and give me a moment to let Maria know you're here."

I sat on an old musty sofa and waited anxiously for approximately ten minutes before Maria entered the room. Her entrance was slow and she had her head tilted to one side, squinting as her eyes adjusted to the dimness of the room. Maria was even prettier than I remembered. She had model-like high cheekbones, lush full lips, a radiant smile, and brown eyes that sparkled even in the dimly lit room. Her light complexion was accentuated by auburn hair, which cascaded down to her petite ass. She smiled at me shyly.

"Hello," she said.

I simply nodded, unable to speak.

Maria sat on another worn sofa located against a wall. I saw a cockroach scamper across the surface of the coffee table between us. I wanted to smash the cockroach, but I pretended not to notice it. I didn't want to make her feel uncomfortable.

"When did you get out?" she asked.

"I've been out about three weeks."

"You were gone a long time, huh?"

"Yeah, I guess I was."

I saw another cockroach scurry on the table in front of me.

"I've heard there's lots of violence in those places," she went on. "How did you survive without getting hurt? And how did you keep from going crazy after being cooped up in a cell for so many years?"

"I have to admit it was tough, especially at first. In the beginning, not being able to talk with anyone for days at a time was the hardest. I thought I would go insane, but after some time, I started to enjoy the solitude. It gave me an opportunity to get in touch with myself."

The things I told Maria that evening were mostly lies, but by the end of the night Maria was talking freely with me.

"You know," she said. "I used to be really scared of you, but you're nothing like I thought you would be."

"You were?" I asked surprised with what she said. "Why were you afraid?"

"Well, rumor has it, you're a pretty mean guy and that you've hurt lots of people, but now that I've had a chance to meet and talk with you, I find you're actually nice, understanding and you seem to know a lot about life."

"Well, Maria," I lied again. "I've never hurt anyone who didn't have it coming or who wasn't trying to hurt me."

"I'm glad to hear that. Hopefully we can become friends," she said smiling brightly as she bid me goodnight.

Walking home afterward made me feel as though the Gods of Love had shined on me. I began dating Maria on a regular basis after that and a few months later we moved into our own apartment. *Doña* Olivia was livid.

"I invited you into my home and you stole my daughter."

Of course *Doña* Olivia was right, but I didn't care about what she thought. I had won Maria and that was all that was important. What was done was done, and if *Doña* Olivia didn't like it, she would have to get over it.

Once we started living as a couple, I told Maria a little about my defection from the NF. I didn't want to scare her, but I had to make sure she understood the seriousness concerning this situation. I explained that I had taken a till-death-do-us-part oath and that she wasn't to trust anyone because sooner or later the NF would come to hurt me. Maria followed my instructions to the letter. She never spoke about my problem with the NF to anyone.

I was always prepared for an unexpected visit from the NF too. I slept with a fully loaded Remington twelve-gauge pump shotgun by my bed and a thirty-eight semiautomatic Smith & Wesson under my pillow. But not knowing when the NF would attempt get their revenge was nerve-racking. If not for the temporary relief I got from heroin, I would have had a nervous breakdown for sure.

Eight months after Maria and I started living together, Maria did me wrong. She spent the night with the father of her daughter Lisa. When I found out what she had done, I wanted to kill her, but of course I didn't. I struggled with my emotions, but ultimately decided to stay with Maria even though she had been unfaithful. It was a difficult decision for me because I had never dealt with infidelity. A few months later, Maria told me she was pregnant. Later we found out she was going to have twin boys. I wanted to be happy, but I didn't know if the babies were mine. So I simply pushed her betrayal into the pit of my gut like I did everything else that I couldn't take care of with violence.

A YEAR AFTER SB42 passed, Chicken Man was released from D.V.I. Since I had dropped out of the NF, I knew he would jump at the opportunity to get revenge on me for humiliating him while we were in West Hall a few years before. One day, one of my homeboys approached me with some serious news.

"Hey Homeboy," *Loco* said, "That punk Chicken Man was in the *barrio* last night asking about you."

"Was he alone?"

"Naw man, he had his sister Carmen and two other guys with him."

"*Oralé*, Homeboy, thanks for the information."

The following week I looked for Chicken Man every day. I wanted to break his legs or bust his head so he would stop looking for me, but he was keeping a low profile and I couldn't find him. A few days later, on the morning of August 31, 1977, I stopped off at Mama's to pick up a pair of clean socks before meeting up with her at the courthouse where she was waiting for me. I had to appear in court that morning for assaulting *Doña* Olivia. The lady had come to my house one evening a few weeks before ranting about how much of a loser I was. When I asked her to leave, she had responded by slapping me across my face, not once, but five times. I didn't believe in hitting women, but if a woman wanted to act like a man and put her hands on me, I didn't have a problem reacting with violence.

Therefore, when *Doña* Olivia hit me I had retaliated by punching her out. I broke her nose and blackened both her eyes. She had filed assault charges on me and I had been arrested. Posting the twenty thousand dollar bail, I was out on bond pending litigation of the case.

As I entered Mama's house I called out to *Neto*, my younger brother, but got no response. *Neto* had called me the night before and told me he was coming over to my house. He said he needed to talk to me, but he had never shown. Entering the bedroom where he slept, I saw why he hadn't responded when I called out to him. His body was lying on the floor in a pool of coagulated blood. He was shirtless and the stab wounds on his body were clearly visible. Later, an autopsy determined he had been stabbed forty-seven times.

I had witnessed many killings during the time I was in prison, but I wasn't prepared for the sight I encountered that morning. I stood frozen for a few seconds at the doorway of the bedroom looking down at my brother's lifeless body as snap shots of *Neto*'s life rushed through my mind. I remembered how young *Neto* had been when I left to prison. He had been around twelve when I went away and eighteen when I had returned. Sadly, we hadn't spent any time with each other because on the day of my release, *Neto* had surrendered into the custody of the Tulare County sheriff to begin serving a year in the county jail.

I had visited *Neto* a few times during his incarceration and had picked him up on the morning of his release two days before.

"You know, Jess," he had said with complete admiration that day. "Thanks for visiting me while I was in jail. If it wasn't for you and Mama putting money on my books and you coming to visit me once in a while, I would have felt completely abandoned."

I had wanted to embrace him and let him know that I loved him, but I didn't know how to express those emotions. Now he was dead and I would never be able to tell him how much I cared.

Coming out of my daze, I stumbled toward the bathroom, using the walls to steady myself. When I got to the toilet, I puked my guts out. After I finished vomiting, I splashed cold water on my face trying to wash away the image of my brother's mutilated body. Afterward, in a trance, I walked outside toward *Pato* and Maria who were waiting in my car.

"What's the matter?" *Pato* asked.

"*Neto*'s dead. I think he overdosed."

Pato got out of the car hurriedly and jetted inside the house. A minute or so later he came back and cautiously told me he didn't think *Neto* had overdosed.

"There's too much blood."

I didn't comprehend what he was saying. I was in shock. Everything seemed surreal. It was as though I was looking at what was happening from a distance. I saw *Pato* walk inside the house to call the police. I don't remember how long it took them to arrive to Mama's house. I lost all sense of time. What I did know was that I had to tell Mama about my brothers killing. I asked *Pato* to drive me to the courthouse where Mama was waiting.

When we got there, I could tell by the way Mama arched her eyebrows that she knew something was wrong. Mama could always read me like a book. She didn't wait for me to walk over to where she stood. Instead, she walked over to meet me as I approached her.

"What's the matter?" She asked.

There wasn't an easy way to tell her about *Neto's* homicide.

"*Neto's* dead, Mama."

"What did you say?"

I didn't respond. I just stood there helpless with the picture of my brothers' lifeless body carved into the recesses of my conscious.

Mama got a crazy look. Her face contorted with anguish. The blood drained from her face and her cheeks paled. Her lips quivered and her eyes fluttered wildly. She lost her equilibrium and her knees buckled. I caught her before she hit the sidewalk and held her tightly as she screamed.

"No! No! No!"

Hearing Mama's piercing cry and seeing the sorrow on her face made me want to cry, but I held my tears in check keeping in mind that no matter what, "Men Don't Cry."

Holding her in my arms I wished I could protect her from the heartache she was experiencing, but there was nothing I could do but hold her as she shuddered grievingly. The following day would be her birthday.

Life sure was cold.

The day after *Neto's* murder Maria delivered twin boys by cesarean section. Some members of my family wanted me to name one of twins after my brother *Neto*, but both Maria and I agreed that if we did, the, that particular twin would not have his own identity. Since they were identical, we gave them names with the same meaning, yet were pronounced different. One was named *Angel* and the other *Santos*.

It was tough for me to handle everything that was happening, but I dealt with it by using more heroin than I ordinarily did. I would wake up in the morning and immediately take a shot. I'd take another injection by midmorning, then again at noon, and yet another by mid-afternoon and then another and another.

I don't know how my family members dealt with *Neto's* murder. I mean, I had heroin to lean on, but they had nothing except their own strength. What I do know is that everyone was extremely sad because *Neto* was only twenty years old when he got killed. He had had his entire life to live. They were also on edge and had trouble sleeping at night because no one knew who had killed *Neto* and everyone was afraid the killers would come back and hurt someone else in the family. It wasn't until a week or so after *Neto's* homicide that the police received an anonymous tip from a woman indicating it had been Chicken Man and two others who had brutally taken my brother's life.

The tipster turned out to be Carmen. Chicken Man's sister. A few days after she called the police, Carmen walked into Woodlake police headquarters with her lawyer and gave homicide detectives a statement naming the three guys involved in *Neto*'s murder. The cops arrested one of the suspects in San Jose, California, another culprit was apprehended in Fresno, and Chicken Man was taken into custody at Ontario Airport as he was about to board a plane bound for Mexico. All three were returned to Tulare County to stand trial.

After Chicken Man and the other two suspects were apprehended, and the sequence of events concerning *Neto*'s murder began to unfold, many members of my family looked at me as though his murder was my fault. No one accused me directly, but I could tell by the accusatory stares that they held me accountable. I blamed myself for his death too. After all, if I hadn't gotten into the NF, this might never had happened. I finally got the courage to speak to Mama and told her I was sorry for what happened.

"You shouldn't feel guilty *Mijo*. It wasn't your fault."

Still, the guilt gnawed at me and I didn't want anyone else in my family getting hurt or murdered because of my lifestyle, so I decided to leave the state.

I told Maria I was leaving for Texas to meet my real father. She didn't want me to go, but there wasn't much she could do to make me stay and I couldn't take her with me. The next day I bought enough heroin to last me a few days. I knew I would have to find a heroin connection quickly once I got to Texas because heroin didn't care if you moved somewhere else. The Gorilla, as I called my heroin habit, needed to be fed no matter what. And so it was that I boarded a plane bound for Texas.

WHILE I WAS IN PRISON, I had often imagined how it would be if I ever met my biological father. In my fantasies, he would always embrace me and explain his reasons for walking out on Mama and me. In my illusions I would forgive him and we would "live happily ever after." Of course, as is the case with most fantasies, they rarely, if ever, come true.

When I landed at the airport in McAllen, Texas, my biological father was there to meet me in a cream colored 1968 Chevy station wagon. I immediately saw the resemblance between us. I had his eyebrows, his large nose, and the same intense look. He didn't hug me or say much as he helped carry my suitcases to his car, but once we were on our way to his house, he began to ask about my involvement in crime.

"You know what, *Jesús*. I don't know how you were raised, but I was told you were in prison for stealing. Is that true?" he asked glancing at me.

I nodded.

"No, *Señor*. I won't allow thieves to live in my house. So you're going to have to get a job and earn your money honestly. I don't want any problems with the police, understand?"

His words cut deep. I couldn't believe he was talking so raw to me after only meeting a few minutes before. I took so much offense to what I considered insults, that for a brief moment, I entertained the thought of socking him on his mouth.

In the penitentiary no one had ever spoken to me so disrespectfully and gotten away with it. The only reason I didn't punch him out was because I had been taught by my older homeboys to respect my elders no matter what and beating my father would be totally out of line.

My real father was a tall man with a deep masculine voice and a permanent scowl on his dark complexioned *Mestizo* face. My aunt *Lupe*, his older sister, told me my father was a stubborn man who did what he wanted and no one could tell him anything. She said that on weekends he would go across the border to Reynosa, Mexico to drink and carouse with other women for days at a time, yet here he was pointing his finger at me for the way I lived. I thought he was nothing more than a hypocrite. He might not have stolen merchandise out of stores like I did, but I'm sure he stole his family's peace of mind.

Early the next morning, I told my father I was going to the unemployment office to see about getting a job.

"You should go to the corner of 18th street instead," my father said as I prepared to leave the house. "A lot of men go there to find work."

I told him I would, but I had no intention of going to the unemployment office or 18th street. I was really on my way to the local Methadone center where I knew I would find heroin addicts. Methadone, a narcotic pain reliever, similar to morphine, was being used to reduce withdrawal symptoms for people addicted to heroin. Clinics had sprung up throughout cities in the U.S. during the late 1960's. I had found the address of the local clinic in the phone book, which luckily for me, wasn't very far from my father's house.

When I got to the center, I waited outside until I spotted a guy with an extremely thin physique, deep sunken eyes with dark shadows around them, and a sickly yellowish complexion. He was in a rush to get inside the clinic so I decided to wait until he came out to speak with him about scoring some heroin for me; a delicate situation to say the least. I wasn't worried about the guy thinking I was a cop, but I knew he would be concerned about me being a snitch.

"Hey, Homeboy," I said to the guy. "My name is *Dragón* and I need to buy some dope."

"I don't know you," he replied eyeing me suspiciously.

"I know that, *Esé*. I just got in from California yesterday. I had to leave because the cops are looking for me up there," I lied.

I had to make my being there believable or else he wouldn't help me out.

"If you score for me I'll turn you on to a free shot and fix my dope in front of you so you don't have to worry about me taking any of the dope with me and giving it to the police."

"*Oralé*," he said cautiously. "How much do you want to buy?"

"A fifty dollar bag."

"Do you have a car?"

"Naw, I walked here."

"Let's go in mine."

We climbed into his car and took off. He drove through the Mexican part of town until we came to a house hidden among a grove of trees. I gave the guy my money and he disappeared into the grove. He came back in a matter of minutes and we fixed right there on the spot. Afterward he told me his name was *Flacó*.

"Listen, *Bato*" (in Texas they pronounced *vato* with a B not with a v), "I usually have stuff myself, but I fixed it all last night. If you want to buy some more stuff later, here's my number so you can call me," he said as he handed me a piece of paper.

"*Oralé*," I replied.

That day, and for the next three months I stayed at my real father's house until I got arrested for shoplifting Polaroid film out of a Piggly-Wiggly Grocery Store in Alamo, Texas. Since he had told me how he felt about thievery from the beginning, I didn't believe he would bail me out, but I called and asked if he would at least cosign my bond if I got the money. Just as I suspected, he said no.

Later, I called Mama and asked her if she would lend me the one thousand dollars, ten percent of the ten thousand dollars required to post bail and cosign for my release because my father had refused to do anything to help me get out of jail.

"Not only will he not sign to get me out," I said as I spoke to her on the phone from the Hidalgo County Jail in Edinburg, Texas. "But he gave the police information that got me into deeper trouble."

"He did what!?" Mama exclaimed. "I'm going to call that *cabrón* and make him get you out. Don't worry. I'll take care of everything, even if I have to travel to Texas myself."

Mama and my real father hadn't spoken to each other since he had walked out on her after he had gotten her pregnant with me. I don't think Mama would have ever talked with him had it not been for my incarceration. In her anger, however, Mama threw caution to the wind and called my father to confront him about his refusal to bail me out of jail.

When they spoke, my father told Mama he didn't want to sign because he didn't want to be liable for paying the additional nine thousand dollars in case I fled Texas without appearing in court. Mama, on the other hand, told him that even if I did leave him with a nine thousand dollar debt he had gotten off cheap since he had never done anything for me while I was growing up.

"The least you can do is to get him out of jail one time," Mama said. In the end, Mama won, and he signed.

When I walked out of jail a few days later, father was waiting in the lobby. As he drove to his house, he told me I would have to find another place to live. He complained that my criminal behavior had caused too much friction between him and his wife, Lupe. I was going through heroin withdrawals and not paying much attention to what he was saying. My only concern was to relieve the agony I was suffering, so I simply nodded my head.

It was too late to call *Flacó* so I toughed it out until morning. That night, I suffered both physical and emotional torture. I don't know which were worse; the cramps, vomiting, hot and cold flashes, or the torment of not being able to purge the image of my brother *Neto*'s mutilated body from my consciousness. Without heroin, I could clearly envision him lying on the floor dead and picture the pain on Mama's face when I told her about his murder.

As soon as there was light the next morning, I went straight to *Flacó's* house to get fixed. *Flacó* must have been watching through his living room window, because before I had a chance to knock, his door swung open. I could tell by *Flacó's* droopy facial expression and the way he stood at the doorway scratching his scrotum that he was under the influence of heroin. Knowing this gave me hope because I knew it wouldn't be long before I would get fixed and all my pain would disappear. I had never met anyone whom I considered God, but at that precise moment, *Flacó* was God. He had what I needed.

It didn't matter that he looked anorexic and that his facial bone structure was clearly pronounced because he seldom ate as a result of his constant use of heroin. It was of no consequence to me that his eyes were devoid of light and sunk deep into their sockets with dark circles around them. I didn't care that the veins on his arms were marked by dark scar tissue that made them look like railroad tracks.

He was my Savior.

"*Órale, Dragón*," he slurred, as he opened the door. "You look bad, man. Where you been?"

"I've been in jail," I replied weakly.

"Come inside and let me fix you up, homeboy."

I followed him into his shooting gallery located at the back of his house. I could hardly wait to feel the warm euphoric sensation of the brown powder treasured by heroin addicts. I handed *Flacó* twenty-five dollars that he quickly stuffed into his pant pocket. He then pulled out his magic works and began to prepare a fix for me. I watched him pour the brown granules into a tablespoon and draw water into the syringe. Squirting the water into the spoon he then struck four matches and held the fire underneath the spoon to dissolve the fine particles of heroin into liquid. The smell of burning sulfur made me want to puke, but I held on, shivering, while needing to defecate and throw up at the same time. I tied a dirty red bandana around my left bicep to build up my blood pressure and waited anxiously for *Flacó* to finish preparing the stuff.

When he completed dissolving the powder, *Flacó* dropped a small piece of cotton into the cooker to use as a filter, and then drew the liquid into the syringe. Once done, he handed me the hypodermic filled to the top with the brown solution. I snatched it from his hand and put the syringe between my teeth as I slapped the vein on the crook of my arm to make it stand out even more. When the vein was clearly visible, I stuck the needle into it. Immediately, blood shot up into the syringe indicating I had made a direct hit. I slowly pushed the plunger down to inject the liquid into my bloodstream. At once, the drug took effect. I felt the warmth of it begin at the tips of my toes and spread rapidly throughout my entire body. Straight away every ache in my body, the nausea, the hot and cold flashes, the guilt about my brother's murder, and the image of Mama's anguished face vanished! I handed *Flacó* the syringe and took a seat on a well-worn sofa to enjoy my high. I sat for hours with my head on my chest comatose to the world.

After the effects of the heroin began to weaken, I left *Flacó's* house and found temporary refuge at a homeless shelter. There, I began to think about the way I was living and how my lifestyle had hurt so many people. I also thought about how my father had booted me out of his house so coldly. I found myself swimming in an ocean of misery, thoroughly soaked with grief. I wanted to cry, but I didn't know how to shed tears. Instead, I reacted in anger and decided to leave Texas vowing never to return.

A few days later I bought a Greyhound ticket and enough heroin to last me until I arrived in California. As the bus traveled down the highway, my heart throbbed with sorrow. I tried to rid myself of my emotional torment by slamming as much heroin as I could without overdosing, but the dope only brought temporary deadness to my despair. I wasn't equipped to handle this type of pain. So I stuffed my emotions inward and returned to California with a bottomless void in my soul. I felt like a weak punk for allowing my father to hurt me so bad.

After that, I didn't let anyone touch my heart for years. I made my heart hard like penitentiary steel so nothing could cause me so much pain ever again.

WHEN I GOT BACK to California, after three days and two nights on the road, Maria and the kids were waiting for me at the Greyhound depot. I don't know how she knew I was arriving when I did, but I was glad she was there. I hadn't fixed since the night before and it was now noon. I was beginning to get heroin sick and needed a shot quick! Giving her a hurried hug, I jumped into the driver's seat of our 1966 Chevy Caprice and drove as fast as I could to my Homeboy Alex's house to get fixed.

"I'll be right back," I told Maria when we got to his house. She gave me a knowing look but didn't say anything.

Knocking on the door, I waited for Alex to open up. I knew he was home because his car was parked in the drive way and Alex never went anywhere unless he drove.

"Hey, Home-Squeeze," he said smiling as he opened the door. "Where you been, *Ese?*"

"I've been in Texas. You have any dope?" I asked.

"*Simón.* You need a shot?"

"Hell, yeah! I haven't gotten well since last night."

"Well, come inside. I have everything laid out."

Alex led me to a back room of his house with nothing more than a small wooden table and two steel chairs. On the table lay a small container of water, a cooker made out of a wine bottle cap, some matches, and a syringe. Alex handed me a piece of tin foil that held Mexican Tar heroin. (Tar heroin had recently been introduced in California and had replaced the powder stuff still being used in Texas). I hurriedly unfolded the foil and scraped the sticky Tar onto the cooker to prepare for injection. It didn't take me long to get the stuff ready and slam it into my vein. In seconds, I felt normal again.

"Listen Homeboy," I told Alex after I finished. "I gotta get going. I have Maria and the kids waiting in the car, but we'll get together soon and catch up on the latest news, cool?"

"*Oralé*, Homes."

I spent the next couple of days with Maria and the kids, but then hooked up with a couple of hoodlums from Visalia. Hollywood, who got his nickname because he always wore dark prescription Ray-Ban sunglasses, became my partner in crime. He had grown up a criminal and was a heroin addict just like me. I had met him during one of my incarcerations.

I had never met Leonard, the other guy who became my crime partner, but Hollywood, whom I trusted to the fullest, said Leonard was reliable and that was good enough for me. Leonard was currently out on bail for escaping from the Farmington, New Mexico County Jail.

"We hog tied the cop, locked him in a cell, and bolted out the back door of the detention center," he said. "But we didn't stay on the streets long because the guy who escaped with me got drunk and beat his wife for being unfaithful to him while he was in jail. Can you believe that shit? Had I known he only wanted to break out to beat his lady, I never would have escaped in the first place. I posted bail after I was rearrested and have been on the streets for the past year. I just pled guilty to a two-to-ten year prison term in New Mexico last week. In thirty days I have to turn myself into custody to begin my prison sentence. The judge gave me a stay of execution so I can get my personal affairs in order before."

"That's the house right there," I told Leonard, changing the subject. "Pull into the driveway."

Before my brother's murder, a guy I knew had told me about the valuable coin collection in this particular house. I had cased the house and learned that the owner left every morning for about an hour. I had had every intention of burglarizing the house, but after my brother's homicide I had left to Texas.

As Leonard drove into the driveway, I noticed that the homeowner's car was gone. I got out of our car and walked cautiously to the house and knocked hard on the front door. When no one answered, I took a set of channel locks from my back pocket and easily snapped the lock and slowly opened the door and listened for any noise that would indicate someone was home. After making sure no one was there, I signaled Hollywood and Leonard to join me. In seconds, they were at my side.

We hurriedly stepped indoors and spread out inside the house. Hollywood and Leonard unplugged the TV, stereo, and other electrical appliances. I went straight toward the bedroom where my friend said the owner kept his coin collection. Stepping into a large walk-in closet in the master bedroom, I found what I was searching for. The small safe was in a corner of the closet with the doors open. I wondered why the owner of the house had bought a safe only to leave the door ajar. I swung the door completely open and pulled out one of the drawers. Inside were seven Double Eagle twenty dollar gold pieces. One of the Double Eagles dated back to 1849. There were other coins and jewelry inside as well. I didn't have any doubt we could get a substantial amount of money for this merchandise. I had a fence (a guy who buys stolen property), so getting rid of this stuff wouldn't be difficult.

The fence was a shifty lawyer who represented drug dealers. One of his clients, a guy named Marcelino, introduced me to the attorney at a party.

"If you run into any gold, jewelry, or valuable coins, make sure you come to see me," he had said that night.

I lifted the safe and carried it outside and placed the strong box in the trunk of the car. I saw Hollywood and Leonard carrying a huge TV out of the house.

"Forget about that," I told them as I slammed the car trunk shut. "We have plenty goods right here," I said as I smacked the trunk with the palm of my hand.

They dropped the TV on the spot and we drove off. It seemed we had gotten away scot-free until Leonard started to complain about leaving the TV and other goods behind.

"How are we going to make any money when we don't have anything to sell?"

"Listen, *Ese*," I replied somewhat angrily. "I already told you that the merchandise in the trunk will bring us lots of money. Shit, if we don't make at least twenty thousand dollars, we're not making a penny."

Before Leonard could respond I saw a sheriff's patrol car heading our way. Instinctively, I knew we were in trouble. I found out later that there had been a rash of residential burglaries in the area and that the cop on patrol that morning was on a special team specifically developed to curb the burglaries.

"That cop's going to pull us over, watch," I said matter-of-factly.

Sure enough, he flipped a U-turn and began to pursue us with the red lights on his patrol unit spinning round and round. Leonard started to speed up as though he was going to attempt to outrun the cop.

"What the hell you doing, *Ese?*" I asked. "We can't get away from him in this bucket. Pull the damn car over." Leonard followed my instructions.

Once we stopped completely, the officer walked over toward our car and peered inside cautiously. I saw he had his hand on his gun ready to pull it in case anyone made a wrong move

"You have driver's license?" He asked Leonard.

"Why did you stop us?" Leonard asked as he handed the cop his license.

"Because you don't have a '78 sticker on your license plate."

What a fucking idiot! I thought, rolling my eyes in exasperation. I couldn't believe we had been using an unregistered car to commit felonies.

The fact that the car was not registered was all the probable cause the cop had needed to stop us. In the meantime, I was trying to decide if I should give the officer an alias. I knew more cops would be arriving soon. Since I was well known by police, I realized that if I gave this officer a bogus name and was recognized by another policeman, it would give them more suspicion to pursue this traffic stop. As I struggled with my dilemma, two more patrol cars showed up. I decided to give the cop my real name.

When the officer told Leonard to get out of the car and began to search him, I slipped the key of the trunk into my mouth swallowed it. I couldn't let them uncover the stolen property stashed in the trunk. We would be gone for sure.

In the meantime, the officer who made the initial stop ran our names through police headquarters to find out if any of us were fugitives. As a fate would have it, a detective thirty miles away heard my name over his police radio and immediately radioed the onsite officer to inform him that I was a burglar. He told him that we were probably responsible for the burglary that had just been reported nearby. I think the onsite officer had been away from his car when the transmission had been aired and had missed the police broadcast. During this time police officers didn't carry radios on their person like they do today. We were arrested on the spot. I knew right then I was on my way back to prison.

It took eight months before Hollywood, Leonard and I were convicted and sentenced to state prison. Hollywood received a sixteen-month sentence with credit for time already served and was released from prison six months later.

Not long after he was let loose, I read about Hollywood in the Visalia Times, Newspaper while I was in Soledad State Prison. According to the article, Hollywood had attempted to rob a Savings and Loan office in Merced, California. The robbery had gone bad with Hollywood almost crashing into an officer responding to the silent alarm triggered by an employee of the S&L. Since Hollywood didn't want to get arrested, he sped off onto Freeway 99. The chase had escalated into a shootout and culminated with Hollywood's capture. Fortunately for Hollywood, no one had been shot. Later, I heard through the prison grapevine that he was sentenced to fifteen years.

Like Hollywood, Leonard received sixteen months for the burglary charge. He was transported to New Mexico where he served both his California and New Mexico sentences concurrently. When I ran into Leonard six years later, he told me he had been in Santa Fe Prison during the riot of 1980. Leonard said he was lucky to be alive. I could tell by the way his eyes clouded over when he talked about the riot that it had been much worse than the media had reported, but I didn't press him for details.

Right before I got sentenced, Maria came to visit and served me with divorce papers. I didn't try to convince her to stay with me. I had chosen to live in a world of uncertainty where women would come and go. Not long after Maria announced her decision to leave me, I was sentenced to three years for the burglary charge, plus two years for my prior convictions.

On March 7, 1979, at the age of 28, I was flown to Chino State Prison in Southern California to begin my second prison term. I didn't think I would make it out alive this time. After all, I was going to a prison controlled by the Mexican Mafia, and I was a known member of Nuestra Familia. Worse still, I was now a dropout of the NF and no longer had their backup. In fact, I was on their hit list too. I wanted to ask for protective custody (PC) when I got to Chino, but my pride wouldn't let me. There was no way I could look myself in the mirror if I asked to be protected by the Man.

My pride would get me killed for sure, I smiled ruefully.

Chino State Prison, officially known as California Institution for Men or CIM, opened its gates in 1941, and covers approximately 2,500 acres. It consists of four separate facilities located three miles south of the city of *Chino*, California. Although this prison was the reception center for newly committed felons from Southern California Counties, CIM had been designated the reception center for anyone sentenced to prison from as far north as Fresno County. Tulare County was within those parameters. That's why I was sent there instead of the Northern Reception Center located in Vacaville.

I arrived at CIM around noon and was given a new prison number, C02449. I had just sat down to eat my sack lunch after going through the tedious booking process when a CO called out my name.

"De La Cruz!"

"Right here."

The officer walked over and looked at a mug shot he held in his hand to make sure it was me.

"Put your hands behind your back," he said.

I did as instructed and he expertly snapped a pair of handcuffs around my wrists tightly. Grabbing hold of my cuffed wrists, he led me down the prison's long dimly lit corridor toward Palm Hall, the unit where high-risk inmates are confined.

"Escort, move out of the way!" the guard hollered at inmates in our path.

When we arrived to Palm Hall, the officer shouted, "incoming" into a porthole on the steel door of the unit. A cop inside unlocked the first door and we stepped into the sally port. Two more doors were opened before I was steered and deposited into cell 102 at the front of the tier. As we walked there, I saw the all too familiar mirrors sticking out through the bars from some of the cells located down the tier.

"Is that you, *Dragón?*" A voice asked.

"Who wants to know?" I asked suspiciously.

"It's Shadow."

Shadow had acquired his name because he was extremely dark. I had met him during the time I had been at DVI. We had become close friends. I hadn't seen him since my release in '76. He was serving a life sentence for murder and had been in prison for eleven years. Shadow had dropped out of the NF too after one of his blood brothers had been killed by the organization.

"*Oralé, Carnál!*" I exclaimed, relieved to know someone I knew lived on the tier. "It's been a long time, *Ese.*"

"*Simón.* You couldn't stay out, huh?"

"You know how it is, homeboy; had to come home sooner or later."

"The hell with that shit, *Ese*. This ain't my home. If I ever get out of this fucking hole, I'm not ever coming back. And you can take that to the bank!"

I didn't respond to his fervent outburst, and after catching up on the latest prison gossip, I told Shadow I would talk with him later. I was worn out from the trip and needed to rest. Lying down, I thought about what Shadow said about getting out and never coming back. His fiery response to my statement about "coming home" had caught me off guard. As far as I was concerned, breaking the law was what I did for a living and going to prison was part of the job description.

Not wanting to think about something that was so foreign to me, I closed my eyes. Sleep came quickly, but when it did, I dreamt about falling into the dark pit again. Like always, I fell rapidly into the darkness of the hole, yelling as I plummeted downward.

As always, I woke up gasping for breath, trembling like a wino going through delirium tremors. The dream never failed to unnerve me. After regaining my composure, I got angry that a dream could disturb me so much.

What's the matter with you? I asked myself. You starting to get weak or something? It's too late to start thinking about changing anything now. You're in prison again, and you have to concentrate on staying alive. What's more, you can't change even if you wanted too. This is the hand you were dealt, so you have to play it out. Besides, you don't know how to live any other way.

I was housed in Palm Hall for three months and then transferred to the California Training Facility, or CTF, located in Soledad, California. I always got a kick out of the names of California prisons.

California Training Facility, HA! The only training anyone got was on how to become a better criminal.

I arrived at Soledad in June of '79 and it was déjà vu. Soledad looked just like DVI. As soon I walked into R&R, I was placed in a small wire-meshed cage and interrogated by a Special Service Unit (SSU) officer concerning my NF status. The SSU had been established by C.D.C. to address the growing prison gang problem and to identify gang members; the active and the inactive, or dropouts. There were so many members dropping out of their gangs and asking for protection that Protective Housing Units (PHU) had been established to accommodate all the P.C. cases. I didn't ask for protection, but was placed in PHU anyway.

PHU had been transformed into a self-sufficient entity. It was a prison within a prison. The unit had a side door leading to a small recreational yard where inmates could play handball, cards, lift weights, or just sit and talk trash. Stainless steel tables capable of sitting four men had been installed in the center of the unit and served as a dining/recreation area. Food carts filled with large pots of food prepared in the mainline population kitchen were rolled into the unit for breakfast, lunch and dinner. There were five long benches and a television at the end of the unit that served as a TV room.

There was a gunner on the second tier armed with a shotgun and a 38-caliber pistol to squelch any acts of violence, which often erupted on the spur of the moment and without much provocation. PHU was a dangerous place that housed treacherous people. Anyone dumb enough to think guys who dropped out of their gang were weak often wound up seriously hurt or dead.

I constantly struggled with the fact that I was locked up with rats, child molesters and guys who had been my sworn enemies. Guys who I would have stabbed without any hesitation now lived in the same unit as I did.

Every day my conscience mocked me whenever I looked at myself in the mirror for walking out on the gang.

"You're nothing but a lowlife coward. Look where you ended up, tough guy," the voice would say.

It took months before I came to terms with the fact that I was living with what is considered scum by prisoners on the mainline population. I spent most of my day in a fetal position and didn't come out of my cell for weeks. I didn't eat much and as a result, lost so much weight I looked anorexic.

Luckily for me, there were a few good dudes in PHU who had been in the NF with me. They would bring me food and spend time talking to me. If it wasn't for those guys, I might have lost my mind from the pressure of having to live in protective custody. Gangster, a guy from Salinas, spent lots of time talking to me and trying to help me understand that it wasn't my fault I had had to leave the gang.

"I remember some of the things you did for the NF. You were a diehard. It was the NF who had let us down. They lied to us about everything."

"Man, I would have given up my life for them in an instant," I would reply sadly.

Little by little, Gangster pulled me out of my depression and I was able to forgive myself for dropping out of the Tip.

In January of 1980, I was transferred to CIM South. Up to this point, CIM South was the best prison I had ever been in. The institution had large, single cells, a gym, a swimming pool, and a large track surrounding a big yard. There was also plenty of freedom within the two large razor-wire topped cyclone fences that surrounded the prison. Since there weren't very many jobs, most guys spent their time telling each other stories about their criminal escapades or talking about what they were going to do once they got out. I never said much myself. I mostly listened and watched. I had developed the habit of not talking while I had been confined in the Hole at DVI and single celled in Soledad. Besides, I didn't like exposing myself to others and that's exactly what people did whenever they started running off at the mouth. I knew a guy, by the name of Wino, from San Jose, California who had gotten so caught up with one of his stories that he had told his cellmate about a murder he committed while on the streets. Wino told his cell partner every detail about the murder right down to where he had buried the murder victim's body. His cell partner didn't waste any time before he called the Santa Clara County District Attorney where the murder had taken place and cut a deal. Not long after, the snitch was released and Wino was prosecuted and sentenced to life.

Gabby, another guy serving time at the White Elephant (another name for CIM South) was probably the best storyteller I ever met. He couldn't keep quiet even if his life depended on it. That's why he was called Gabby, but he liked to call himself the "Mad Gab."

Gabby had robbed everything from local drug dealers, neighborhood Mom & Pop stores, supermarkets, and banks. He was, as he liked to put it, "an equal opportunity robber."

"I like to walk into a market dressed professional like, you know. Dress slacks, a long sleeve shirt and shiny shoes. I always have my hair neatly combed and my face smoothly shaved so as not to arouse suspicion," he would say. "I usually walk around until I locate the manager. Most of the time, he's one of those dorky looking guys who wears glasses and combs his hair swooped to the side. I usually say something like, "Excuse me sir, can you help me?" The manager looks at me briefly and asks, "How can I help you, sir?"

Lifting my shirt to show him the gun tucked into my pants I say, "Can you cosign this?" The look on his face after I show him the butt of my gun always makes me want to cum in my pants." Gabby always concluded his stories laughing boisterously.

Gabby used to say he was going to go on a robbing spree when he got out and make lots of money, but I don't think he robbed for the money. I believe he enjoyed the power he had when he pulled his gun on people.

True to his word, Gabby got out in the summer of '82 and immediately started to rob. When he was apprehended three months later, he was charged with seven bank robberies and three murders. I heard through the prison scuttlebutt Gabby had been acquitted on all three of the murders and on five of the bank robberies, but had been found guilty on two bank robberies and sentenced to forty-two years. Years later, while I was serving time at Soledad prison on another prison sentence, I heard Gabby killed a guy at Leavenworth Federal Penitentiary in Kansas and that was the last I heard about Gabby.

CHAPTER NINE

WHEN I WAS AT CIM, I met a young woman I had written while I was in DVI in '73. She had never answered my letter back then, but came to visit me with my sister Lydia that first Sunday after my arrival at CIM South.

The first time I laid eyes on Linda, she was standing near the vending machines in the visiting area. She had a bright smile and thick wavy auburn hair that hung down to her waist just the way I liked it. Linda was dressed in a pair of tight-fitting designer jeans that hugged every curve of her body. She wore black summer sandals that exposed her bright red polished toes, which matched her silk red blouse. She had on a stylish cut black suede jacket that accentuated her physical attributes. Like the song says, she was truly a "sight for sore eyes to see."

Linda had three sons, Gary, Larry and Jerry. Gary, the oldest, had a hard time accepting me as his mother's new man, but eventually he came around. Larry and Jerry were identical twins, and started to call me Daddy Jess right after I got with their mother. They often came with Linda to visit me on weekends. For the next year, our relationship intensified, and we decided that I should parole to Linda's house in Los Angeles. I had made up my mind to quit using heroin when I got out. I was tired of doing time and by now the shine of becoming a gangster had worn off.

On May 21, 1982, I paroled from CIM. I wasn't as nervous about getting out this time as I had been the time before. I felt as though I had a sense of direction and wasn't in the dark about the latest trends on the streets. Television had kept me informed about what was happening in the free world during this incarceration. Special reports about Rock Cocaine had kept me up to date concerning the destruction it had caused in many communities, especially in Black districts. But, Rock Cocaine, like all drugs, was an equal opportunity destroyer. A friend of mine who had once been a heroin addict told me that Rock's high was much better than heroin.

"When you take that first hit," he said, it's like you're rocketed into another dimension. The problem is you never get the same feeling as that first hit, but you keep hitting the pipe trying to get there, you know. Rock intensifies everything and often makes you hallucinate. You don't sleep or eat trying to get more money to buy more Rock. And before you realize what's happening, you're caught in a vicious cycle, stealing and robbing only to give all your money to the drug man. Rock's grip is powerful. You do things you never would've done if not for the craving of Rock. It's unbelievable. I know a guy who started giving his booty to the connection for a hit. But, all that being said if you were to ask me if I'm going to smoke Rock Cocaine when I get out I'll have to say, hell yeah; all day long!" He concluded.

I was at a complete loss by what he told me concerning Rock Cocaine and the affect it had on people who smoked it. I couldn't understand why someone would use a drug that made them see things that weren't there? The main reason I used drugs was to escape and I surely wasn't going to use a drug that forced me to see the very things I was trying to forget.

It was a bright spring morning when I walked out the prison's main gate. I spotted Linda waiting in the parking lot standing next to her mother's 1974 Thunderbird. When she saw me, she rushed over and gave me a tight hug and light kiss on the lips. It felt good to be out. I turned and flipped the main tower guard a bird as I got into the car and we drove away. I didn't know if I could survive without breaking the law, but I figured that so long as I didn't use heroin, everything would be okay. The problem was that I wasn't sure if I could stay drug free. I had never been on the streets without using heroin ever since I started injecting it back in '69, but I was going to try.

Life without heroin was pretty boring, but I stayed busy so as not to think about it too much. I spent the first few days on the streets with Linda and the kids. The first weekend I was on the streets, Linda's parents took us to the City of Pasadena where *Tierra* (a popular Chicano music group at that time) was performing. I had never been to a concert before. I enjoyed the music, but it made me nervous to be around so many people.

A week or so after my release I got a job working in a warehouse. The job wasn't much, but it kept me occupied, off the streets, and with honest money in my pocket. Then one day, after I had been working for about a month, I was called into the office and told that my services were no longer needed. I didn't understand why I was being fired and the supervisor didn't give me any explanation. He just let me go as if I didn't count. I walked away devastated and feeling like a failure. As I left the warehouse, I became incensed and went to a bar and got drunk and wallowed in self-pity. When I staggered home that night, Linda was waiting for me.

"Where were you?" She asked.

"I was at the bar getting drunk," I slurred. "I lost my job."

"Why?"

"How should I know? They didn't give me a reason. They just excused me as though I was nobody."

"It's okay, honey," Linda said soothingly. "We can live off my welfare check."

"What are you talking about? I'm not going to live off you. I'm the man around this house and it's my responsibility to take care of you and the kids. If I have to start breaking the law to support you, then that's what I'm going to do. I tried to do the right thing, but I they kicked me to the curb. Well, I'm not working for some chickenshit punk for nickels and dimes anymore," I concluded, seething with drunken rage at what I considered society's injustice.

Linda hugged me, trying to calm my temper, but I had made up my mind. I was going back to crime.

"I'll show them," I said, before I passed out.

The following day I went to *Maravilla*, one of the oldest *barrios* in East Los Angeles. My intent was to hook up with *Wito*, a guy I met while at CIM. I had heard through the criminal grapevine that *Wito* was making big money and I thought he might be able to help me get on my feet.

When I found *Wito*, it didn't look like he was doing so swell. *Wito* was a potbellied guy in his mid-thirties who wore his unruly hair down to his shoulders and dressed in shabby, outlandish, secondhand clothing. I soon learned that *Wito* dressed the way he did as a front to keep the cops from paying close attention to him. Later, he took me to his house located on the west side of LA and flashed me a large wad of money.

"What you doing to get all that money," I asked.

"Selling dope," he said, as he opened a black duffle bag filled with plastic bags containing Mexican Tar heroin. It must have been around a pound of the stuff in that bag and looking at all that dope made my mouth water, and body tingle as I remembered the warm euphoric feeling brought on by heroin.

"You want a fix?"

"Hell yeah, man!"

Wito didn't use himself, but he had bags of syringes, ten to a bag, in case any of his customers wanted to taste the quality of his product. *Wito* gave me a smidgen about the size of a match head of the Tar.

"This is quality stuff," he said as he scraped the Tar onto the edge of the cooker. "It doesn't take much. I don't want you to overdose on me. Besides, if you need more, I have plenty."

I had shot heroin a few times while I'd been in prison, but it had been a few years since the last time I fixed so I had to be careful. Many guys released from prison made the mistake of trying to inject as much heroin as they had been using before they got busted. They often overdosed and sometimes died. Therefore, I didn't complain about the amount *Wito* gave me. I quickly prepared it and shot the stuff into my vein. Even before I finished slamming the heroin into my vein, I felt its familiar warmth engulf my body and the potency of the heroin made my knees buckle. I held onto the table and quickly sat on a couch against a wall in the room.

"You alright?" *Wito* asked.

I nodded then laid my head back and let the dope take over. I must have dozed off for quite some time because when I snapped out of my high, it was dark outside.

"*Oralé, Dragón*, how was it?" *Wito* asked.

"It's good stuff."

"So you want to work with me?"

"Hell yeah, man!"

Wito gave me half an ounce of uncut heroin on consignment to start my operation. The following day I contacted five guys I knew from *Maravilla* and made each one a profitable proposition. For a hundred dollars I would give them eight twenty-five dollar bags so they could double their money. It was a good deal and before long, I was raking in the dough.

Linda and I were happy and life was good.

A few months later, while driving down Brooklyn Avenue, now Cesar Chavez Boulevard, in East Los Angeles, I saw Pancho, a guy who had spent time in prison with me. I pulled over to the curb and called out his name. Pancho suspiciously peered inside my car trying to remember me.

"It's me, *Esé, Dragón*."

"*Oralé, Carnál*. I didn't recognize you. Looks like you're doing great," he said, as he ran his hand over the fender of my black 1980 Buick Regal.

"I'm doing alright. How are you doing?"

"I'm doing bad, sleeping in an abandoned car and hooked like a side of meat at a slaughter house."

"Well, jump in and let me get you well. I've got some stuff with me and I'm due for a shot. Afterward, we can get something to eat and talk business. Maybe I can convince you to work with me. You interested?"

"*Simón, Esé*! At this point I'm ready for anything."

Pancho climbed into my car and we sped off to get high. He started making deliveries for me that afternoon. The world of crime and drugs is a small place and everyone who bought drugs off me already knew Pancho, so I didn't have to bother with introductions. Not long after, I expanded my operation and started making even more money. Everything was working out great until the day Pancho didn't show up to make his deliveries. I had to make them myself. I tried to contact Pancho on the telephone throughout the day, but to no avail.

Going home that night, I had a premonition something bad was going to happen.

It was late when Linda and I went to bed, but it seemed as though I had just fallen asleep when I was awakened by someone smashing the front door of our house. There was a lot of shouting when I came out of my sleep and at first I thought I was dreaming, but then I saw the guns pointed at my head and realized it was a drug raid by sheriff's officers. Cops were everywhere in my house. They had snatched me off the bed and slammed me to the ground. Officers were screaming at me not to move, which I found ludicrous since they had my arms twisted and pinned behind my back while an officer had his knee on the back of my neck.

After being handcuffed, I was yanked to a sitting position as officers searched my house for drugs. I wasn't worried about them finding my stash because I kept my heroin supply buried in my back yard wrapped in plastic bags. I had sprinkled black pepper around the grass where it was buried so the sheriff K9's wouldn't be able to sniff it out. While I was lying there smug, the police were out back digging. They uncovered my Mexican Tar heroin without any help from their K9's. Pancho had given me up.

"We got you now, punk," one of the cops said with a smug look on his face as he held the dirty plastic bag that contained the heroin.

Linda wasn't arrested, but I was transported to the 3rd Street Sheriff's station in East LA and fingerprinted, photographed, and placed in a dimly lit cell. I realized right then I was on my way back to the penitentiary. It took four months before I cut a deal for three years in state prison. It was July 1985 and I was thirty-four years old.

On the morning I was transferred to CIM, I ran into Old Man Mike in the chow hall. As it turned out, Old Man Mike and I ended up seated next to each other on the bus ride to CIM. We didn't talk much because Old Man Mike was having difficulty breathing. He had been diagnosed with emphysema during the time he had been in the county jail. I watched him as he sat slumped over, periodically heaving as he gulped air into his lungs. I wondered if the emphysema would kill him before he got out of prison.

"Chingé, su madré!" Old Man Mike said abruptly.

"What's the matter?" I asked.

"Man, I just want to make it to the streets again so I can shoot dope one last time."

"Damn, aren't you ever going to change, you old bastard?"

Old Man Mike laughed eerily. "What for? It's way too late to think about that now. I should've thought about changing when I was your age."

"Fuck you, old man."

When we arrived to CIM, I couldn't believe how crowded it was. Everywhere I looked rooms had been transformed into housing units. The library, gym, and some of the hallways were filled with double bunks. The prison system was bursting at the seams with prisoners even though the state had built three prisons since the last time I was paroled in 1982.

I wasn't locked up in Palm Hall with the other dropouts this time and I wasn't housed on the CIM mainline very long either. Instead, I was sent to CIM West, a facility located next to the reception center that housed inmates in dormitories. I was scared about living in an open area where anyone could sneak up on me and stick a knife in my back. And for a fleeting moment, I thought about telling prison authorities I was from Northern California so they could lock me up for my own protection, but that thought was gone just as quick as it had come. There was no way I was going to ask for protection. I don't know which was worse, the stress of being on your toes all the time, ready for the unexpected, or sitting in a cage 24/7. What I do know is that I had to use all my observational skills to ensure no one could hurt me without getting hurt themselves.

Since I had been out of state prison for approximately three years and had discharged my C02449 number, I was given a new one, D10514. My "Central File" containing all my criminal and institutional history wasn't available to the correctional counselor in charge of my case. So when she interviewed me I gave her as little information about my past as possible. She knew I had been in prison before, but because of my age she told me she was going to suggest I remain on the CIM West permanent work crew. Inmates on the permanent work crew maintained the institution. I don't think she would have made that type of recommendation had she known about my past *Nuestra Familia* affiliation. Anyone associated with any prison gang, especially the NF, was subject to automatic lockdown. It didn't matter if the person was out of the gang or not.

I enjoyed my three-month stay at CIM West, but one Friday afternoon, when the transfer list came out, I saw my name on the DVI column. I realized right then and there that the party was over. DVI was not Disneyland like CIM West. DVI had always been one of the most dangerous institutions in California.

Since I was from Northern California, I knew I would be in serious trouble once I got to DVI because it was now controlled by *Sureños*. The *Sureño-Norteño* dispute was serious. Many guys from both sides had been maimed or killed. The conflict had begun during the summer of '73 when a guy named *Pato* from Wilmington, CA, and a small group of guys from Southern California attacked a couple of NF soldiers at DVI. The NF had retaliated immediately by stabbing six guys from Southern California the following day.

The only reason I hadn't gotten stabbed while I was in CIM West was because many of the guys housed there had served time with me in the LA County Jail and because most of the guys at CIM West weren't seasoned convicts like the ones being housed at DVI. The inmates at DVI were hardcore and serving long sentences. Most of them would just as soon take your life as look at you.

I arrived at DVI in July of '85 to begin my third prison term. The temperature was way over one hundred degrees. I was housed on the third tier of West Hall. During my two-week stay in orientation, I wasn't allowed out of my cell except for a fifteen-minute shower three times a week. Ten days later, I was taken before a housing committee for permanent placement on the mainline. I walked into the small committee room a nervous wreck and took a seat. I wanted to tell the committee I didn't belong in this institution, but my pride got in the way.

"Inmate De La Cruz, D10514, comes before this committee for permanent housing placement. De La Cruz is a thirty-four year old Hispanic male, transferred from CIM-West. His controlling case is sales of a controlled substance. He was sentenced out of Los Angeles County. His sentence is three years."

"Is all the information mentioned correct?" another committee member asked.

"Yeah," I replied.

"So you're from Los Angeles County?"

"No."

"What do you mean?" the committee member asked confused.

"I'm from Tulare County."

"Tulare County? But you came from *Chino*, and you were sentenced out of LA County." he said.

"I got arrested in LA, but I'm not from there."

"Well, you know who runs this institution, don't you?" one of the members asked.

"I thought you did," I replied ruefully.

They all laughed uncomfortably at my response.

"This is a Southern Penitentiary," he continued.

"But it's located in Northern California, isn't it?"

"Does that mean you want to go out to the mainline?" he asked.

I wanted to say hell no, I don't want to stay. Instead, I said, "This is where you sent me, right?"

That evening I was moved out of orientation and housed in H-Wing. My cellmate turned out to be a guy from Mexico, or Border Brother, as they're called in prison. He was a first termer who didn't know much about the politics concerning the North and South conflict between Chicanos in California prisons.

We got along and after a few days he began to look up to me because he knew I was an OG. Not wanting to put him in crossfire, I told him as little as possible about my past. I instructed him not to say anything about what we discussed in our cell if anyone asked. I told him that the less he knew about me the better off he would be.

The next three and a half months were extremely strenuous on my psyche. Every day I wondered if someone would expose me as a dropout of the NF. I dreaded waking up and having to go out among the general population. I knew that every inmate on the mainline was a potential enemy.

Nothing happened until one cold winter morning in November of '85. I had gone out to the yard to get some fresh air and exercise. As soon as I walked onto the yard I sensed something wasn't right. I couldn't quite put my finger on exactly why I felt so uneasy, but there was an underlying tension on the yard. I scanned the area trying to uncover what was wrong, but didn't notice anything out of the ordinary. I glanced toward the weight pile and saw a guy I knew watching me intently. When I looked his way, he nodded and brought his index finger to the bottom of his right eye and then pointed at me—the universal prison sign for " be on the lookout for danger. It's coming your way."

At that precise moment, I caught a glimpse of three youngsters moving stealthily in my direction through my peripheral vision. Nonchalantly, I looked their way so as not to let them know I knew they were trying to creep up on me. When I turned my attention toward them, they immediately stopped and acted casual but as soon as I turned away, they continued to move slowly toward me. I watched them out the side of my vision as they wound their way toward me. In that instant, I decided to make my move. I wasn't going to let these youngsters take me out without a fight.

I causally walked over to where I had buried a ten inch piece of steel which I had honed into a razor sharp knife on a grinder in the machine shop a few days after I was placed on the DVI mainline. I had concealed the knife in the ground next to the horseshoe pit and marked the spot with two rocks on a small grassless area of the yard. Keeping an eye on the three youngsters, I sat down and dug out the knife without being detected by the tower guards. I then walked to the bleachers at the far end of the yard, climbed to the top row, leaned against the rail and waited, tensed and ready for battle.

From the top of the bleachers I clearly saw the three youngsters make their way toward me. I don't think they knew I was strapped or that they were going to have to put in work in order to get a piece of me. I had my knife out, hidden behind my right leg. As they got closer I could tell one of them had more courage and carried himself with more self-assurance. My instincts told me he would be the one to make the first move when they decided to strike. I trained my eyes on the other two culprits as though I wasn't paying him any mind, but kept the self-assured youngster in my peripheral vision and a deadly calm came over me as they got nearer. I knew then that I was ready.

"What's up?" I asked coolly.

They didn't respond and looked at each other nervously. It was a brief awkward moment. Even the self-assured youngster didn't know what to do, but then they dramatically brandished welding rods that resembled ice picks. I flashed my knife to let them know I was ready to get down, too. My ruse about acting as though I didn't know what was going on had worked. Their facial expression was one of total surprise. They looked at each other, at a loss about what to do next.

It's one thing to move on someone who doesn't know he's going to get hit, but when the element of surprise is taken away, the move requires experience and skill, attributes these youngsters didn't have just yet. But I made it easy for them.

"Hey," I said smiling uneasily. "We just got naked baby. We're getting ready to fuck now."

My statement had the intended effect, and the self-assured youngster swung at me, aiming straight for my neck. I was expecting him to make the first move so when he swung, I shifted my upper body slightly. I sensed the power of his blow as his arm shot past, narrowly missing my neck. In one fluid motion I brought my knife up swiftly and stuck him in his solar plexus. In doing so, I exposed myself to the other youngster who took full advantage and stabbed me. I felt the rod enter and exit smoothly between my ribs. The other youngster just stood there with his mouth wide open. I was thankful that he had panicked, or else the outcome of this skirmish might have been much more injurious for me.

The guy I knifed immediately went into shock. I saw his eyes glaze as he hunched over holding his stomach. I grabbed the rail of the bleachers for support and kicked him viciously on his face. He stumbled backward, but the other two grabbed him before he fell. They left hurriedly with their wounded friend cautiously glancing back toward me to make sure I didn't run up on them and stab them in the back as they departed.

I didn't have any intention of continuing the knife fight and once they were off the bleachers, I sat down and looked at my blood-soaked jacket. I couldn't believe the tower guards hadn't seen what had just taken place. As I contemplated my next move, I heard the panic alarm go off. Everyone was ordered to get on the ground and the tedious process of searching each inmate as he entered the main entrance into the prison corridor was initiated. When my turn came, a guard noticed I was wounded and escorted me to the infirmary where I was patched up. The youngster I stabbed was taken to an outside hospital where he stayed for about a week. I heard through the prison grapevine he had almost died. Fortunately for both of us he recovered.

After being medically attended, I was placed in segregation. The youngster I had wounded was also put in the Hole, although the administration never connected his stabbing to mine and recorded them as two separate assaults.

On a cold, damp, 1985 December morning, I was transferred to the California Men's Colony (CMC) located in San Luis Obispo, California. CMC had originally been built to house older inmates, but it now accommodated prison gang dropouts, guys on gang hit lists, child molesters, and rats. Guys who had been actively involved in the NF during the time I was in the Tip were at CMC. *Quate*, who I hadn't seen since he left the Tip when we were housed in West Hall in 1974 was there. I ran into him on the yard once I got out of orientation.

"What the hell were you doing at DVI?" *Quate* asked somewhat agitated when I bumped into him on the yard.

"That's where they sent me."

"That was really dangerous and sort of dumb, if you ask me. Someone could've killed you."

"They tried," I replied, lifting my shirt to show him my stab wound. He just shook his head in amazement.

I settled down to the daily routine at CMC and got a job in the prison laundry. I hooked up with a friend of mine named Santos. He was out of Los Angeles and an original member of the NF. He had been stabbed in '72 after he had been transferred from Soledad to CIM to testify for a couple of *EME* members who were being prosecuted for murder in Los Angeles County. The subpoena was just a ploy by the *EME* to get Santos alone so they could kill him, but there was nothing Santos could do. He surely couldn't go to the guards and tell them what the *EME* intended to do. No way! That was snitching.

Santos had been transferred to CIM back then and had been stabbed the day after his arrival by two *EME* soldiers. As a result of the attempted murder on Santos, the war between the NF and the *EME* got more intense and the NF retaliated the following day by killing Cheyenne, one of the *EME*'s most respected leaders housed in Palm Hall at that time. Only once did Santos ever talk to me about that incident.

"I feel bad about being known as the guy who started the war between the NF and the *EME*, but there's nothing I can do about it now. That rep follows me like a dark shadow, you know."

"I can only imagine."

Santos's guilt was legitimate. After all, many men, women, and even children had died as a result of this war between two criminal organizations. I wouldn't have wanted to have that weighing on what little conscience I had. It was bad enough I had to live amongst these lowlife's without having to live with that too.

One morning while Santos and I were eating breakfast, an older White man sat on our table. I glanced over at the White guy completely bowled over that he'd had the audacity to sit on our table. Santos could see by the disgusted expression on my face that I felt disrespected by this guy's intrusion and leaned toward me.

"You know who this guy is?"

"Come on homeboy," I replied sarcastically. "How would I know this old bastard?"

"That's Singleton. The guy who chopped a young girl's arms off and left her to die on the outskirts of Modesto after he raped her, remember?"

My heart began to pump faster as I recalled reading about this depraved son of a bitch in the newspaper. I felt the heat radiate off my face as my anger rose. Turning slowly and deliberately toward the White man I told him.

"Listen, you perverted fuck. Get your punk ass off my table and don't ever sit even remotely close to me again."

Singleton looked at me with murder in his eyes and was about to respond, but he must have seen the ugliness in mine because he simply got up and moved. He never sat next to me after that.

That evening when I lay down to sleep, I was riddled with guilt again at having to live surrounded by people like Singleton. I wondered how anyone could enjoy hurting children. I thought it would be great if society would allow anyone wanting to do so, without prosecution, the opportunity to rid the world of deranged people like Singleton, but there were too many sicko's like him. Besides, I didn't believe society thought very highly of me either. To the general public, a crook was simply a crook.

On December 16, 1986, I was set free again. Unlike before, there was no one to pick me up at the gate this time. I had lost contact with Linda and Mama had gotten disillusioned with me going in and out of prison. I was on my own, without anywhere to live and no immediate plans. My future looked grim to say the least. I didn't have any idea what I was going to do. Standing in line waiting anxiously to board the bus taking me to Los Angeles, my insides trembled. I wanted a drink of booze to calm my nerves, but a no-drinking policy for inmates being released had been implemented and was being strictly enforced. Leaving the bus depot to buy alcohol was now considered a parole violation and grounds for a swift return to prison.

An hour or so later, when the bus made a brief stop to pick up passengers at a town along the way toward LA, I rushed to a liquor store not far from the depot and bought a half pint of Smirnoff Vodka and a pint of orange juice to wash the vodka down. Hurrying back to the bus with the bottle tucked into my pants, I went straight into the restroom located at the rear of the bus and locked the door. Twisting the cap off the vodka bottle, I took three deep breaths, held my last breath, and guzzled the entire contents.

The vodka burnt my throat as it went down. I took a sip of the orange juice to quench the fire, exhaled, and threw the empty bottle into the trashcan. I walked back to my seat just as the bus departed. Not long after, I felt the warmth of the alcohol hit my stomach, and with the warmth came a little relief from my fear.

My bus arrived downtown LA around six in the evening. By then I was drunk. I had bought another bottle of Vodka when the bus made another pit stop, but the alcohol hadn't completely relieved me of the stress of being on the streets. I required something stronger and convinced myself that I needed a shot of heroin.

I walked over to the Grand Central Market on Fourth and Broadway, an area where I knew people congregated to make drug connections. Sure enough, as I turned onto Fourth Street I saw the drug dealers. They were squatted against the wall trying to blend into the darkness so the police couldn't see them.

When I got closer, I could tell by the look of their elongated gaunt faces, the dark circles around their eyes, and their sickly yellow complexion, that these guys were heroin addicts who sold dope to support their habit. I walked over and asked one of them if he had any dope for sale. He eyed me up and down slowly trying to determine if I was a cop. The guy squatted next to the one I asked looked me up and down too. I must have passed the test because I saw the one that must have been the shot caller nod at the other one as if giving him permission to sell me drugs.

"How many bags you want?"

"Give me three ten dollar sacks of heroin and three of coke. I also need an outfit and a place to get down."

"Hey, an outfit and a place to get down are going to cost you extra," one of the drug dealers said in a heavy Mexican accent.

"No problem. I'll give you each a bag of dope for your trouble."

They readily agreed and we left to an undisclosed area where their car was parked. I climbed into the front seat and went first. Pouring the contents of the heroin into the cooker, the powder quickly dissolved into liquid. I then poured a bag of powered coke into the cooker, too. I mixed the coke with the heroin and concocted what had come to be known as a Belushi (named after the actor John Belushi who died of the same lethal mix). I had never liked coke, but I was drunk and only interested in relieving the panic eating at me. I tied myself off and stuck the needle into my vein. As soon as the drug hit my blood-stream, it literally took my breath away and all my anxiety disappeared in a snap. I lost track of time as I went in and out of consciousness. I woke up only after one of the guys shook me awake to ask me if I wanted to take a leak.

"Yeah," I replied, groggily stumbling out of the car to relieve myself.

When I finished pissing and tried to get back into the car, one of the guys grabbed me from behind and slammed me to the ground. The impact knocked the wind out of me. Being under the influence of drugs had affected my sense of awareness and defense and before I could react, I was completely incapaci-tated. One guy held a knife pressed to my throat while another pinned my arms to the ground and another sat on my legs. I didn't recognize the guy holding my arms, he hadn't been with us when I'd fixed the Belushi. He must have been picked up.

What I did know was that this punk was a mean dude. He kept telling the guy holding the knife, "Kill him, homie! Kill him!"

I was too drugged to panic. I remained calm and coolly told the guy with knife he didn't have to kill me.

"I'm not gonna call the cops and nobody will know about this except us. You don't have to worry about going to jail. But if you kill me, the cops will have to investigate my murder and once they find my body there's no telling what will happen. There's no sense in complicating things by killing me, you know. My money is in my left sock. Take it."

I could see by the strained look of his face that he was thinking about what I said and it must have made sense to him.

"I'm gonna give you a pass," he said. "But if you get up before we leave, I'm going to cut your throat, understand?"

I nodded.

With a bob of his head he signaled for the other two guys to let me go. All of them walked slowly back to their car making sure I didn't get up. I did exactly as I was told and didn't move a muscle and they jumped into their car and left. I didn't get up until the taillights disappeared around a bend on the road. When I finally stood up, I looked around trying to determine my location and realized I was on a hill of some sort. I was completely disoriented, but I could see the lights of the city down below from where I stood.

It was pitch black as I descended off the mountain. I couldn't see anything. After walking a bit, I came upon two youngsters hanging out in their front yard. I asked them where I was. The teenagers told me I was in *El Séréno* and that *El Séréno* Boulevard was at the bottom of the hill.

Following their instructions, I walked down a winding road and soon reached the Boulevard. I walked into a hole-in-the-wall drinking establishment and asked the bartender if I could use the telephone. The bartender nodded in the direction of the phone. I called my friend Charles who lived in the city of Whittier.

"Hey, Charles," I said when he answered. "It's me, Jess."

"Hey, Little Brother, how you been?"

"Well, I got out earlier today and I already messed up. I got high and can barely function. I got robbed too. I was wondering if you could pick me up and let me stay at your pad for the night."

"Where you at?"

"I'm in *El Sereno*."

"I'll be there in forty-five minutes to get you. Just sit tight."

I had lived at Charles's house prior to getting arrested and had kicked a monstrous heroin habit during the time I was there, something I had never done while on the streets. He had tried to help me get straight and had introduced me to Christianity. He taught me some of the principles of the Bible and spoke about Jesus Christ and how He had changed his life. Charles didn't drink, use drugs, cuss, gossip, and prayed all the time. I had tried to change, but in the end, weakened and left to resume using heroin and breaking the law. Fortunately, Charles hadn't given up on me and arrived about an hour later to pick me up.

On the drive to his house I nodded in and out of consciousness. I slept in his van that night although Charles offered me a bed inside his home. The following morning, I found a couple of dollars next to my pillow. Charles must have put the money there after I'd passed out. I quickly got dressed and left before he woke up. I walked to Whittier Boulevard and boarded the 72 bus line which would take me to East LA. Along the way I got off the bus, walked into a store and stole a combination television/radio and a Polaroid Camera. I sold the goods to a man who worked in a body and fender shop for eighty-five dollars then continued my trip to East LA.

Arriving on the corner of Brooklyn and Mednik, I got off the bus and walked to Jerry's, a heroin addict who had done business with me during the time I had sold drugs a few years before. Jerry's house was located on Hamel Street and known to law enforcement officers as *"Casa Morales,"* which was Jerry's last name. The house was a shooting gallery and drug distribution center. Local drug dealers hung out there to sell their product because heroin addicts from all over Los Angeles came to *Casa Morales* to buy heroin. Every dealer paid Jerry or his sisters Virgie and Carmen a percentage of whatever they sold at the end of each day. If they didn't pay, they weren't allowed to come back and do business there.

Jerry and I had always gotten along before I went to prison this last time. I was hoping things between us hadn't changed. As I walked to Jerry's, I scrutinized every car that drove by. I wanted to make sure potential enemies didn't sneak up and hurt me. When I arrived to Jerry's house, I took a deep breath and knocked on the door. Someone inside cracked it open just enough to see who was outside. I couldn't tell who was looking at me, but then I heard the chain on the door being released after which the door opened slowly. Jerry stuck his head out to see if there was anyone around then motioned me to step inside.

"What are you doing here?" he asked apprehensively. "Everyone is mad as hell at you for sticking that dude while you were in the Joint."

"Yeah, I guessed as much, but I was hoping I could kick it here for a few days until I figure out what I'm going to do."

"Listen, you know we're cool, but I don't need all the added heat I'm sure to get from the homeboys if I let you stay here. It's bad enough I have to duck and dodge the police."

"*Oralé*, I understand."

Jerry must have felt bad about not being able to let me stay so he offered me a shot of heroin. After I finished shooting up, I told Jerry about getting robbed the night before.

"So you're broke?" He asked.

I nodded.

He then gave me thirty dollars and said that's all the money he could spare. I told him it was cool and we shook hands before I left to the bus stop on the corner of Brooklyn and Mednik. I caught the 72 uptown to the Greyhound depot. I had decided to head to Visalia to visit my Mama.

On the bus ride to the depot I thought about my present circumstances and realized my future was bleak. I didn't have a clue about what I was going to do out here in the free world. I'd only been out twenty-four hours and already had gotten drunk, used heroin twice and been robbed of all my money. As much as I wanted to deny it, I knew I was already hooked on heroin and that it wouldn't take long before it drove me into doing whatever needed to be done to obtain relief from the torment of withdrawals. I hadn't walked out of prison with the intent of using drugs, but the fear of being out in the world with nowhere to go was so powerful that I hadn't been able to resist using heroin to relieve my worries. Heroin had lured me to it just like flies are drawn to feces. I leaned my head back, closed my eyes, and tried not to think anymore.

Arriving in Visalia late that night, I called my sister Gracie to pick me up at the Greyhound depot. Gracie had gotten married and was living in Farmersville with her husband Lupe, a man from Mexico who she met at a downtown grocery store. Since I was already on the run from my parole officer, I couldn't stay with Mama. The cops in Woodlake knew me all too well and would surely arrest me on the spot.

Farmersville is a sleepy farming community without much excitement. But a few days after I got there, I made contact with *Bella*, the woman who had been at the river when I stabbed the man who had intruded in on our party. It seemed like ages since then and a lot had happened in both of our lives.

Bella had recently been released from prison for the second time. She had turned out to be a very attractive woman. Her body was thick, yet tight from the rigorous workout regiment she had implemented into her daily routine while in prison. She had long, silky, auburn hair that hung to her lower back. Her dark brown eyes were intense and her lips were full. *Bella* had perfectly set teeth that were as white as freshly fallen snow. As soon as she saw me, she rushed over and hugged me.

"It's been a long time, baby. You ready to get busy?" she asked, smiling seductively.

"Hell yeah, girl. Let's do this."

We walked over to her house and had wild sex. She was an attentive lover and made sure I was satisfied. Afterward, we lay in bed smoking and reminiscing about the past. *Bella* had married a guy from my neighborhood, but she had recently divorced him because he had done the unforgivable of turning Rat trying to avoid going to prison. He had made an agreement with the District Attorney to purchase drugs off some local drug dealers and testify against them.

"That punk got me started on dope so I would get off his back about him using. He was right too. I did stop nagging him once I started using. Shit, I couldn't very tell him to quit if I was doing it, too. But then he went and turned snitch and left me to fend for myself."

I could tell *Bella* had been hurt badly by her ex-old man turning Rat and abandoning her.

"It's all right though," she continued. "I'll survive without his punk ass."

"Sure you will," I replied.

The next night, *Bella* and I began robbing Mexicans who worked in the fields. We knew most undocumented workers didn't deposit their money in bank accounts because they were afraid that by doing so they would get caught and get sent back to Mexico. So they usually kept their money stashed in their socks, which made them easy crime victims. They seldom, if ever, called the cops to report that they had been robbed. These were hardworking men, who went to *Las Angelinas,* a drinking establishment on Main Street to have fun on Saturday nights. *Bella* and I usually entered the bar separately so as not to arouse suspicion or make any potential victim nervous about approaching *Bella* because I was with her.

To get the men's attention, *Bella* would wear low-cut blouses that showed off her ample breasts and tight skirts that hugged her round bottom and clung to every curve of her body. I would watch her from a distance as she flirted with a likely target, whispering in his ear as she rubbed her body against his. Most men couldn't resist her advances. *Bella* would always signal me with a slight nod whenever she had a man on the line. After her signal, I would exit the bar and wait at a designated spot for her to bring him where I could relieve him of his money.

I would hunker down in the dark and wait with my predatory instincts on alert. I would watch *Bella* maneuver our prey to where I was hiding. As soon as they were close enough, I would swiftly pounce, slam him to the ground, knock the wind out of him, and stick my knife to his throat. In a low menacing voice I would tell him to give me his money.

With eyes wide and his body trembling with fear, the victim would always comply with my demands and hand over his valuables. I would whisper in his ear threateningly that if he reported me to the police, he would end up getting deported because he didn't have legal documentation to be in the U.S. I used their ignorance about immigration against them. Our mode of operation worked for the next three weeks, but then *Bella* was taken into custody for parole violation and everything changed. *Bella* had been in jail for a few days when I attempted to rob a man at one of the local bars downtown. I drank a huge amount of alcohol earlier in the day trying to fill the emptiness I felt, not really caring about the consequences of my actions as I staggered to the bar.

Arriving at the drinking establishment located at the east end of town, I immediately spotted a likely prey. I had seen him around and we had spoken with each other briefly on a number of occasions. Wanting to get him outside, I asked him for a ride to my house. He readily agreed to take me. He had just purchased a pickup truck and was excited to show it off.

Walking outside, we climbed into his new Chevy truck. As he reached to turn on the ignition, I swiftly pulled out my knife and placed it to his ribs.

"Give me all your money," I said menacingly as I pushed the knife firmly against his ribs.

The look on his face was one of pure shock, but he complied. It wasn't until I told him to get out of the pickup that he began to resist. He grabbed the steering wheel and pleaded with me not to take his truck. I didn't have any compassion for the man and told him to get out, but he refused to give in. I got angry and stuck him with my knife between the ribs. Unexpectedly, he floored the gas pedal and rammed his truck into the bar. We ended up in the middle of the dance floor truck and all. He then jumped out and began to yell that I had stabbed him. Someone inside the bar called 911 and the cops were there before I could get away. I was taken into custody and booked on robbery and assault with a deadly weapon charges. Two weeks later the allegations were dismissed because the victim never appeared in court.

I wasn't home free, though. I had to answer to the Parole Board. A revocation hearing isn't like court, where you're guaranteed due process of law. The simple fact that you have been arrested is enough to get you sent back to prison. The Parole Board's motto is, "Where there's smoke, there's fire." And in my case, I was guilty as sin.

As a result of my arrest, I was sent back to prison for a flat year. It wasn't so bad considering I could've gotten at least twenty years had the victim shown up and testified against me in court. So I didn't complain.

I ended up at Solano State Prison. Solano was part of the prison building frenzy California was currently experiencing. California had built four new prisons in as many years, Mule Creek State Prison, known among convicts as Jack Ass Creek, Corcoran State Prison, New Folsom, later renamed Sacramento State Prison, and Solano.

These prisons all looked alike. The cells had solid steel doors as opposed to bars like San Quentin Prison did. The windows were long strips of glass that couldn't be opened like in the older prisons. Every building was grey, which made the prison look even drearier. All the buildings had a control tower set smack in the middle of each building that allowed guards to operate every door with a push of a button. If a fight broke out, there were gun ports at every control booth for guards to stick their guns out and shoot whoever was involved in the disturbance. Signs that boldly read, "Officers Shoot to Kill" were posted on all buildings.

Nothing much happened during the year I spent at Solano, and in the summer of '88, I was released again. I caught a bus to Visalia, knowing I was to report to a parole officer in Los Angeles, but I wasn't going back to LA and putting myself in harm's way again no matter what. It was at this time that I ran into my old buddy *Poncho*.

He had recently been released from Oregon State Prison after serving sixteen years out of a twenty-year prison sentence. It became apparent that we no longer had a close connection to each other. Too much had happened in our lives. Both of us were now addicted to heroin and had become suspicious of everything and everyone after being exposed to the deception, treachery, and manipulation which comes hand in hand with the criminal lifestyle. We had both learned that friendships and brotherly love doesn't exist in the world of drug addiction and crime. Making money by any means necessary to feed our heroin habits had become the driving force for everything we did, and nothing else mattered.

CHAPTER TEN

I DIDN'T LAST VERY LONG on the streets this time either, and in October of '88 I was arrested for armed robbery and assault with a deadly weapon again. I sat in the county jail for two weeks waiting to appear for a preliminary hearing.

During the time I spent in jail, I sweated bullets. I knew I was facing a lot of time if I was convicted of the charges. The district attorney had offered me a seventeen-year deal when I had appeared in court. I had told him he was crazy to think I would accept that type of offer.

"Well, De La Cruz," he replied when I gave him my response. "If you go to trial and we convict you, I'll make sure you get the maximum thirty-seven years this type of charges carry."

"Seventeen is just as bad as thirty-seven," I replied. "There's no way I'm getting out either way. So let's put twelve in the box and roll 'em."

That was my way of telling the DA, I was willing to gamble with a jury.

As it turned out, the victim didn't appear in court to testify against me and the charges had to be dismissed. After the dismissal, I was sitting in the bullpen waiting to be transported back to jail when the holding tank door swung open. I was asked to step out and led by two Marshals to an office where the investigating officer of the case that had just been dismissed was waiting. The detective was a tall, bald headed, mean looking man.

"Let me tell you something, you little punk," he said, spitting venom. "The next time I see you on the streets, I'm going to take you out."

I knew he was talking about killing me and didn't doubt for one second that he would carry out his threat. Knowing he wouldn't do anything at that moment, I tilted my head to one side and looked him in straight in his eyes.

"Well," I said mockingly. "I'm sorry to disappoint you Detective, but I don't think you'll ever get to carry out your wish because my criminal career in Tulare County is over."

The detective didn't respond. He just stood breathing hard, fuming at the thought that I had gotten away. For a moment, I thought he was going to spring across the desk and strangle me on the spot, but after a few seconds he nodded to the other cops and I was escorted back to the holding tank.

A few days later my parole officer revoked my parole, so I was transported to DVI and housed in East Hall. East and West Halls were no longer lockdown units as they had been back in the mid 70's. The cellblocks had been converted into a receiving center to house the large number of guys being sent to prison. Back in the day when I first started coming to the penitentiary, there were only a "chosen few" who were sent. But now, the State was sending everybody.

A couple of months later I was moved to the mainline, which was no longer controlled by *Sureños*, although they were still trying to retain power. The day I hit the yard, two guys approached me from Southern California. One guy, the shot caller for the *Sureños*, did all the talking.

"*Oralé, Esé,*" he said. "*Soy el Flacó.*"

I nodded slightly.

"The *Carnáles,*" he was referring to members from the *EME*, "have given me the okay to let you *vatos* from the *Norté* do your thing so long as you guys don't get out of line."

"Is that right?" I said sarcastically. "Well, I'm sure everyone from the *Norté* appreciates your gracious gesture. But I think you should know how I see things so we can all be on the same page, you know? I was here in '85 when there was no one from Northern California. I didn't let you Southerners control me then and I'm surely not going to let you tell me what to do now, especially since there's about the same number of guys on both sides. I think it would be wise for us to get along, although that's entirely up to you. But if you move on anyone from the North, I'm going to make sure you get hit first when we retaliate."

Flacó didn't respond, but I could see from the piercing look he gave me he didn't like what I had said to him. I continued to rub it in even more.

"The party's over," I concluded smiling exaggeratingly.

He walked away without responding and life at DVI resumed. The *Sureños* watched us, and we kept an eye on them. Things went well as far as the *Sureño-Norteño* conflict was concerned, but there were two factions from Northern California that were creating dissention between *Norteños*. The Northern Structure (NS), an offshoot of the *Nuestra Familia,* and the Fresno Bulldogs were having trouble getting along.

I really don't know where the problem between these two groups began, but I think it was because the Bulldogs didn't want anyone telling them what to do and the NS wanted control of all *Norteños*. I had just enough juice at that time to convince both sides to put their disagreements to one side so we could reach a common goal: take control of DVI from the *Sureños*.

Things worked out for a couple of months and everyone at DVI seemed to be getting along. But violence in the penitentiary is always lurking in the background ready to pounce on any unsuspecting victim. As is common in prison many guys have a tendency to loosen up when things are running smoothly. Since I had been coming in and out of prison for years, I had learned never to let my guard down.

One day, as I was making my morning yard observations, I spotted *Diablo*, as he was called, walking the prison yard checking out the surroundings. He reminded me of a lion sizing up his environs before he leaped on his prey. I watched from a distance as he walked around the prison track and then I decided to walk in his direction. I wanted to look him in his eyes to see if I was reading his body language correctly. When I passed him by, I saw the hunger. It was the same look I'd had years before when I was working toward becoming a gangster. *Diablo* had come down from Folsom and was being housed in J-Wing.

"You see that dude standing over there against the handball court wall?" I said to my sidekick LT as I nodded toward *Diablo*.

He nodded.

"That's the guy who's going to make the next move for the *Sureños*. Tell the homeboys living in J-Wing to keep an eye on him. He's looking to make a name for himself."

"*Oralé, Carnál.*"

A few days later *Diablo* stabbed a *Norteño* named *Chico* from San Jose during shower release. *Chico* didn't die, but it wasn't because *Diablo* hadn't tried to kill him. As soon as *Diablo* made the hit, he was taken to segregation and the entire institution was locked down. A few days' later Black and White inmates were allowed to continue normal programming. Chicanos from the North and South were kept locked down.

About two months later the administration slowly began to release Chicanos from both sides out into the mainline. The guys they considered less of a threat were cut loose first. I was in the last group to be released. During the time we were locked down, I made preparations, with the help of a Black convict I knew from back in the old days to get some weapons ready. I had asked the Black dude to stash them on the yard for me so we could retaliate on the *Sureños* as soon as we were released. There was no way I was going to let them get away with moving on *Chico*. It was like a slap on the face and I wasn't about turn the other cheek.

On the day I was released onto the yard, I met up with my sidekick LT. Midget from the Bulldogs and *Choco* from the NS were also in on my plan for revenge. As the four of us huddled making final preparations, I could see the *Suréños* were apprehensive. They kept pointing toward us. I told everyone not to take any overt action against them. I wanted to make our move during yard recall as we walked back to our cell units inside the corridor, away from the guns. I figured that if we moved on the *Suréños* when everyone was clustered together, it would be difficult for anyone to get charged with a new case. My rationale was that even if someone got blood on their clothing, they could argue that the blood had gotten on them because they had been in proximity of the violence.

Things didn't turn out the way I planned. Prior to yard recall, the *Suréños* made their move. A group of about twenty of them came storming toward us as if they wanted to let the guards in the gun towers know something big was about to happen. It was a protective custody move, or PC move, as we called it. *Flacó* was smart. He knew he was about to get hurt, so he told his people to attack us knowing the guards would stop them before anything happened. It all turned out as he expected. Everyone was forced to lay face down on the ground and one by one every Chicano on the yard was escorted to the hole. A few days later *Flacó* paroled.

I was taken before a classification committee a few days later and given a six month SHU term for participating in a riot. I didn't argue that there had never been a riot. I simply resigned myself to serve the six months. Besides, I had more pressing concerns. There were a number of active NF members being housed in the 'Hole' as well and if they followed the rules, they would have to move on me. After all, I had dropped out of the Tip, and the organization by-laws stated dropping out carried an automatic death sentence. I figured they would try to divert my attention by acting as though they were happy to see me so someone could stab me.

I struggled with my pride about going out onto the K-Wing recreational yard those first few days. On the one hand, I would be considered a coward if I didn't go out. Yet, if I opted to go out it would be like going into an arena filled with hyenas. In the end, my pride won and I decided to take my chances and go to the yard. I would have to be ready because I knew they would try to kill me.

My heart pounded in my ears as the Man escorted me to the yard that first day. My body was tense and my mouth was dry when I reached the entrance gate. As the Man took off the cuffs, I saw Low Rider Bob, Old Man Leo, and Hector, all seasoned members of the NF, already on the yard. I had been close to all three guys when I was in the Clique, but I knew they were diehard members and that they lived by the rules. I didn't think they would do anything that first day though. It would be a game of cat and mouse and I would have to be careful not to let them sucker play me into believing everything was all right.

I walked over to where they were and Low Rider Bob smiled.

"*Oralé, Carnál,*" he said. "It's been a long time, huh?"

"*Simón, Ese*" I nodded.

He then casually walked over to me and gave me a big hug with Hector and Old Man Leo following suit.

"Hey, *Ese*," I said to Low Rider Bob and the others. "Don't be hugging on me man. The tower guard's watching us and I'm sure he's going to report this to the gang coordinator. I don't want to be labeled a member of the Tip again. If they do that I'll never be able to walk another mainline again. You guys know I'm no longer in."

"Hey, *Carnál*," Low Rider Bob answered. "You'll always be one of us. We know where your heart's at."

"I love you guys, but I don't want to be involved in an organization that kills the very people who carry the weight. I'll help you out against *Sureños*, but I won't go against anyone from the *Norté*."

"It's cool, *Carnál*. We're not asking you to come back. And don't worry about anything happening to you while you're here either." Low Rider Bob replied smiling slyly.

"*Oralé*," I said apprehensively. The game had begun.

I stayed on the yard for two months without anything happening. Every time I went to the yard I was on edge, waiting for someone to move on me, but no one ever did. Then one day, I was escorted to an office on the second tier. When I arrived, I saw the gang coordinator, Lieutenant Jones, a fat, ruddy-faced, pickled nose man, waiting for me. After I was cuffed to a chair, Jones and I sat facing each other saying nothing for at least a minute. I think he was waiting for me to start talking first, but I didn't say anything and simply watched Jones as he sat on his big ass staring at me while chewing on a nasty cigar jutting from his mouth. Finally, he started in on me.

"I think I made a mistake with you," Lt. Jones stated matter-of-factly as he manipulated his cigar from one side of his mouth to other.

"In regards to what?" I asked, knowing very well he was talking about my NF affiliation.

"Well, you've been on the yard for the last two months and you haven't gotten hit by the NF," Jones replied pryingly.

"And you say that to say what?" I asked, not wanting to bite into any of his bait.

"You tell me."

"So, what you're saying is that because I haven't been stabbed or become one of your institutional snitches that I'm still involved with the NF? Is that it?" Lt. Jones didn't answer. He just sat there chomping on his cigar and staring at me with an expressionless look on his face. His lack of response and the fact that he was trying to play with my mind got me mad, so I dug in on him.

"I suppose that means you must be incompetent." My remark had the intended effect on Lt Jones. His facial muscles twitched slightly and I could see by the way his face turned redder than it already was that he got angry. I pressed on.

"After all, you're the one who cleared me of any involvement with the NF."

I had him, and he knew it. He cleared his throat and leaned toward me and tried another tactic.

"I know you're not involved anymore, De La Cruz, but the administration believes you are."

I knew he was bullshitting. He was the one in charge of investigations so whatever he said was all it took for anyone to be marked or cleared of gang involvement.

"All you have to do is tell us what Low Rider Bob and the others are talking about on the yard and you won't be put on the active list again."

"You must have bumped your head! I'm not putting myself in more danger than I'm already in to help you people out. Besides, where do you get the idea that you can disrespect me by asking me to be your snitch? And just so you know, I will never work for you guys no matter what! So don't ever think you'll turn me. You ain't got it like that. Furthermore, I'm not going out to the yard anymore. I don't care how long I have to stay in my cell to prove I'm no longer in the Tip. You know that if I don't go out to the yard, it's an automatic green light for anyone to move on me. But I don't give a fuck. I'm out of that shit, and have been for a long time. I can't explain why I haven't been hit either, and believe me I was expecting them to move on me every time I went out to the yard, but no one ever did. Nevertheless, I'm not going to let you folks label me an NF member again."

I was escorted back to my cell, and later that evening, when I was allowed on the tier to shower, I walked up to Low Rider Bob's cell.

"*Oralé, Carnál,*" I said.

Low Rider Bob simply nodded.

"Earlier today, Lt. Jones questioned me about my involvement with the NF. He asked me why I hadn't been hit even though I dropped out of the Clique back in '76. He asked me to be his rat. I told him to go fuck himself. I knew they would try to label me a member again if you guys didn't move on me. That's why I didn't want to go out to the yard in the first place. The only reason I went out there was because I didn't want anyone to think I was weak. But, I won't be going out there anymore until I find out what they're going to do with me. I'm only telling you what's happening because I respect you and don't want you to think I'm a coward."

"Hey, *Carnál,* I know you got plenty of heart. Maybe even a little too much," he smiled ruefully. "Go ahead and do what you have to do. If anyone on the tier says anything bad about you because you're not going to the yard, just let me know and I'll take care of it."

Later that night, as I lay on my bunk, I tried to figure out why I hadn't gotten hit and why Low Rider Bob was raising his hand for me even though I had walked away from the Clique. I knew plenty of guys who had been whacked for much less, yet here I was without a scratch. It was just as confusing to me as it must have been for the administration.

For the next four months I stayed in my cell without going to the yard. I wasn't bothered by not being able to go outside, I had been in solitary many times before and I was used to isolation. I spent my days working out, reading, or watching television.

I had always hated sports because as a kid I had never been able to get involved, but I had gotten into watching football, basketball, and baseball while I had been in the Hole. On the evening of October 17th, 1989, as I sat on my bunk watching the Oakland A's and San Francisco Giants prepare to compete for the World Series Championship title, I felt my bed begin to move; subtly at first, then harder and harder. I heard a banging noise coming from underneath the bed and in a matter of seconds the noise got louder and realized it was an earthquake.

As the seconds passed, the television screen went blank. The quake had knocked out the electrical power. I stood up and walked shakily over to stand beneath the door sill of my cell. I could feel the building literally sway as the earth rocked. Many of the guys in the cellblock yelled for the guard to let us out, but the guards had already evacuated the building. I knew we were stuck, and no matter what, we wouldn't be cut loose. I didn't want to die stuck in a cell without having a fighting chance. I never felt so helpless and frightened in my life as I did that day standing in the doorway gripping the bars of my cell.

When the power was restored the next day, I learned that the earthquake had measured 7.1 on the Richter scale and that it had only lasted fifteen seconds, although it had seemed like an eternity to me. I watched the televised collapse of the Nimitz Freeway that crushed 42 people to death. Newscasts reported a total of 63 deaths and 3,757 injuries. For the next few days all everyone talked about was the devastation of the *Loma Prieta* Earthquake.

It took a while before things got back to normal at DVI, but a few weeks after the quake, life returned to its usual routine. The swing shift officer asked me if I wanted to be a tier tender. I accepted his offer in exchange for a shower, extra food, and the opportunity to socialize with the guys on the tier. One night, while playing the dozens with one of the guys, I heard someone in a cell down the tier from me laughing loud and hard. I walked over to find out if the guy was okay and found Joe doubled over laughing hysterically.

"You okay?" I asked as I stepped in front of his cell.

"I'm cool," he said, stopping long enough to catch his breath. "I just get a kick out of the way you joke around."

I didn't think my jokes were so funny as to merit the type of reaction as the one Joe was demonstrating. But Joe was a strange dude. He always had a far off look in his eyes as though he wasn't mentally all there. And although he was always smiling and cheery, his merriment seemed hollow as though he was laughing at something private. Something no one else could touch.

I watched him for a few minutes, and then he did something that took me completely by surprise. He offered me his sister's address and asked if I wanted to write her. I don't know why he did it, but since I was stuck in the Hole with nothing better to do, I took Joe up on his offer to write his sister Rosie.

I went back to my cell that evening and wrote her a long, elaborate letter making sure to dot all my I's and cross all my T's. Nevertheless, she didn't answer me for quite some time. In fact, it took at least two months before she wrote back. In her response, Rosie said she was having family problems and apologized for taking so long to answer. I wrote back and told her I understood and we began a brief correspondence. I sent her a picture I had taken in the yard and she sent me pictures too. She was an attractive lady with a winning smile. I told her in one of my letters that I would like to get to know her on a personal level. Rosie wrote back informing me she had five kids, and was a grandma twice already. She said it would be a big responsibility for any man to take on such a task as raising five kids and asked me if I was such a man.

I wrote back saying I could handle anything. She sent me her phone number and ten days before my release I spoke with her on the phone. We talked for ten minutes. Then she agreed to pick me up when I got out.

On the day of my release, Rosie was waiting for me at the main lobby of the prison with one of her friends. I was afraid about being on the streets and not knowing what to do in the free world, but I didn't want Rosie to know I was scared. I walked nervously toward her and found myself at a loss for words. Luckily, Rosie took the initiative with the formal introductions and hugged me. Taking my hand, she then led me to her car. We climbed inside and left for her house. Once there, she cooked me a meal fit for a king. She made homemade flour tortillas just like Mama used to make and *Huevos Rancheros* and served me a large plate and sat down to watch me eat. It was then that I told her I would have to meet the wife of one of the guys still in DVI.

LT and I had made arrangements for his lady to meet me so I could buy heroin for her to smuggle into DVI. After I was done eating, Rosie and I retired into the living room and drank beer. Rosie didn't drink much, but I downed beer after beer. By the time LT's lady called that evening, I was buzzed. She said she was on her way, but needed directions. I put Rosie on the phone and she told LT's lady how to get to her house.

When LT's lady arrived, I jumped into her car and we drove to Pilgrim Street, an area where drug dealers hung out. As soon as we got there, I saw dope fiends congregating on the sidewalk. They were hanging out as though they had a license to break the law. I knew they were drug addicts because all of them had the same predatory look, waiting to devour any unsuspecting victim who came into their world. The type of world I was familiar with. They saw me coming and two of them rushed over to me.

"What you need, Homeboy?" one of them asked.

"I got it right here," another said as he opened his mouth to show me balloons stuffed inside. The balloons were wrapped into small balls that held heroin. I knew that's what was inside the balloons because I had stuffed balloons in my mouth when I used to sell heroin back in the day. The balloons were in his mouth so he could swallow them quickly whenever the cops searched him. I told him that I wanted three grams, a ten-dollar bag of heroin, and a syringe (the ten dollar bag and syringe were for me). He nodded and walked rapidly to a tree not far from where we were standing. He dug into the dirt and pulled out a plastic sandwich bag filled with small packets of aluminum foil, and quickly walked back. I handed him my money and he handed me three balloons he spit out of his mouth and one packet from the plastic bag. "Balloons in his Mouth" also handed me a new syringe. The deal was completed within a matter of seconds, but before I left, I told him that if he sold me bad stuff I would be back to look for him. He started to reply, but I raised my hand to stop him.

"I'm not saying you're ripping me off, homeboy. I just want you to know I'm not the type of guy who lets anyone get over on him."

"No problem," Balloons in his Mouth replied. "Everything's all good."

LT's lady dropped me off at Rosie's house and left for Vallejo. I felt good knowing I had kept my word to LT by sending him some dope. Many guys released from prison swore they would send drugs back to the penitentiary, but rarely, if ever, did anyone come through once they hit the bricks. Most of us had a built-in forgetter in the brain. We forgot everything that didn't benefit us.

Rushing into Rosie's house, I went straight to the kitchen, grabbed a tablespoon to liquefy the heroin on, and headed for the restroom. I quickly dissolved the heroin into liquid. I drew it into the syringe, tied myself off, and slammed the junk into my vein. As soon as I shot up, I felt whole again. The uneasiness I had been feeling from the moment I hit the streets disappeared into nothing. I loved the feeling, even though I knew I had started the journey back to prison.

I spent the next couple of days getting high and taking it easy at Rosie's house, but on the fourth day I told her I had to leave.

"I have to visit my Mama. I haven't seen her in over a year and my grandma's in the hospital and not expected to live."

"Well," Rosie replied. "Just remember you can come back anytime. And if you don't have a way back, call me and I'll go get you, okay?"

I nodded.

Rosie drove me to the Greyhound depot where the bus was about to leave.

I hurriedly bought a ticket to Visalia and climbed on board. I waved at Rosie as the bus drove off and laid my head against the seat. I fell into a deep nod and before I knew it, I was in Visalia. I saw Mama leaning against her car waiting for me as the bus pulled into the parking lot of the depot. She looked frail and had a worried look on her face.

"How are you, Mama?"

"I'm okay but your Grandma's very sick."

The next day I went to visit Grandma at the hospital. She was sitting up on the bed when I walked into her room.

"Hey, Grandma. How are you?"

"Tired, *mijo,* tired."

Grandma went on to tell me she didn't think she would live much longer and just as she prophesized, she died three days later. After Grandma's funeral, I called Rosie and asked her to pick me up. She was there the following day and I went to live in Stockton, California.

Rosie had five kids, and adjusting to life with an instant family was difficult, but with the help of heroin, I handled the transition with ease. I used heroin daily and my habit grew larger and larger every day. I still hadn't reported to my parole officer and I was sure a parolee-at-large warrant had been issued for my arrest.

One day, after I had been living in Stockton for about three months, I went to Pilgrim Street to buy my morning shot of heroin. While there, I hooked up with Peanuts, a guy I knew from the penitentiary. After we each bought our dope, we walked behind an old Victorian house located on the block to inject the heroin we had just purchased. As I squatted preparing the heroin, I heard the distinct sound of a police car driving up on us. Instinctively, I threw the cooker, syringe, and water in three different directions. The cop climbed out of his car and commanded us to put our hands on his car. We complied.

The policeman knew Peanut, and after searching him and finding nothing illicit on his possession, he told Peanut to hit the road. The officer had never seen me and asked for my name. I gave him an alias. He ran the name through police headquarters and the name came back without any criminal record.

"I can't believe you've never been in jail," he said shaking his head, as he handcuffed me and put me into the backseat of his police car. He drove me around for a few minutes then asked me to tell him who I really was.

"I already told you who I am, but I'll be whoever you want me to be," I replied sarcastically.

"Oh," he said, looking at me grimly through his rear view mirror. "You want to be a smartass, huh? Okay, punk. But I have something for your wise ass."

He floored the gas pedal and drove straight to police headquarters. Once there, he snatched me out of the car and hustled me inside. He placed me in a small holding tank that smelled of urine and vomit. The smell made my nose cringe. The arresting officer brought his superior, a cop with sergeant stripes, over to the holding tank so he could view me. I was reminded of the animals held in cages at the zoo. The cop who busted me told the sergeant that I hadn't broken any law, but that he had a gut feeling I had given him a false name. The sergeant suggested he fingerprint me and have the paddy wagon transport me to their alcohol Detox Center located at the County Honor Farm. There, I could be held without actually being booked into custody until my fingerprints came back to determine my true identity.

The arresting officer followed the sergeant's instructions. I was finger-printed, photographed, and put into the back of the police paddy wagon. There were two other men in the paddy wagon who were totally drunk and smelled as though they hadn't showered for weeks. I sat as far away from them as I could while we were driven around the city. When I was finally taken to the Detox Center, I convinced the guy working at the desk to cut me loose. He wasn't a cop and agreed to set me free so long as I could get a ride home. He let me use the phone and I called Rosie.

"Hey, Babe," I said anxiously. "You need to get to the County Honor Farm and pick me up before the police find out I'm a parolee-at-large."

"I'm leaving right now," Rosie replied, hanging up the phone.

I waited nervously for her to arrive. She was there within minutes just as she said, but as I walked down the ramp to her car I saw headlights turn onto the Honor Farm property. It was the police paddy wagon. Before I had a chance to get out of there, an officer jumped out of the paddy wagon with his gun drawn.

"Hold it right there, De La Cruz," he said. "Put your hands up and don't move."

I was busted.

I was transported to the San Joaquin County Jail, an old brick building bursting with inmates sleeping on the floor and cockroaches everywhere. I was reminded of our old house in *La Rana*. I copped a spot in a corner of the cell and laid down to rest. I knew this would be the last time I would be able to sleep for a while. I would have to kick the gargantuan heroin habit I had de-veloped while I had been on the run from my parole.

The following morning I awoke nauseated and in a cold sweat. I felt my stomach rumble and then the vomit came up and I puked my guts out. The agony had begun. For the next couple of days, I paced my cell and tossed and turned while lying on my bunk. Every bone and muscle in my body hurt. It seemed as though it was getting harder to kick.

A few days later, I placed a collect call to my parole officer in Los Angeles. She accepted my call.

"Hey, Mrs. Montgomery," I said, thoroughly irritated. "I told you I'm not going to live in L.A. under any circumstances. Too many guys know who I am and it will only be a matter of time before I end up dead or with a life sentence for killing one of them. Either way I lose. I want my parole transferred to Stockton while I'm serving my time for this violation."

"Whoa," Mrs. Montgomery countered. "I never said anything about any violation." Her response gave me a glimmer of hope that I wasn't going back to prison so I kept quiet and let her continue talking.

"But I want you to come to L.A., so we can transfer your parole properly. I'm lifting your parole hold and releasing you into the custody of a Stockton parole agent named John Hall. He has agreed to work with me on your case. He will pick you up tomorrow morning and take you to the bus depot. You better be in my office within twenty-four hours of your release or the next time you get arrested I'll make sure you get violated with the quickness, understand?"

"Yeah, sure," I replied, completely surprised that she was cutting me loose.

The following morning I was escorted to R&R and turned over to Mr. Hall, a short, stocky Black man with cropped hair that glistened in the sun as we walked to his car.

We didn't talk much as he drove toward Stockton on Interstate 5, but he did tell me he wasn't going to take me to the bus depot.

"It's up to you Jess. You know what you have to do if you want to remain on the streets. I'm not going to babysit you"

When we got to his office he gave me fifty dollars so I could pay for my bus ticket to L.A., and let me use his phone to call Rosie.

Rosie showed up twenty minutes later and we were gone. I told Rosie about having to go to L.A. She didn't want me to go, but I explained that it was necessary if I wanted to transfer my parole to Stockton. She grudgingly agreed.

I was still going through heroin withdrawals, but I didn't use that night. I knew I would have to piss in a bottle for Ms Montgomery and that if the urinalysis came back dirty, I would be sent back to the penitentiary for sure and my transfer would be squashed.

When the bus pulled into the Greyhound depot in downtown L.A., I walked to Sixth and Broadway and caught the number 72 to Alhambra where the parole office was located. The office was closed when I got there, but I waited fighting the urge to go buy some heroin to ease my aching bones and relieve the hot and cold flashes I was experiencing. As soon as the doors opened I walked inside. A female secretary behind an enclosed window asked if she could help me.

"I'm here to see Ms. Montgomery."

"Is she expecting you?"

I nodded.

"Have a seat and I'll see if she's here."

Not long after, a buzzer sounded and the main door swung open. Standing before me was a diminutive but shapely Black lady.

"Are you De La Cruz?"

"Yeah, that's me."

She smiled brightly and stretched her hand out so we could shake. Her grip was firm and warm and her skin was smooth. She led me into her office and offered me a seat.

"So we finally meet face to face," she said arching her eyebrow.

I smiled apologetically.

"You want to live in Stockton, huh?"

I nodded.

"Tell me why I should let you."

"Well, first of all, I don't have any business in LA. I don't have a place to live or a job, whereas in Stockton, I met a woman who has offered me a place to live and I'm sure I can find a job."

"It sounds good, De La Cruz, but you'll have to stay in L.A. for at least a week until I get the paper work for your transfer approved."

"Where am I going to stay in the meantime?"

"I'll take you to one of our halfway houses downtown."

With that she escorted me to a lavatory down the hall from her office and handed me a small plastic bottle so I could test for her. The urine test registered negative for drugs.

Not long after she drove me to an old hotel that had been converted into a halfway house for parolees. I was assigned to a room on the second floor with nothing more than a small bed and sink. It reminded me of a cell. I stayed there a couple days until my transfer came through. When I got back to Stockton, I was placed on Mr. Hall's caseload. He had agreed to handle my case until I was assigned a permanent parole agent. By this time I had cleaned up and was no longer shooting heroin. Mr. Hall asked me if I wanted to get into a pilot program.

"It's a new drug called Neltraxan. It comes in pill form and you have to take it once a week. The drug is supposed to take away the urge to shoot up, but even if you inject heroin you won't get high. In fact, it will make you very sick if you do. If you really want to stop using dope, Neltraxan might give you the edge you need to get over the hump."

I didn't really want to stop using, because I didn't like the emptiness I felt in my soul when I wasn't high. But I didn't want to continue going in and out of prison anymore, and using heroin was a sure ticket back to the penitentiary. Therefore, I agreed to get on Neltraxan. It worked for me, too. I even got a job in a packing shed weighing diesel trucks loaded with apples. Life was good. Rosie and I were getting along great and then one day she dropped a bomb on me.

"I have a big surprise for you, Jess," she said smiling brightly. "You're going to be a father."

At first I didn't understand what she meant, but then it came to me. She was going to have my child. I couldn't believe it. Here I was, forty years old, and as far as I knew I had never fathered a child. I was stunned, but in a good way. I always thought a child would keep me out of prison, but I always believed that being afflicted with polio had affected my ability to have children.

For the next week I was delighted about the prospect of being a father. But then I remembered that I was a heroin addict and that I would have to change my way of living if I wanted be a part of my child's life. I started to stress about how I was going to teach my child to be honest when I had never practiced honesty. Realizing the enormity of the task ahead of me, I started using heroin again to help me deal with the pressure of being a father. I even used heroin on the morning my daughter Jessica was born.

Holding Jessica in my arms that morning after the nurse had cleaned her up, I felt as though she'd brought significance into my life. I held her to my chest, with tears streaming down my face. I wondered how I was going to be able to teach my daughter the important things I knew nothing about. Rosie looked at me with a puzzled expression.

"What's wrong with you?" she asked. She had never seen me cry.

"What's wrong? Can't you see? Do you want our daughter growing up like me?" Rosie didn't understand. She had been raised in foster homes after her mother had died when she was nine years old and didn't see anything wrong with how we lived. To her, the man of the house was supposed to break the law and go to prison periodically.

"I don't know how I'm going to stop going to prison or using drugs, but before this baby is old enough to understand, I'm going to change." I knew this was a powerful statement, one that I wasn't sure I could keep.

I went to prison ten days after my daughter was born for a parole violation. Luckily, I only served ninety-three days before my parole expired. On the day of my release, Rosie was waiting for me on the prison parking lot with Jessica in her arms. She lifted Jessica in the air as I walked over to them. I saw Jessica kick her little legs, wave her small arms as though she was excited to see me. When I got close, I took hold of her and held her to me. She placed her small head on my shoulder and for a minute neither one of us moved enjoying each other's closeness. I felt an immense love for my child.

But even though I loved her and wanted to stay out, I couldn't stay clean. I started using and breaking the law the day after my release. Rosie got tired and kicked me out of the house a few weeks later. I stayed here and there after that, but every morning for the next year or so I took Jessica to the park or to the store or simply spent time with her. Then one day, when she was around two, I got arrested for petty theft and was sent to prison again.

During this incarceration, it was challenging to do my time. The three years I served seemed endless. I hadn't been able to fill the void in my soul with hate like before. Jessica's birth had touched a part of my heart that had never been exposed to feelings. I had never felt the utter defenselessness of loving someone as deeply and unconditionally as I did my daughter. There were times I wanted to cry, but I never did because in prison tears are a sign of weakness, which could bring retribution from other prisoners.

I struggled constantly with emotions that were uncomfortable and foreign to me. I fought to hold my sadness inside until my release date. I sat on my bunk with mixed emotions as I waited for the man to come cut me loose. On one hand, I was happy to be getting out so I could see my daughter again. On the other, I was afraid of what lay in store for me. I thought about how I had been arrested more times than I could count and questioned why I had survived the countless confrontations with death and many incarcerations I had encountered. Many of the guys who had been raised with me were long gone: dead from drug overdoses, cirrhosis of the liver, or at the hands of rival gangs. The ones who were still alive were either on the brink of death or stuck in the land of the walking dead serving life sentences.

Was there a God?

I pushed that question out of my mind quickly, not wanting to complicate things more than they already were. Then suddenly, I heard a voice speak to me. It was so clear I looked around to make sure no one else was in the cell with my sleeping cellmate, *Huéro*, and me.

"What are you going to do once you're set free, Jesse?" the voice asked gently. "You're going to have to change your way of living or eventually end up in prison for the rest of your life."

Shut up, I wanted to scream.

Going in and out of jail and breaking the law was the only way I knew how to live. Besides, I tried to convince myself, everyone I knew was doing exactly what I was doing. In my circle of friends the guys who hadn't gone to prison were considered strange. The thought of spending the rest of my life in prison had periodically entered my mind, but it had never bothered me as much as it did today. In fact, before this incarceration, I remember thinking it wouldn't be so bad to be among the people I considered my friends. If I would be allowed to get high every once in awhile and get laid every three months like some of the married cons were allowed to do, it wouldn't be so bad. Three hots and a cot, without any responsibilities except staying alive, what more could a man ask for?

"How about your daughter?" the voice asked.

She was almost five years old and I hadn't seen her in three years. There wasn't any way I could continue being a criminal and still be involved with my daughter.

Furthermore, what had started out as something to gain respect and recognition long ago had turned into a violent lifestyle, which I didn't know how to break away from. I felt trapped in a rat maze without a way out. After my first prison sentence back in '72, the dream of becoming a gangster had turned into a nightmare. And every time I had ended up in prison, it was as if someone opened a door into a violent world that deprived me freedom, privacy and individuality. On the other hand, being released was like another door being opened, but this door led to drug addiction and homelessness.

Damned if you stay and dammed if you go, I thought.

My cellmate *Huéro* finally woke up. I could see by the expression on his face that he would miss me. *Huéro* never voiced his sentiments, but I knew what he was feeling. Like *Huéro*, I had developed close relationships while in prison and had seen friends depart to the streets, leaving me with a sense of loneliness that tore at the very core of my being. I understood it wasn't so much that *Huéro* didn't want me to leave. It was more that he wished he could go with me. During the time *Huéro* and I had spent in our cramped cell, we had become close friends. We had shared our dreams and stories about our families. I had told him about Jessica and how much I missed her. I had opened up to him and told him I didn't want to come back to prison. He hadn't responded. He had simply looked at me despairingly, unable to say anything encouraging. We both knew it would be next to impossible to stay out.

I was older than *Huéro* and had spent more years in prison than he had, but he understood the difficulty of changing our way of living.

"I don't know, *Dragón*," he said during one of our many conversations. "You've been doing this a long time. This is what you know. I mean, if it wasn't for the stuff you taught me I don't think I would have made it in here."

I had passed on the information I had gotten from Big *Indio*, schooling *Huéro* on the aspects of prison warfare, telling him what to watch for when there was tension on the yard. Sadly, he was right. I couldn't give him any advice on how to stay out.

"*Oralé, Carnálito*," I told *Huéro* as I prepared to leave. "Take care of yourself and watch your back."

"*Simón, Carnál*. You know I'm going to handle my business," *Huéro* answered, doing his best to maintain his tough guy image.

"I hear you, Homie," I replied, turning away quickly and swallowing a lump in my throat to keep from busting out crying. What's wrong with you, getting all sentimental and shit, I thought.

"Come on, De La Cruz, we don't have all day. They're waiting for you at R & R, so get moving," the Man commanded.

"Yeah, yeah," I answered. It was the same ole game of hurry up and wait.

As soon as I began walking to R&R, I heard another voice reverberating in my ear. But unlike the gentle voice I had heard earlier, this voice was cruel and judgmental.

"What you going to do once you're set free, *Dragón*?" the voice asked sarcastically. "What do you expect to accomplish this time? You don't have a place to live, a car, a job, or any skills to offer a potential employer. You don't know how to do anything except how to use drugs, drink alcohol, and commit crimes. Who are you trying to kid about wanting to change?"

By the time I arrived to R&R, I was a nervous wreck and my stomach was doing somersaults. I sat down on a long wooden bench with the other men being paroled. I wondered if they were going through the same mental chaos and fears as I was. I couldn't tell what they were thinking by the expressions on their faces, but I knew we were experts at hiding our true feelings. I surely wasn't going to ask anyone if he was afraid of hitting the streets. I didn't want to be ridiculed for being scared of getting out. Besides, I had a reputation to maintain. So I sat there fighting the urge to keep from shouting that I was terrified about what lay in store for me once I got out.

Waiting to sign the necessary papers to be freed felt like an eternity. One main question replayed itself in my mind: How will you stay out?

I was at a crossroads in my life, but I didn't know how to cross over to the other side. I had outgrown the need to earn respect and it was no longer important to prove I was someone to be reckoned with, but how was I going to unlearn my bad habits and live lawfully within society? It would require a lot of work to get rid of the garbage I had acquired during my criminal involvement. I wasn't sure I could do it.

"Well, De La Cruz," Officer Miller said. "I guess it's that time again. I don't understand why the state continues to let people like you out into the free world. All you do is create unsafe communities for law abiding citizens," he continued, shaking his head in disbelief. "Sign on the dotted line and I'll see you in six months."

I don't know how he knew I'd be back? Perhaps he could see the fear written on my face and knew it would be a short time before I would return to the security of prison. I looked at this pathetic man with that terrible scar across his face and almost told him to go fuck himself. But knowing this type of remark would be an infraction of institutional rules that would keep me in Folsom an additional thirty days, I kept my mouth shut.

The time to walk out of Folsom's main gate finally arrived, and as the other parolees and I stepped out into the free world, I heard the clanging of the huge steel door slam shut behind us. The loud sound echoed in my ears.

One of the guys in the group recited a popular inmate rhyme:

"Out the gate by eight, in the spoon by noon, and back in the pen by ten."

Everyone laughed except me. I didn't find his poetic bullshit amusing.

I moved faster than usual to the waiting van taking our group into Sacramento. It was a clear, cloudless, April morning with the sun shining brightly.

I glanced up at the castle tower and noticed a guard watching our group intently. He kept a vigilant eye on us as he held his carbine cleverly pointed in our direction as though he was ready to shoot one us if we made a wrong move.

Glaring at him, I wanted to yell. "Hey, punk! We're being released. There's no reason to point your fucking gun at us." I wanted to shout at him how much I detested the society he represented. I wanted to force him to experience the despair of the convicts I was leaving behind. More so, I wanted him to suffer the emotional panic I was undergoing at that moment. But I kept my hatred and fear locked up.

I climbed into the van, inhaled deeply, and took a hard look at Folsom, and prayed silently that I would never have the misfortune of being confined there again.

When I first began serving State time, twenty-seven years earlier, I had heard about Folsom, but I never thought I would end up here.

During the time I was in Folsom, I had read about its history in books I found in the prison library. I had seen photos that showed Folsom at different stages of its construction way back in 1880. I could only imagine the amount of time and sweat it had taken Chinese workers to build this sorrowful place.

Folsom State Prison had housed California's first Death Chamber and ninety-three men had been hung on its gallows. Most of the hanged men had been buried in the cemetery located behind the prison. The gallows at Folsom had been dismantled when the state began using the electric chair at San Quentin.

Before that morning, I had never paid attention to Folsom prison's picturesque setting outside the gates. There were well-painted houses with expansive, neatly trimmed lawns, and colorful flowerbeds maintained by inmates from the prison ranch population (a separate institution from the main prison which housed less dangerous inmates).

As the van pulled out of the main parking lot and onto the road leading off of the institutional grounds, I found myself terrified about my future. I didn't have anything except the clothes on my back and two hundred dollars in my pocket. I overheard a couple of the guys discussing what they were going to do once they got to their hometown. I think their chitchat was their way of handling the stress of having to live on the outside. No more relaxation. Life's in session and there's no recess.

I didn't say anything on the ride into Sacramento, but I clearly heard that sarcastic voice in my mind again.

"You're not going to change on me now are you?" it scoffed.

I tried to shut it out, but the voice continued to nag me. I had no doubt that if I listened to it, I would be pulled back into the self-inflicted cycle of re-incarceration.

Looking out the window of the van I saw a billboard that read,

"You are now leaving Folsom. Thank you for coming and please come again." The inscription on the sign was thanking people for visiting the City of Folsom, not Folsom State Prison. I found the advertisement amusing in a sick kind of way.

When we arrived to the depot, Officer Miller gave us a speech on how we were expected to behave until we departed to our individual destinations.

Some of the parolees started to protest, but then thought better of it. Everyone knew the rules. We knew it wouldn't do any good to complain. In that moment, I realized how ironic it was that many of us involved in crime claimed no one could tell us what to do. Yet, every time the Man told us we couldn't do something, we obeyed. In the penitentiary someone was always running our lives. They told us when to wake, eat, shower, and sleep. Once released, we were assigned a parole officer who continued to control our lives. It was as though we couldn't live without someone directing our every move. Most of us didn't have the vocational or social skills needed to make it out here. We hadn't learned how to pay bills or how to socialize without the use of drugs or alcohol. Every time someone was released from prison, the state gave them two hundred dollars and expected them to stay out. Most of the guys who went to prison had substance abuse problems, but even if the parolee stayed clean, two hundred dollars wouldn't take him far. I looked at the other parolees and wondered if they were thinking the same thoughts as me.

A few minutes later my bus arrived. I got in line, climbed aboard and soon was on my way to Stockton. I turned my thoughts toward my daughter Jessica. I hadn't seen her since my incarceration three years before. I had missed watching her grow from a baby to a toddler. I was looking forward to holding her in my arms like I had done when she was a baby.

I looked out the window of the Greyhound and saw a crew of farm workers in a field of grapes and was reminded of a time when I had worked in the fields with my family long ago. I couldn't believe how quickly the years had passed.

Where had the years gone?

I saw a sign on the highway that read, "Lodi City Limits." Only nine miles before I reached my destination and my dread grew more intense.

CHAPTER ELEVEN

A FEW MINUTES LATER we arrived in Stockton. Disembarking from the bus, I knew the time to step into the real world was at hand. I walked tentatively onto the Center Street sidewalk, and looked north. There wasn't any reason for me to go in that direction. North Stockton represented the good side of town. To the south, two blocks away, lay the infamous "Mariani's," the city district infested with criminals, drug addicts, winos, and prostitutes. As much as I wanted to stay away from that area, something within urged me that way.

I strolled over to that contaminated part of downtown and for the first time in my life, felt ill at ease walking through the desolate conditions—garbage collected on the curb, graffiti on the old paint-chipped buildings, with their filthy windows. In the past, I would have jumped into crime without any reservations, but this time, it was different. As I walked aimlessly, my mind felt as though I was in a Texas hailstorm, being pelted by granules of doubt and fear without having anywhere to run for cover.

I got a headache from thinking so much, so I did what was familiar to me to alleviate my problems. I walked into a nearby liquor store and bought a twelve pack of beer. I knew I couldn't drink it all, but I wanted to drown my dread. I snapped open a beer and took a big swig. Like always, the alcohol tasted nasty. But it didn't matter. I invited alcoholic oblivion.

I walked around the corner of the store and bumped into *Chuco*. He was considered an OG. Someone had given him the moniker *Chuco* because the name described someone who paid special attention to the way he dressed. *Chuco* always wore his clothing neatly pressed and creased. His Stacy Adams shoes were always polished to a glossy shine. He was always cleanly shaven and there was never a single slicked-backed hair on his head out of place. I must admit, the guy stayed sharp. *Chuco* appeared genuinely happy to see me.

"*Oralé, Carnál,*" *Chuco* exclaimed, as he shook my hand. "How are you doing, *Dragón*? It's been a long time. Did you just hit the streets?"

"Yeah, I got off the bus about ten minutes ago. You want a beer?" I extended one to him.

"*Oralé,* why not? I'll take a cold one. Got to celebrate your home coming, *que no?*"

"Yeah, I was thinking the same thing before I bumped into you," I lied.

Chuco popped open his beer and took a long drink. Afterward, he burped, wiped his mouth and asked, "So how does it feel to be out?"

"It feels strange. You know how it is, Homeboy, it's all about program in the penitentiary. And now here I am without anywhere to go, you know what I mean."

"*Oralé, Dragón,* what you talking about, Homeboy? Getting' out ain't nothing for guys like us. We've been doing that shit for years. You're probably just going through the, I just got out of the penitentiary blues," he laughed as he did a little shuffle. "Hell, before you know it, you'll be back in the groove and rollin' like Nolan," he said as he slapped me on my back.

Chuco was on a roll and I could tell by the way he scratched his nose and slurred his words when he spoke that he was under the influence of heroin and talking out the side of his neck.

"I hear you, homie," I replied.

The truth was, I was frightened about being out, but I couldn't tell *Chuco*. *Chuco* then proceeded to bring me up to date on the latest neighborhood gossip.

"It's the same ole thing, *Carnál,*" *Chuco* said. "*Pato* and *Flacó* overdosed a few months back when a batch of pure stuff hit the streets. I never tried any of that stuff myself, but I heard it was quality shit. What a way to go, *que no.*"

I nodded.

"What's really cold is how a robbery went bad and now Junebug and *Négro* are serving life sentences at the Bay."

The "Bay" was short for Pelican Bay State Prison, a Supermax prison designed to house documented gang members and inmates considered incorrigible by CDC. Inmates housed there were locked up twenty-three hours a day and only allowed to spend one hour out of their cells in a small cement enclosed yard. They weren't allowed to socialize with other inmates. There were only three ways an inmate ever got out of Pelican Bay.

He paroled, he died, or he debriefed.

Debriefing was a term coined by CDC. It was sophisticated word for "snitching." If an inmate told CDC what they wanted to hear concerning the gang he was accused of being connected with, the inmate would be transferred out of the Bay.

"Junebug and *Négro* had the robbery all planned out," *Chuco* continued.

"They were supposed to go in and out, but some guy working in the store decided to act like Superman. The guy resisted and the Homeboys had no choice but to shoot him. After they killed the guy, it was all over. The police surrounded the store and arrested them. At least *Pato* and *Flacó* don't have to feel anything anymore, but Junebug and *Négro* will spend the rest of their lives in the land of the walking dead. You hear what I'm saying? That sure is cold." *Chuco* said, shaking his head.

"Yeah, I hear you."

I shivered at the thought of spending the rest of my life in prison like Junebug and *Négro*.

I took another drink of my beer and tried not to think anymore.

"Well," *Chuco* said. "I've got to get going. I have to make some money to feed the monkey on my back. Thanks for the beer, Homeboy," he said, as he walked away.

I finished my beer, and opened another. Realizing it would be dark soon, I guzzled it down. I needed to find a place to spend the night. I didn't want to get caught on the streets of the *barrio* after nightfall. It was dangerous, even for a guy like me.

I walked over to the Southside of Stockton and found a motel on Charter Way. It was one of those motels that had seen better days, where the management didn't ask questions. Their only concern was collecting the twenty-five dollar fee for the room. I walked into the office and inquired about a vacancy. I was in luck. They had a room. I paid the clerk and he gave me a key to a room located at the farthest corner of the building.

Stepping inside, I switched on the television set on a rickety table, opened another beer, and sat down to watch the news. The room reeked of stale cigarette smoke and body odor. After drinking another two beers, I decided to go to *Memo's* bar down the street. I had been locked up for three years and now I wanted to have some fun.

The alcohol had done its job and relieved my anxiety.

Memo's bar was like many Mexican drinking establishments in south Stockton. There was a jukebox in one corner blaring mariachi music, with four provocatively dressed women working as barmaids.

As I walked across the bar to a table against a far wall, everyone eyed me suspiciously. I chose that spot so I could observe every move made by the patrons. I lived in a dangerous world and had learned long ago never to give my back to anyone.

One of the barmaids walked over to my table and asked me what I wanted to drink.

"I'll take a Budweiser."

When the barmaid returned with my beer, I paid her. She smiled at me and left. After taking a big drink, I scanned the room and saw a man staring at me. Even when I looked away I kept him in my peripheral vision and saw that he kept watching me. I began to worry that maybe I had done something to him in the past. Before I went to prison, I had robbed many drug dealers and this guy looked like he could be one of the connections I had held up. I decided to find out who he was and walked over to him.

"Aren't you, *Dragón?*" he asked.

"Yeah, that's me. Why? What's up?" I asked, ready to fight.

"You don't remember me?"

"Naw," I replied, eyeing him suspiciously. "Where you from?"

"You used to buy dope from me on Pilgrim Street. Remember?"

"Yeah, I remember now, *Chino*, right?"

"*Simón, Ese.* Where you been?"

"On vacation."

Chino smiled knowing I meant I had been in the penitentiary.

"Well, you're out now. Here's something to help you relax," he said, as he spit out a small marble like object and handed it me. It was a balloon that contained heroin. I didn't want to take it, but something compelled me to reach for it and put it in my mouth. Afterward, I tried to make small talk with him for a little while longer, but the heroin in my mouth urged me to go back to the room and inject it into my vein. So I bid *Chino* farewell and rapidly headed back to the motel room. On the way, I stopped a street hooker and bought a new hypodermic syringe from her.

Once I got to the motel room, I locked the door and hastily prepared the heroin and slammed it into my vein. I hadn't forgotten how to do it. Shooting up was like riding a bike, you never forgot. As always, the drug immediately took effect, but this time the high was different. It didn't fill the isolation eating at me. I sat on the lumpy chair in the middle of the room late into the night nodding in and out of consciousness until I passed out. But before I slipped into nothingness, I remember thinking I had begun the downward spiral that would lead me back to prison.

That night I dreamt of being in a huge steel lung. Like the one I used to be placed into when I was a kid in the hospital after I contracted polio because I couldn't breathe. But in this dream, I wasn't a kid anymore. I had grown up. And I'd been placed into the machine because I couldn't breathe as a result of the fear of being on the streets. The panic was suffocating me. This machine was different too. It wasn't providing me with oxygen; it was feeding heroin into my veins. I didn't know who put me into the huge apparatus, but then I saw that it wasn't a nurse who was in control of the machine. It was Chino, the guy from the bar. He saw me looking at him and started to laugh uncontrollably. I could hear his depraved laughter as he manipulated the control buttons on the machine that were feeding me the heroin. I struggled to break out, but the more I tried to break free, the harder it became for me to escape. I was trapped inside this monstrous instrument just as I seemed to be caught in a life of crime.

I woke up gasping for breath with the familiar aftertaste of heroin in my mouth. I got up from the floor where I was when I came to and walked into the bathroom. I didn't have a toothbrush so I tried to wash the nasty heroin taste out with plain water, but it didn't work. I couldn't get rid of the nasty tang. Then, I heard the wicked voice speak to me again.

"You know what do, *Dragón*. Drink another beer. Shoot some more dope. Everything will be all right. Just do it!"

I knew that if I did what the voice suggested, heroin would run me ragged again. But I didn't have the strength to resist it. Heroin was too powerful for me. So I gave in and prepared the heroin left from the night before and injected it to ease my apprehension. The heroin did its job. It gave me the courage I needed for the time being. I knew it was only temporary, but heroin was all I had to lean on.

After I shot up, I got ready and left to visit Jessica. Along the way, I stopped at a payphone and called Rosie to let her know I was headed to her house so I could see my baby girl.

As I walked there, I wondered how I was supposed to stay out of prison when I couldn't even stay clean for one day. There was even a possibility I could get arrested later that day at my required visit to see my parole officer.

I was so immersed in my thoughts that I didn't realize I had arrived at my daughter's house. She must have been waiting for me because before I knew it, she was running down the porch steps yelling, "Papa, Papa," and flinging herself into my arms causing me to stumble backward. I caught her and brought her close to my heart and enjoyed her closeness. She wrapped her small arms around me tightly and laid her small curly-haired head against my chest like she used to do when she was a baby. Being in her presence left me speechless and the void in my soul was temporarily filled. After a while, she broke away and looked me in my eyes with a beaming smile fixed on her face.

"Are you going to stay with me all day, Papa?" she asked, smiling brightly.

"No, baby, I can only stay a few hours, but maybe I can come back to see you after I report to my parole officer." The smile on her face vanished and instantly turned into a sad frown. I looked at my baby and felt an overwhelming need to cry.

Rosie and I didn't talk much, but we were cordial. I told her I was going to take Jessica with me for a few hours. She said it was all right. Jessica and I walked hand in hand to the "Dip," a neighborhood park. We spent several hours there. She seemed happy. I pushed her on a swing. We climbed the monkey bars, sat on a teeter-totter, and slid down the huge slide. I spun her on the merry-go-round, then chased her around the table. She laughed boisterously whenever I caught her. But then it was time to leave.

"Jessica, we have to go baby. Maybe we can come back later, okay?"

She didn't respond. She simply nodded and hung her head. It troubled me to leave my daughter, but there was nothing I could do. When we arrived at her house, I picked her up and she hugged me tightly as if she knew I might not return. Holding her in my arms I sensed her heartache and it made me want to cry. I gently pulled her arms from me and placed her on the sidewalk and kissed her. I walked away slowly and glanced back to see if she had gone inside, but she hadn't. She was standing right where I left her, gazing at me with her head tilted to one side. When she saw me look back, she waved at me forlornly and my sorrow grew even more. I waved back, but turned my head quickly. I didn't want to see the sorrow on her face. her distress. I set my mind on what had to be done next— meet with my parole officer.

I didn't know if I would see Jessica later because I reeked of alcohol. Plus, I was also under the influence of heroin. There definitely was a strong possibility I would be back in custody before the end of the day. I'm not even sure why I kept my appointment with my parole agent. I had never reported before when I had been released, yet here I was, walking that day into possible incarceration.

What an idiot, I thought, as I entered the parole department office, but I continued inside.

"May I help you?" the receptionist asked.

"I just got out of Folsom yesterday and I'm here to report."

"All right," she replied. "Please fill out these forms while you're waiting and I'll tell your agent you're here. Can I have your CDC number?"

"J-27449."

I sat down and began to fill out the forms she had given me. Then I thought about how stupid I was for being there. Just as I was about to leave, the main door of the office swung open and a tall, thin, blond woman who looked to be in her mid-fifties called my name.

"De La Cruz."

"Yeah."

"Come in," she said with a bright, vitalizing smile. "It's good to meet you." It seemed as though she was trying to make me feel at ease, but I knew she was the enemy and that I couldn't trust her. She led me down the hall to her office, and as we walked there, I kept thinking she was going to send me back to prison for being under the influence of heroin. I felt my stomach churn from nervousness as we stepped into her office. I had a strong urge to puke, but I held it down.

"My name is Ms. Jones," she said, once we were in her office. "I've been assigned as your agent. We're here to discuss your parole conditions."

I nodded.

"Listen, De La Cruz," Ms. Jones began. "I can smell alcohol on your breath and I can tell by the pinched look on your face that you're under the influence of heroin, too. You just got out and already you have given me two reasons to send you back. However, today is your lucky day. I'm not going to send you back to prison this time, but if you ever come into my office in your present condition, I will send you back in a snap! Do I make myself clear?"

I nodded.

I was truly surprised she was giving me a break. And then, when I thought things were starting to look up I said:

"Ms. Jones, I need to throw up."

"What!?"

I couldn't make it to the toilet so I grabbed her trashcan and puked my guts out. As I threw up, Ms. Jones looked on with disgust. I finished quickly and apologized.

"Don't ever do this again, Jess," she said sternly. Then she escorted me to the bathroom where I dumped the vomit into the commode and rinsed her wastebasket. We returned to her office where she gave me the conditions of my parole.

"You're not to drink alcohol or use drugs. You must obey all laws and register as a drug addict with the Stockton Police Department within the week. And you're not to come in contact with any law enforcement agency or associate with known criminals," she concluded.

Wow, does she honestly believe I will be able to abide by all these stipulations?

Shit, the only people I knew were criminals, and the police were always messing with me for one reason or another. It never occurred to me that the only reason the police harassed me was because I was always breaking the law, hanging out in crime-ridden areas, and associating with known criminals.

I walked out of the parole office and went straight to my heroin connection convincing myself that I needed relief from the pressure Ms. Jones had dumped on me concerning my parole stipulations. I bought a twenty-dollar bag and rushed to a secluded area to inject the stuff into my vein. Three days later, I was out of money, hooked on heroin and angry with myself for allowing drugs to dominate my life again.

How could I have been so stupid to get caught up in this crap for the umpteenth time? I didn't have the answer. What I did know was that it felt as though I was being pulled into a dark shaft and that however hard I tried, I didn't have the courage or strength to keep from being sucked in. I knew I would have to start stealing to support my habit and that if I got caught, I could kiss the free world goodbye forever.

I stopped attending my weekly appointments with my parole officer, so she issued a parolee-at-large warrant for my arrest. I was going down fast.

One day, I was sitting under a huge oak tree located near the homeless shelter where I had been staying. Hobo, appropriately nicknamed, was cooking asparagus over an open fire in a beat up pot that pretty much resembled my life. He was telling jokes to the others gathered around the fire. Everyone was laughing up a storm. I didn't find anything Hobo was saying funny at all and watching those men act as though everything was fine made me angry. Not at the men, but at the lifestyle. I couldn't believe these guys were convinced it was all right to live akin to packrats, having to scrounge for food and shelter.

After all, I knew that every man under that huge tree was running from something. Most of us were running from the law. But mainly, we were running from ourselves. I was acquainted with some of the men there and knew most them had problems with drugs and alcohol. Everyone was homeless, carless, moneyless, everything less, yet here they were laughing and carrying on as if they didn't have a care in the world. Looking at the place where I had ended up and the tattered clothing I was wearing made me ashamed of what I had become.

I wondered what had happened to the guy I used to be. The one who had once been a real gangster with a nice place to live, plenty of money, a nice car, and nice clothing to wear? I had always dressed well, making sure the creases on my pants and shirts were razor sharp. Now I wasn't even wearing underwear. I had thrown my boxer shorts away because I had gotten tired of washing them in the shower of the homeless shelter every night, like I'd done in prison. If someone had told me years earlier that I would end up homeless, I would have socked them in the mouth for disrespecting me.

Psychologically drained from the stress and humiliation of living such a shameful life, I walked back to the shelter. I took a quick shower and laid down to rest. I tried to sleep, hoping sleep would bring temporary escape from the emotional strain I was experiencing, but sleep wouldn't come. I tossed and turned. Finally, after battling with my mind all night, I made a decision. First thing in the morning I would turn myself into the parole department so they could send me back to prison. Going back wouldn't be so bad once I kicked my two-month heroin habit and I got my health back. At least I would be back in my world where I would be calling the shots. I knew I would miss Jessica terribly, but I didn't know what else to do.

At 6:00 AM, after injecting my last piece of Tar heroin, I walked over to visit Jessica one last time. Along the way, I stopped at a store and bought a forty-ounce bottle of King Cobra beer and sat down to drink at a park located two blocks from Jessica's house. I knew it would be difficult for my daughter to understand why I had to go back to prison again. I grappled with finding an easy way to tell her that I didn't know how to live out here without drugs. Even with the drugs and booze in my system, I still felt weighed down with grief. Jessica was the only bright spot in my life and going back to the penitentiary would snuff that light out. Looking towards the sky I suddenly yelled out at God in anger and desperation.

"Why are you treating me so bad? I know you didn't put me on this earth to be miserable."

I needed to blame someone other than myself for the mess I had created, and I didn't expect to get an answer to my question, but out of the nowhere, I heard a voice speak to my heart.

"I'm not treating you this way, son," the voice said gently. "It's you who's mistreating yourself so cruelly."

At that moment, it felt as if I had been struck by a Mack Truck and for the first time I realized the voice was right. I had been crueler to myself than I would have ever been toward my worst enemy. I had always been skeptical about believing in God and had never been religious, but there had been times when I'd had brief periods of wanting to believe in something. However, false pride had always held me back from surrendering. But on this day, I realized I had hit rock bottom and in utter defeat I raised my arms in total surrender.

"God," I asked. "Help me do what needs to be done so I can change. Teach me to live right."

Nothing miraculous happened right then and there, but I had a gut feeling that my plea had been answered. Since I didn't know what God intended to do in my life, I continued with the plan to turn myself into the parole department. In the meantime, I stopped at a neighborhood store and bought another King Cobra for the road. When I walked out of the market, I ran into a guy who worked as a liaison between the court system and drug treatment centers in San Joaquin County. I didn't know Mike personally, but he seemed to know me.

"Where have you been?" he asked.

I merely shrugged my shoulders.

"Are you ready?"

"Yeah," I answered, totally crushed. "I'm ready."

"Get in," he said, nodding towards his car.

Taking one last swig of the beer I had just purchased, I threw it into some shrubs on the side of the building and climbed into his automobile.

Mike drove me to a drug treatment center located on the outskirts of town. The center was situated on hospital grounds surrounded by great towering eucalyptus trees that gave the place a sense of peace and serenity. When Mike and I arrived, there were men and women milling around the center complex of the treatment center.

"Hey, everybody," Mike said. "This is Jess. He'll be staying here for the next three months. I want you guys to help him feel welcome.

Some of the residents nodded at me. An older gentleman in his late fifties named Fred walked over and introduced himself. He had a bright smile, a thick head of gray hair, and a glow that I found intimidating. I had never met anyone as friendly as this man and his openness quite frankly scared me.

"How are you?" he asked, sticking out his hand.

"I'm all right," I answered apprehensively, as we shook hands.

"That's good," he smiled. "Listen, Jess. You're going to hear a lot of stuff in the next few months. Some of the things are not going to make any sense to you at first, but just hang in there and remember that you don't have to change everything all at once."

I didn't understand what he was talking about. Actually, I thought he was crazy, but I didn't say anything. I just nodded.

After going through the admission process, I went to lie down on my bunk in the dormitory where I had been assigned. I prepared myself for the agony of heroin withdrawals that would be coming soon enough.

The following morning I was awakened by the beginning stages of heroin withdrawals. My stomach ached, my muscles throbbed, and I had a slight case of the runs. I knew the pain would get worse if I didn't get a shot of heroin or on the twenty-one day Methadone program as Mike had promised. Mike had promised me that if I stayed at the center, he would get me into the program. Mike kept his word. At 8:00 a.m., he took me to the clinic where I was given a medical examination and a dose of Methadone. Not long after I took the medicine, I felt normal again.

During the next few days I heard program residents talk about such things as being honest and cleaning house. I didn't know what cleaning house meant, but later I found out it meant getting rid of "emotional garbage." I listened to these people pour their hearts out. I heard a guy talk about praying for his enemies. He spoke openly about the things he had done before changing his life, like stealing from his family to get drugs, and not keeping his promises to his children. His candor frightened me.

How can these people be so open about matters that were so personal? I didn't think I could do what these guys were doing because guys would surely line up to snitch on me if I was totally honest about what I had done in the past. I would be their get-out-of-jail-free card whenever they got busted again. Perhaps I would only disclose some of the things I had done and keep the serious acts to myself.

When I had been at the center for nineteen days, I seriously contemplated leaving. The methadone wasn't working anymore. During that time, I often wondered if changing was worth all the pain. It was a constant mental battle for me to stay put. I wasn't sure if I could handle everything these people were suggesting either, but I had never been a quitter. I knew I had to try to find another way of living or else I was going to wind up in prison and never see my child again. I couldn't handle that, so I stayed and continued to work on changing my lifestyle.

A month or so after I had been in the program, I went to the Social Security Office to apply for SSI. Not long after I applied, I was sent to a M.D. so he could determine whether or not I was physically able to work as a result of being stricken with Polio. The Social Security Administration also required me to see a psychiatrist concerning my mental stability. I was a little offended that they would think I was crazy, but I realized I had to go through the process if I wanted to receive any financial assistance. In the end, both doctors indicated that I was disabled and I was provided a monthly Social Security check. I didn't get angry because the psychiatrist said I was definitely mentally and emotionally impaired. As long as I was getting some type of income, they could say whatever they wanted.

One morning after I had been at the center for approximately forty-five days, I went into the main complex to get some coffee. Afterward, I stepped outside to enjoy the quietness of the morning. As I sat thinking about how lucky I was to be alive, I suddenly, and for no apparent reason, started to weep a gut-wrenching cry that I couldn't control. It began as a deep guttural groan that made my entire body shudder. I didn't know why I was weeping, but the tears flowed as if someone had turned on a faucet that couldn't be shut off. I sat moaning like a child for a long time, but when I finished, it was as though I had released years of fermented emotional pain that had turned to sludge deep in my gut.

I went through three months of learning what it was like to live without drugs and alcohol at the center. We had daily group sessions during the mornings and afternoons. Sometimes, people from the outside world came and shared their experiences with us. One particular guy shared that he was grateful for the "snitch" that got him busted. He went on to say that after he completed treatment, he had thanked the cop who arrested him, the District Attorney who had prosecuted him, and the judge who had sentenced him. I thought he was crazy and didn't think there was any way I could ever thank anyone who had helped put me in jail. But as time moved on, I slowly but surely started to chip away and destroy the principles taught to me by my criminal mentors.

The hardest thing I had to deal with was my violent urges. Ever since I could remember, I had been physically aggressive. In street life, you had to be ruthless and respond to any disrespect quickly and violently. In this new way of living, however, violence wasn't acceptable and I had to be careful not to slap, punch, or stab anyone.

One day, two weeks before I completed the program, I woke up at my usual time. Like most mornings, I began my daily routine by brushing my teeth, taking a shower, and shaving. I had already brushed my teeth and showered and was preparing to shave when Frank came in to get ready for the day as well. Frank was a big guy built like a heavyweight boxer. He even had a set of boxing gloves tattooed on his right shoulder. We had been in prison together on a number of occasions. Frank had been admitted to the center about ten days before. Unlike me, Frank hadn't been able to get on methadone and had kicked heroin cold turkey. Something I could never do while on the streets. I had a lot of respect for Frank and shuddered at the thought of what he was going through.

"Órale, Carnal," he said.

"What's up," I replied. "How you feeling?"

"A lot better. I slept two hours last night."

Before I had a chance to respond, I sensed someone standing behind me. I glanced over my shoulder and saw a new guy to the program standing real close to me. I knew he wasn't feeling well so I asked him as politely as I could to give me some space.

"What did you say?" he replied, his voice on edge.

"I said back up," I answered hotly shooting him a cold stare. "I mean, you're almost on top of me."

I didn't like the way he had responded to my initial request and ordinarily I would have swung around and punched him in his mouth, but I was learning not to react violently every time someone got out of line with me. He didn't say anything else so I figured our brief disagreement was over. I finished my business and walked back to my sleeping area to get dressed. As I was getting ready, the man I'd just spoken to walked up to me.

"Hey, man, the next time you talk to me like you're some big shot, I'm gonna kick your ass."

"You're going to do what." I said. "Look dude, you need to be careful about what you're saying."

"I'm not afraid of you."

Pow!

I hit him square on his jaw and dropped him like a bad habit. The guy flipped and flopped on the floor like a fish out of water. Had I been in full gangster mode, I would have stomped his face in, but I didn't. I simply walked away and actually felt bad that I had resorted to violence. I couldn't believe I had actually socked this clown. My only consolation was that I hadn't put boot to him and that I felt awful about hitting him. In retrospect, I considered this growth for me. Staff, on the other hand, thought differently. I was almost excluded from the program, but in the end they gave me a break to complete because they didn't really know for sure if I had socked the guy.

That evening I attended an Alcoholic Anonymous (AA) meeting. The guy sharing spoke about his transformation and what he had done to bring about his change. I began to think that maybe I hadn't changed so much. After all, if my manner of reacting to adverse situations had been transformed, why was I still responding the same way as before anytime someone disrespected me? In the end, I realized that my behavior had been altered somewhat because in the past I would have stuck him with my knife when he got out of line in the bathroom instead of just punching him on the jaw. The change was slow, but it was coming along. I just had to be careful not get arrested for assaulting people.

On the night of my completion from the treatment center, I was awarded a certificate for being a successful survivor of the program, despite my slipup. The dining hall was packed with guests, family and friends of many of the graduates. None of my family was present. They lived too far away. I'm not sure they believed I was staying clean and sober. It was a little heartbreaking not having anyone from my family at my commencement, but I had been alone most of my life and I promised myself to do the right thing no matter how lonely I got.

Jessica wasn't able to come either. Rosie didn't think my accomplishment was all that significant.

"Listen, Jesse,' she said during a telephone conversation, "I know you're playing some sort of game. After you get whatever it is you want, you'll go back to being the same ole' junkie you've always been. You can't fool me."

I didn't blame her for being angry and distrusting. I had used heroin from the very first day we met and throughout the entire time we were together. At first she had accepted my drug use, but when heroin took complete control of my life, and using became my primary focus, she realized drugs were more important than our relationship. I can only imagine how devastated she must have felt losing to a substance that destroyed peoples' lives.

When the ceremonial festivities were completed, I moved into a studio apartment complex where all the tenants were clean and sober. The studio wasn't much, with only a small bed against one of the walls, but it was a place I could call home.

Hell, I thought this place isn't so bad. I've been in worse cells than this.

The following day I started attending AA meetings on a daily basis in order to gain knowledge and learn how others with similar problems had made the transition into mainstream society. I went to meetings three times a day for the first five months after I left the treatment center because I didn't know what else to do. The process of living within the mainstream was slow. Trivial household tasks such as paying rent, PG&E, and doing laundry were responsibilities completely foreign to me. CDC had always taken care of those chores when I had been in prison. Now, at the age of forty-five, I was like a big kid trying to learn how to navigate in the real world.

Once, about two weeks after I moved into my own place, I went to a Laundromat located a few blocks away to wash my dirty clothes. I had never used a washing machine before and although I knew bleach should not be added into to a load of colored clothing and that whites were washed in hot water, I didn't know how much soap to use for one load. To my way of thinking, the more soap you put into the washer, the cleaner the clothes would get. So I put three cups of detergent into the washing machine and sat down to wait for the cycle to be completed. I felt great that I was finally doing things ordinary people did on a regular basis, no longer washing my cloths in a toilet or sink like I did in prison.

As I waited, I noticed that suds were coming out of the washing machine. I looked around to see if anyone had noticed what was happening. I saw a Mexican lady sort of giggling and asked her if she knew why all the bubbles were coming out of the washing machine. She asked me how many cups of soap I had put into the machine. I told her I had put three cups.

"Well," she said. "You're going to have to wash that load three times to rinse the soap out of the clothing. You're only supposed to put about three quarters of a cup per load."

I was embarrassed, but I surmised that I shouldn't feel stupid just because I didn't know how to wash clothes in a Laundromat. After all, I had never done this before and this incident helped me realize just how much I needed to learn.

Two weeks after I completed treatment, I went to an agency named Central Valley Low-Income Housing to apply for subsidized housing. CVLIC, as it was called, was a program designed to assist individuals on SSI to obtain permanent housing. The program paid the majority of the SSI recipient's rent. The program required the applicant to fill out an extensive application. As long as the participant stayed off of drugs and alcohol, CVLIC would continue to assist the individual with their rent. I had to call my case manager on a weekly basis too. It wasn't much work considering all the help I would get once I was accepted into the program. I had to wait thirteen months before I was finally approved and given permission to find my own place, but it was well worth the wait.

About a month after I completed treatment, I bumped into a guy named Frank whom I had met four years earlier at an AA meeting. During the meeting he talked about how alcoholism had affected his life, how he eventually learned to manage his life without drugs and alcohol. I was touched by his sincerity. After the meeting, I asked him if he could sponsor me. He said he would be honored to be my sponsor so we began hanging out and attending AA functions together. He shared a lot of information with me about staying clean and sober and gave me a tremendous amount of self-confidence. One day he asked me if I wanted to take a trip to the Bay Area with him the following week. He said he wasn't working and wanted to take advantage of his free time by doing some sightseeing. I had never been to San Francisco before (although I had served time in San Quentin Prison, which was, technically speaking, in the Bay Area) so I agreed to go with him.

The following week, Frank and I left for San Francisco early in the morning. On the ride there, Frank talked about the things he had done in order to keep from using drugs and drinking alcohol. According to Frank, his problems with substance abuse were rooted deep in his childhood.

"I didn't have a man to teach me how to be a man," he said. "So I found a role model. Someone to look up too, you know. The problem was that the guy I chose gave me the wrong information. As a result, I did terrible stuff to my family, my friends, and to myself. In the end, I turned to drugs and alcohol to fix my problems because they took away my pain. Well, you know what happened then. I wound up emotionally messed up. I didn't go through as much stuff as you did because I never served time in prison. Nevertheless, I believe AA can teach you how to live a much better life than the one you left behind. AA can help you can turn your life around so that you never go back to prison. CDC doesn't have to stand for California Department of Corrections anymore; it can mean Choices, Decisions, and Consequences—a whole new concept."

It sounded great. His past and mine were very much alike. I was impressed with all the effort he had put into changing his life, but I wasn't sure I could stay clean and sober. It was evident that the things he was doing were working because he had been clean for ten years. I decided to take him up on his suggestions and continue to work on improving my life.

Frank talked all the way to San Francisco and I simply listened. He impressed me with all his knowledge about living within the law and doing the right thing even when he knew no one was looking. I was so captivated by his conversation that before I knew it we were crossing the Golden Gate Bridge. I had only seen pictures of the bridge, but in real life, it was breathtaking.

Frank drove across the bridge and into the city of Sausalito. We parked at the Marina, ordered espresso, and walked over to the rail to take in the magnificent view. I looked across the Bay and saw Alcatraz sitting all alone in the middle of the Bay. As I stared at it, I was reminded about a guy I had met in 1985 during one of my many incarcerations in the Los Angeles County Jail.

The guys' name was *Hueró* Dutchmen. He had served thirty years in the Federal penitentiary system for taking part in the killing of a Federal agent. He had been a prisoner at Alcatraz during its closure in 1963.

Hueró had been on the streets about a year after his release from Atlanta Federal Penitentiary and had been arrested for being under the influence of heroin. He had been sentenced to serve ninety days in the L.A. County Jail.

During that time, I was an inmate trustee in the jail. Trustees were given the added privileges of using the phone anytime we wanted because we were the inmates who swept, mopped the tiers, and handed clothing to the inmates in the cellblock. Other inmates weren't allowed out of their cells very often so it was next to impossible for them to use the phone. *Hueró* saw me on the tier one day and called me over to his cell.

"*Ese, Carnálito,*" he said. "You think you can call my old lady and tell her to come visit me?"

"Sure," I replied. "Just write her name and phone number on a piece of paper and I'll take care of it."

"You want her to bring a visitor for you, too?" He asked, as I was about to walk away.

"Sure, that sounds good."

"Give her your name and booking number and tell her I said to bring one of her friends. And tell her not to forget to bring some money."

When I called his lady, the first thing that caught my attention was the sound of her voice. Her voice oozed sensuality. I had never spoken to anyone who talked like she did. She agreed to come visit him that evening and promised to bring someone to visit me as well. I hoped that whomever she brought would look half as good as she sounded.

Sure enough, around six, *Hueró* and I were called out for our visit. We walked down to the visiting area together and waited anxiously for our visitors to come in. I hadn't seen anyone from the streets in over four months and many of the women in the visitors' galley looked good. I was hoping the woman coming to visit me would be attractive and have lots of money. Every inmate dreams about meeting a woman who will send him money so he can buy goodies at the jailhouse commissary.

As I sat there waiting, I saw two transvestites walk into the visiting room. One sat in front of *Hueró* and the other sat in front of me. I was stunned. I looked over at *Hueró* and saw that he was genuinely happy to see this person. Out of respect for him, I didn't walk out or say anything disrespectful to the gay guy. I looked around to make sure no one saw me visiting with a drag queen. After all, I had a reputation to uphold. When visiting was over, *Hueró* and I walked back to our housing module. *Hueró* smiled brightly and looked as though he was thrilled that his significant other had come to visit him.

"Hey, *Carnálito*," he asked excitedly. "How did you like your visit?"

"It was cool." I lied.

Tears streamed down my face as I stood gazing at Alcatraz remembering that incident of long ago. I grieved for men like *Hueró* who had spent so much time in prison that they had forgotten what it was like to have a relationship with a woman and had to turn to another man for intimacy.

"Hey, Jesse," Frank said, as he noticed the tears spilling down my cheeks. "You're not guilty."

"Why not?"

"By reason of insanity," he replied easily. "You did insane things in order to survive in the crazy world you created."

I had never considered myself insane, but the more I thought about my life and the things I had done, the more I had to agree with Frank. His simple explanation seemed to relieve me of much of the remorse concerning many of the things I had done during my involvement with crime and drugs. Ever since I had been drug free, I had been plagued with guilt trying to forgive myself for some of the terrible things I had done to others in the past, but I hadn't been able to do so. That afternoon, however, I walked away from the marina and left most of the guilt and shame that had hung like an old musty woolen suit in the dark closet of my conscience.

On the drive home, Frank asked if I had given any thought to the type of work I wanted to do.

"No," I answered. "I've been focusing on staying clean and out of prison."

"Well, you might want to consider going to college."

"College?" I asked in amazement. "I didn't think people with my type background could go to college."

"Sure, why not? You have just as much right to attend as anyone else, and from what I hear, education is the gateway to a better way of living."

What he said made sense. If I was going to succeed out here in the free world, I would have to start working on what I intended to do with my future.

"I'll go check it out next Monday," I replied wondering if I could handle college.

Like most everything else in this new way of living, I didn't have a clue about school and the thought of school scared the hell out of me, but I convinced myself to give education a shot. I didn't have anything to lose and maybe going to school would give me a sense of direction. I hadn't been in school for almost thirty years, so I didn't have any idea what was in store for me, but I was going to find out.

The next day, a clear cloudless Friday morning, after attending my aftercare class at Recovery House, I was waiting for the Number 1 bus to get back into Stockton, when my parole officer, Ms. Jones, drove up and parked.

"Hi, Jesse," she said. "You waiting on the bus?"

"Yeah."

"You want a ride into town?"

"Sure."

I was surprised that I had said yes without hesitation. In the past, I never would have accepted any favors from anyone remotely connected with law enforcement—especially not from a parole agent. But I felt different now that I had gone through treatment and learned that parole agents and others involved in monitoring the law were just doing their jobs.

"Let me take care of some business inside and I'll be right back," she said smiling brightly.

She walked into the treatment center office and came back in a matter of minutes.

"Get in," she said as she slid behind the wheel of her state car.

I climbed in and buckled up. We sat in silence, each of us caught in our own thoughts as Ms. Jones drove down Mathews Road toward Interstate 5. I enjoyed the humming of the car engine as I looked out over the nearby scenery. I noticed a ranch house, which sat alone in the far distance surrounded by nothing more than a huge field of freshly plowed earth.

The house and the freshly plowed clean earth reminded me of the newness of my life. I was overcome by an immense sense of gratitude, especially toward this lady who had shown me so much kindness when she hadn't sent me back to prison after I had thrown up in her office. Or when I had given her three positive tests and absconded for over thirty days. She could have sent me back to prison and been done with me. Instead, she had taken a chance and allowed me to get treatment for my drug problem.

"Hey, Ms. Jones," I said choking up.

"Yeah, Jess."

"I want to thank you for giving me an opportunity to live," I said humbly.

Smiling brightly, Ms Jones turned slowly and looked at me.

"You're welcome," she said.

CHAPTER TWELVE

THE FOLLOWING MONDAY MORNING I awoke excited about my impending trip to the local community college. I wanted to do everything I could in order to succeed in this new way of living, but I wasn't sure I could handle the pressure of attending college. I had dropped out, or rather, I had been expelled from high school in the tenth grade because of my involvement in a fight that escalated into a full-fledged riot. Therefore, I didn't know anything about school except that it was a place completely foreign to me.

Shaking off my fear, I showered, got dressed, and walked to the corner bus stop. When the number 52 bus arrived, I jumped on board. Traveling to the school made me feel the same way I used to feel when I was on the "Gray Goose" being transferred from one prison to the next. The difference was that once I arrived at the designated prison, I always bumped into an old acquaintance that would ease my nervousness by letting me know who was at the prison. Here, I wouldn't know anyone and I was sure everyone would be able to see I was an ex-con.

Once I got to the college, I swallowed my fear and pushed on. I took care of every detail to ensure my enrollment in school was complete. After two trips to campus, filling form after form, and taking an assessment test, I was formally enrolled. One of the secretaries told me I could register for classes for the coming semester.

"You can use one of those phones right there," she said pointing to five phones on a shelf against a far wall.

I picked up a phone, dialed the extension and registered for Psychology 101, English 1A, Sociology 1B, English 33A and a PE class.

Once I was done with registration, I walked across campus to catch the 52-bus home. As I made my way to the bus stop, I was moved by the picturesque landscape and architecture of the college. There was an abundance of Maple, Sycamore, Pine and Cottonwood trees throughout the campus. The lawn was covered by a green blanket of grass set on a background of rolling hills and huge well-kept parking lots. There were multicolored shrubs and flowers everywhere. I could see dust particles illuminated by the sun as it shone through the trees and wondered how I could have been so blind that I had never noticed the beauty of this campus. After all, I had been to the mall located across the street on many occasions when I had been shoplifting. It was amazing how sightless I had been to many things, which had been here all along.

Things seemed to be going great and I was beginning to think that maybe I could do this school thing. I was enjoying the panoramic scenery of the college when out of nowhere I heard a voice scream in my mind.

"Who do you think you are? Do you honestly think people are going to forgive you for the things you've done? You must be dreaming." The voice's mocking laughter reverberated in my head.

The voice unnerved me, stopped me dead in my tracks. I literally shook with fear in the middle of the parking lot. I fought to get a grip, reminding myself that I was a tough guy, the kind of man who could handle any situation. But this indefinable panic was truly out of my control so I turned to a power greater than me.

"Hey," I said aloud. "Help me out here. Give me the courage to walk through this."

Without hesitation I heard a gentle voice speak to my heart. Like the other voice, I didn't know where it came from, but it was there when I needed it.

"What can these people do to you, Jess?" it asked. "These people can't hurt you. You've been where flies don't even want to land. You can do this, and if you hang in there, I promise to help you."

Straight away, I felt better and decided not to let anything sidetrack me from my present course of action. Taking a deep breath, I shook off my fright and caught the 52 downtown and went straight to an AA meeting where I always felt safe.

Afterward, I walked over to my daughter's house to pick her up so she could stay the night with me. She had been spending a lot of time at my house since my completion from the drug program. I told her I would be starting school in January and she seemed happy, but at this point in her life, I don't believe she understood the importance of obtaining a college degree. She had never been exposed to anything except the criminal lifestyle and was much too young to understand education was the key to a better life. Whether or not she chose to live a proper life as an adult would be entirely up to her, but it was my intent to teach her by example that there was a much better way of living other than crime, drugs, and gangs.

Six months after completing treatment, I was granted full custody of Jessica and she came to live with me. Her mother had started using drugs and had gotten deeper into wrongdoing. It saddened me to see most everyone in my daughter's family caught up in lawbreaking, but I understood the complicatedness of trying to live law abiding lives when breaking the law was the norm. Jessica suffered most as a result of the changes occurring all around her. She was torn between what I was teaching her and what her mother's side of the family was telling her. Her allegiance to her family tore her up. Fortunately, I was winning most of the battles, and Jessica was influenced more by my actions rather than her family's empty words. I constantly fought the negative elements of the barrio trying to keep my daughter from getting involved in illegal activity. In the barrio, kids learn how to make fast money at a very early age and Jessica was no exception.

One morning, Jessica approached me sheepishly and told me her mom had been making her go with her when she went shoplifting, using Jessica to camouflage her intent.

"I don't like going, Papa, because I know it's wrong. But she's my mom and I feel I like I can't say no to her. Please don't be so hard on Mama."

My first reaction was to beat her mother down for implicating my daughter in her crimes, but as I looked at my child I became aware of the fact that I couldn't get crazy with her mom without hurting my baby. After all, she was Jessica's mom, and no matter what, Jessica was stuck with her.

"Don't worry baby," I replied in a gentle voice. "I'm not going to hurt your mom. I'm just going to let her know she isn't to take you shoplifting again. I know you feel like you betrayed your mom, but you shouldn't because what she's doing is completely wrong. Mothers shouldn't be teaching their children how to steal no matter what. I'm proud of you for telling me Jessica and I want you to remember that you can always talk to me about anything, okay."

She hugged me and laid her head on my shoulder like she used to do when she was a baby. I was touched by her gesture and felt an all-encompassing love for my child.

Later, when Jessica went to sleep, I called Rosie.

"What the hell do you think you're doing? If I ever hear you're forcing our daughter to go with you to steal again, I'm going to call the police and do everything I can to put you in jail. Do I make myself clear!?" I shouted.

Of course, I never would have called the police on her, but she didn't know that. As far as she was concerned, I was nothing more than a sellout that had turned "Rat," but I didn't care what she thought, and she never took Jessica to pilfer again. I would periodically check to make sure Jessica wasn't being forced to do those things.

In the meantime, I continued pushing forward with my education and working on improving my life. I wasn't sure what I wanted to do once I finished school, but I knew it was imperative that I continue my educational training in order to gain lucrative employment. With my criminal background, I had no doubt it would require as many degrees as I could obtain to earn a decent living for Jessica and me.

From the very start, college was a remarkable experience and I enjoyed everything about it. Everyday my mind was opened to something new and exciting. Sometimes I was caught off guard and I didn't understand exactly what the instructors were asking. Like the day my English teacher came in and announced that we would be writing an essay.

I was confused by her instruction. I thought she had said we would be doing an *Esé*, which in California Spanish is colloquial for a guy, dude, or man. I was confused because essay and *Esé* are identical sounds. In my bewilderment, I looked around to see how the other Chicanos in the class had responded to her assignment. They didn't seem at all concerned about what the instructor had said. I knew none of these people were tough enough to deal with someone like me so it couldn't have been me she was talking about. I would beat the shit out of anyone who even looked as if they were going to move on me. There were a few tense seconds, but then the instructor explained the assignment. I felt stupid, yet relieved that I hadn't made a fool out of myself by reacting to what I thought she had said. It was then that I realized just how far behind I was in real life. I felt like I was forty-five going on eighteen both psychologically and emotionally.

Most instructors and students treated me with respect and often greeted me with a "Happy to see you, or glad you made it to class," statement. These types of compliments were foreign to me. Where I came from no one made such comments and were only "happy to see you" if you were giving them something. However, there were a few occasions a professor treated me with a total lack of respect.

One particular day my English teacher said, "Okay, class, I hope everyone has an enjoyable spring break, and Jess, be sure you don't end up in jail."

I stood speechless for a fleeting moment, but quickly regained my poise.

"Yeah," I replied. "And let's make sure none of us get into an automobile accident and dies since this applies to everyone," I concluded, looking at her furiously.

No one responded to my comeback, but once outside, one classmate asked me why I let the professor talk to me that way.

"What do you want me to do?" I asked. "Kill her?"

"No," he answered. "But you don't have to take her sarcastic bullshit either. She's been on your case since the start of the semester."

"Hey, listen," I replied. "I appreciate your concern, but this is something I have to live with. After all, I was involved in crime for much of my life and people like Ms Theodore don't trust anyone, much less guys who come from where I come from. They honestly believe guys like me don't have a right to an education and that once a crook always a crook. I'm aware of the difficulties ahead of me and realize it's not going to be easy, but I'm not giving up no matter what. Besides, her remarks are nothing compared to what I've been through already."

"Well, you have much more tolerance than me," my classmate said. "I don't think I could take all the crap she dishes out to you."

"I heard that," I replied smiling ruefully. "Believe me, it's not easy."

A few years later, while I was conducting a presentation on gang awareness at the same community college where Ms Theodore taught, she came into the auditorium with her English class. She sat in the front row. Afterward, she came to the reception and stood in line to comment on my speech.

"You probably don't remember me," she said. "But I want to congratulate you on your lecture."

"Oh, but I do remember you," I replied, smiling. "You're Ms Theodore. I had you for English 1A on Tuesdays and Thursdays at 1:30 P.M. You gave me a B for the class."

She was impressed that I remembered. I didn't tell her I remembered her because she'd been so mean. I wasn't angry with her anymore. In fact, I silently applauded her for having the courage to congratulate me. It must have been difficult for her to give me kudos, but she had done it nonetheless.

There were times when it wasn't easy to stay focused with school, recovery, and the emotional chaos I was experiencing as I worked on changing my lifestyle. Every once in awhile, I wanted to throw in the towel and give up on education and everything else, so I could go back to using drugs and breaking the law. People don't realize how much easier it is for us to give up on ourselves. For some of us, being bad is simpler than being good.

One morning, while driving to school, exhausted from everything associated with college, I tried to figure a way to stop going and still save face. I made a strong effort at trying to convince myself that I could establish a landscaping business that would assist ex-cons in obtaining employment without having to get a college degree. After struggling with the decision to quit, I asked myself if starting a landscaping business was what I really wanted to do. Of course the answer was a resounding no. I wanted to earn a degree that would place me in a position to give voice to the difficulties concerning ex-offenders transitioning from the inside to the streets. And even though I hadn't been in school long, I'd learned enough to understand that without any type of degrees behind me, I would simply be just a typical ex-con. People in positions to make the changes needed in our system would never listen to me. It was then that I heard what I now referred to as the "Good Voice."

"If you do what you're supposed to do," it said. "I will make you a great man in your community."

After that, I didn't resist whenever I had to change old ideas and behaviors, but it was easier said than done to sort through all the garbage I had created during my involvement with crime, drugs, and gangs. I was a challenged every day and had to make adjustments in how I behaved on a daily basis. I had to work extra hard to improve my communication skills so I wouldn't get into trouble by saying things that could offend people. Sometimes I wanted to tell certain people to go fuck themselves, but I held my tongue. I understood I was living in a much different world and if I wanted to ensure a better life for Jessica and me, I would have to swallow my pride and learn to play the game. My motto became, "No Pain, No Gain."

One day, while hanging out with some other Chicano students in the college Quad, I noticed a black man walk toward our direction. I watched him as he leisurely approached us and wondered why he thought it was all right for him to infringe on our space. In prison, all interaction between different ethnic groups is dangerous. My never had dealing with Black prisoners. To be honest, I didn't trust them in prison, and I didn't trust them in those early days of change.

My body tensed as he continued to walk in our direction. For a brief moment I felt as though I was back on the prison yard. I prepared myself for the unexpected. I'm sure the man didn't have a clue what I was thinking when he walked up to us that day and introduced himself to me with an extended hand. I cautiously shook his hand, balling up my other hand into a fist, ready to punch him in the mouth if he tried anything funny. When he let go of my hand, I brought it back quickly as though a snake had bitten me.

"My name is Tom Ferret. I'm the Student Activities Advisor. I've been watching you for quite some time now, and I like the way you carry yourself. I need someone with your self-assurance to manage the on-campus student flea market. Do you need a job?"

"Does it look like I'm looking for a job?"

"Whoa," Tom said lifting his hands out in front of him and backing up a few steps. "I was only asking. I didn't mean any disrespect."

I instantly realized I had messed up by responding to him in a mocking manner and that this man was sincere about giving me a job. It was true that I wasn't looking for employment right then, but this could be an opportunity to create a work history. I had to quit thinking as though I was still in the penitentiary. Not apologizing for my sarcasm I moved on.

"What kind of work are you talking about?" I asked.

"I need a Flea Market manager and if you take the job, you'll have to work every Saturday and Sunday except Easter Sunday, Christmas, New Years or the Fourth of July if any of those holidays fall on a weekend. The hours are long. You'll work between 4:00 am to 4:00 pm. The job pays minimum wage, but it has benefits which we can discuss later."

I told Tom I would think about it and let him know my decision the following week. I had to find out if working would affect my Social Security benefits. I intended to go to school for the next few years and would need income to make sure I could provide food and housing for Jessica and myself.

The following day I contacted the Social Security office and asked if I could work and still receive benefits. The Social Security Representative I spoke with told me I was entitled to earn a certain amount of money before my benefits were affected negatively. The next day I called Tom and told him I would take the post. I started working at the Flea Market the following weekend.

It was a pretty good job. I was in charge of the overall operation and responsible for the large sum of money generated at the Flea Market. The job taught me how to deal with large numbers of people and handle situations without the use of violence although I must admit I sometimes utilized the "shot caller" approach I had applied while in the penitentiary. It was difficult not to respond aggressively when a person was in my face, but I slowly learned to temper my reaction to what I considered disrespectful comments. I worked there for a little over a year until I transferred to the university.

BEFORE COLLEGE I had never been involved in any type of meaningful relationship with any woman. I always loved and respected my mother, and of course Jessica was now the number one female in my life, but truth be told, relationships involving women had always been self-seeking and based on taking whatever I could get from them. I had been married twice and had lived with many women during the short periods of time I had been on the streets, but I didn't know what it meant to truly love a woman. All that changed in the fall of 1998 when I met Anna, a beautiful young lady with thick lustrous black wavy hair, pearly white teeth, luscious lips covered with bright red lipstick, and an intoxicating smile.

I remember thinking she was truly a work of art when she strutted into Spanish class that first day of my second semester. I wanted to walk up to her just like I did in the old days and simply let her know I was interested in being with her. But I held back. I was beginning to understand that just because I had done things in a particular manner in the past; it didn't mean that was the way things were done here. Besides, she was much too young, way too pretty, and probably too smart to get involved with anyone like me. So I resigned myself to enjoy her beauty from a distance. I never talked to her, but sometimes during class she would nod and smile at me.

One day, about midway through the semester, she walked into the classroom and sat next to me. I was surprised, but even more amazed when she handed me a note that read: "When are we going to lunch?"

I quickly jumped at the opportunity to spend time with her and promptly led her out of the classroom down the hallway towards my car. Once there, I drove us to a Mexican restaurant located in the center of the city. I talked all the way to the eating-place without giving her a chance to respond to any of the things I was saying. I had never been much of a talker when I had been involved in crime, but now I couldn't shut up. Anna told me later she had known I was trying to impress her so she had let me talk my head off. On the way to the restaurant, I asked her if we could spend more time together and get to know each other better.

"I don't know, Jess," she replied. "You move just a tad too fast for my liking. I mean, you're nice, but some of the things you say are completely out of line. I hope you don't get offended by my candor?" she concluded. I could see she was trying her best not to hurt my feelings.

She was right, of course, I did move fast. I didn't know how to move any other way. During the drive to the restaurant I had asked her if we would be having sex after lunch. Looking at me as if I was crazy, she heatedly told me we weren't doing any such thing.

"What's wrong with you? Are you crazy? I can't believe you asked me something like that." she exclaimed with complete annoyance.

"What's wrong with asking," I responded feeling dumb. "What's so crazy about wanting to take you to bed?"

"There wouldn't be anything wrong with it if we had known each other for more than ten minutes!" she exclaimed, sarcastically. "And for your information," she continued. "People don't meet each other and immediately go to bed. Well, maybe they do where you come from, but not from my world!"

I apologized for being so brash and for not knowing how to behave around someone with so much class.

"It's all right," she said. "But you really do need to work on your interpersonal skills."

I agreed and kept my mouth shut the rest of the time we were together that day. Being with Anna was fantastic. Her laughter was like a melody and her smile was infectious. I silently prayed I had not ruined any possible chance I had of being with her.

I chased Anna for two years before we became a couple. She told me later that she would often go out of her way to avoid running into me because she knew I would be on her like white on rice. I couldn't help myself. Every time I ran into her my heart would start to beat faster, I would get short of breath, and my hands would get clammy. No other woman had ever affected me in such a way.

During my pursuit of her, Anna moved to Bakersfield, California and we developed a long distance relationship. We called each other every day and spoke for hours every night. In the course of our conversations, Anna taught me many things about how to treat a lady and I learned to care for her deeply. I didn't even know how much I loved her until one day, as I drove on Highway 99 through Manteca, California; I was struck with an emotion so powerful, it nearly caused me to lose control of my vehicle. Quickly regaining my equilibrium, I tried to pinpoint what I was feeling? Then it came to me. I was in love with Anna. I concluded that passing through the city where Anna had lived before she moved to Bakersfield had somehow brought my emotions for her to the surface.

I had heard many stories from AA members about their relationship experiences. They talked about the difficulties they encountered due to their lack of understanding about what love could do to a person, especially to someone who had used drugs and alcohol for long periods of time. Seasoned AA members warned newcomers about getting involved in relationships, explaining how people often relapsed as a result of not being able to deal with the wild power of love. They would often tell the newcomer how love could devastate someone and cause them to lose control of their lives if they weren't ready to handle its intensity. I now understood what they were talking about. If it weren't for what I had learned about love in the rooms of AA, I never would have known what was happening to me that afternoon on the freeway.

That evening, I called Anna and explained what had happened to me while driving through her old town.

"At first I couldn't figure out what was happening. But then it came to me. I'm in love with you, Anna," I said, not holding back.

"Well, Jess," she answered tentatively. "I'm really touched to learn you care so much for me, but I'm sorry to say that I don't feel quite as deeply for you. Please don't be hurt. I'm very fond of you and care about you tremendously, but I don't want you to get the wrong impression about our relationship. After all, you are quite a bit older than I am," she concluded.

"Hey, listen," I said, a little hurt. "This isn't about how you feel about me, but how I feel toward you. I'm just happy I can finally experience these types of feelings," I lied. I actually felt as though she had stuck a knife through my heart.

"Okay,' she replied. "I just want to make it clear that I'm not in love with you in that way right now, but things could change in the future."

I left it at that, and our conversation turned to other things, but I was disappointed that she didn't love me as I did her. I resigned myself to the fact that becoming human and developing feelings was good enough for now.

Anna and I did many things together. We went on trips to San Francisco, Los Angeles, and Tijuana, Mexico on a couple of occasions. We talked about different subjects and almost never argued, but she often got upset with me because she said I was aggressive. I personally only remember being upset with her once while we were dating. As far as I was concerned, our relationship was great, but Anna didn't think I was mature enough. Looking back on it I guess she was right.

"You know, Jess," Anna said to me one day. "All the things you're learning about relationships at this point in your life, I already know."

"I know you do," I replied.

Although I didn't show it, I was saddened by what Anna had said because she was only twenty-two and I was forty-five yet she knew much more than I did about relationships and about life in general.

I would have married Anna without hesitation. Unfortunately, Anna's mother was against our being together and made it clear from the first time she found out we were dating she would never agree with Anna marrying me. In the end, Anna decided it was better we go our separate ways. When our relationship ended, I was left with an ache in my heart so profound that it was difficult for me to sleep at night. Not being able to rely on drugs, alcohol, or hate to dull the emotional discomfort I was experiencing only intensified my pain. Nevertheless, I went through my loss without using any mind altering substances, a difficult task for anyone, but much more difficult for a recovering drug addict.

I felt fortunate to have had the opportunity to learn how to handle the sorrow of losing someone so dear to my heart. It took months to get over Anna, but finally the storm raging in my heart fizzled out and I was left with nothing more than numbness. I didn't let losing her stop me from continuing to improve my life.

IN THE SPRING OF 1999, I earned my AA degree from San Joaquin Delta College. The only family member who attended my graduation was my niece Tina. It made me feel good to know someone in my family thought it was important for them to support me. It was truly a milestone and an exciting experience on the road toward my eventual success and normalcy. Of course, success is measured by different standards for different people and to me, having graduated from college with my Associate of Arts Degree after everything I had put myself through was a huge accomplishment. I knew there was still a long way to go for my complete reconciliation to the free world, but I was one step closer to achieving my educational endeavors. I had applied to California

State University, Stanislaus. When the acceptance letter arrived a few weeks after graduation, I called Mama to share my excitement with her.

"Mama, I'm going to a university."

"Well, I don't know, *mijo*," she replied unknowingly. "Why so much school anyway?"

"Why not, Mama? I mean, it's not going to hurt me. Besides, the state is going to help me financially so what do I have to lose?"

"Well," she replied cautiously. "I guess you're right, but you should start thinking about going to work."

"I'll get a job when I get done with school, Mama," I said, feeling a little dejected at her response.

Her reaction had been a letdown, but I knew she didn't mean anything bad. She just didn't understand the importance of education. After all, Mama had never attended school and had only worked as a farm laborer all her life.

I began my university classes in the fall of 1999 and had a great time learning and connecting my personal experiences with the academic material we were studying. Having survived all the madness I had exposed myself through gave me an inside scoop and made it easier for me to do well during my undergraduate sociology studies. By now I didn't hide my past and I tried to be a positive role model to guys who were still trapped in the criminal lifestyle. I often shared with students and professors alike my experiences in an attempt to give them a deeper insight into the causes and conditions of crime, substance abuse, and gang involvement.

I graduated in the spring of 2001 with my Bachelor of Arts degree in Sociology. This time, my sisters Dee, Lydia, my brother Philip, and most of their children attended the graduation ceremony. Afterward, we had a party at Louis Park in Stockton. There was a DJ and lots of food. During the party, I announced that I had been accepted into graduate school at Stanislaus State. I told everyone that I was going for a Masters of Social Work Degree and intended to continue my climb up the ladder to eventual academic triumph. Many of the people there gave me props for graduating and for having the tenacity to keep moving ahead with my educational goals. I was touched by their sincerity and filled with an incredible sense of worth.

On September 11, 2001, I awoke early to get ready for an orientation being held at the Stockton, California site of Stanislaus State University. Driving to the school, I was so preoccupied with my thoughts concerning graduate school I didn't know about the obliteration of the Twin Towers in New York.

Many of the students at the orientation were in the dark about the terrorist attacks in New York and the Pentagon too. It wasn't until one of the professors received a phone call from his wife who was in New York at that time that we were excused for the day. Rushing to my car, I turned on the radio to find out what had taken place. When I got home, I turned on the television and watched the gruesome scenes splashed across my T.V. screen. It was a horrendous sight, and I felt a tremendous amount of empathy for the many people who had lost loved ones. I didn't understand why I felt so bad and briefly entertained the thought of dropping out of graduate school and return to my old habit of using drugs where I wouldn't be affected by anything.

Later that day, I attended an AA meeting and found refuge from the reeling madness our nation was undergoing as a result of the national catastrophe. I wanted to put my feelings into proper perspective and being around people who had gone through the same type of experience as I had always gave me comfort. Sitting in the meeting, I reminisced about how much my life had changed. I thought about the Oklahoma Bombing and how different the Twin Towers attack had affected me in comparison to that shocking act of violence.

I had been serving time in Soledad State Prison when the Oklahoma Bombing had occurred and clearly remember watching the scene on television and not caring about what happened there. I remember thinking that the bombing didn't concern my family or me so why should I care. This time, however, I was deeply moved by how the passengers on Untied Airlines Flight 93 had sacrificed their lives when they attempted to regain control of the plane. Even though this was an appalling incident, it allowed me an opportunity to measure my emotional growth and I clearly saw I was becoming human and that I now had the ability to feel sympathy towards others.

THE CLOCK on my bedroom wall indicated it was 5:00 AM when I opened my eyes and rolled out of bed. My stomach fluttered with excitement at the thought of graduating from California State University, Stanislaus later that morning, with a Master's Degree. Most of the guys from back in the days when I had been involved in crime had never even completed high school, much less graduated from a university with this type of degree.

I walked over to the bathroom, turned the shower on, and got in. I quickly scrubbed and washed my body. Stepping up to the bathroom mirror, I grabbed my Gillette track two razor and began to dry shave. I never used shaving cream, a habit I had developed after serving years in the "hole" during the time I had been in prison. Some habits are just too hard to break and this was one of them.

As I shaved, I thought about a conversation I'd had with my homeboy *Pato* a few days before. I had called *Pato* after someone from my neighborhood called to tell me *Pato* had been released from prison after serving fourteen years. *Pato* had been one of my principal instructors on the aspects of being a *vato loco* when I was a youngster coming up in the 'hood.' When he answered the phone and realized it was me, I could hear the enthusiasm in his voice.

"*Oralé, Carnál!* I hear you're doing big things up there in 'Stocktone.' Going to college and getting a master's degree no less."

"Who told you I was going to college?" I asked, worried that he would think I was weak for attending school.

"I met a guy from 'Stocktone' while I was in Soledad and asked him if he knew you. The guy got all excited when I mentioned your name. He told me you were in some university working on developing a program to help ex-cons. It makes me feel good to know at least one of us made it out of the madness, you know."

The phone went silent for a few seconds and I thought I had lost the call on my cell phone.

"You there Homeboy?" I asked.

"Yeah, I'm here. Hey, you remember how I used to school you when you were a kid," he continued. "And how you used to look up to me?

"Yeah, I remember."

"Well now you're my role-model. And you give me hope, *tu sabes.*"

I was humbled by his praise and felt a lump in my throat as I struggled to hold back my tears.

"Thanks, Homeboy," I replied softly.

I heard movement in the living room and realized my eleven-year old daughter Jessica had woken up. Jessica had been living with me ever since she was five years old. I had told Jessica bits and pieces about my past and she had seen me burn midnight coal as I studied for exams and wrote term paper after term paper.

"Good morning Dad," she said as she rubbed the sleep from her eyes. "Are we meeting Grandma at the University?"

"Yeah, Baby, so let's get ready okay."

We got dressed and left to meet up with Mama, my niece Tina, and her husband Raul. I was pleased Mama had made the trip to see me graduate although I knew she didn't understand the significance of my accomplishment.

The campus was bustling with excitement when we arrived. There were people everywhere and cars were bumper to bumper. I'd heard through the school grapevine that eighteen hundred students were graduating, but only one hundred and ninety six were receiving Master's Degrees in their chosen fields.

Leaving Jessica with Mama and Tina, I made my way to the section designated for my cohorts. As I walked to find my spot in the long line of students, many graduates exchanged congratulatory pleasantries with me. I smiled and nodded at them in return. I thought about the guys locked up in penitentiaries throughout California, caught in the revolving door of our judicial system like I had been for many years. It troubled me to know that all the guys I knew from back in the day would never have the opportunity to experience the immeasurable joy I was feeling at that precise moment. Most of them would be stuck in their small cells for the remainder of their lives.

I found it unbelievable that not too many years before I had been part of the thirty-seven percent Hispanic Californians in prison, but now was part of the roughly four percent of Americans holding Master's Degrees.

THE ACTUAL CEREMONY was a blur as I sat thinking about my past trying to figure out how I had managed to get to this point in my life. Tears rolled down my cheeks as I remembered the long, painful road I had taken me to get here. I wondered what was so different about me. Why had I been able to escape death or a life sentence like so many of the guys I had grown up with? After all, I had been one of the worst guys from my neighborhood, going in and out of prison for nearly thirty years. Yet, here I was. I didn't have the answers to those questions, but I knew the journey I had taken had affected me in a profound manner. And as I sat there with all those thoughts running through my mind, I wondered if I had more courage to keep working on the enormous changes that still needed to occur in my life. I sat second guessing myself until I was called to receive my diploma.

AFTER GRADUATION came the difficult task of obtaining a job. I started searching as soon as I finished school. For the first few weeks I went out every day and submitted applications. I also submitted at least 100 online applications. A month later, I still didn't have a job. I was lucky to be receiving SSI still. Fortunate too that my housing was still being subsidized by Central Valley Low-Income Housing, or else I would have been on the streets with my (for the moment) worthless Master's Degree.

One day, after I had finished job hunting, I went to pick up Jessica from school. She must have seen the concern on my face.

"You're not going to get a job, huh, Dad." It was more of a statement than a question.

"What did you say, baby?"

"People aren't going to give you a job," she said shaking her head sadly. "I don't understand, Dad. What do they want? I mean, you went to school, you quit drinking and using drugs, and you stopped breaking the law. You even quit smoking and got a Masters. Doesn't that mean anything? I thought you said getting a Masters would help you get a job?"

I looked over at my child and saw hopelessness fixed on her little face. I knew I had to answer quickly and correctly so as not to disillusion her about the importance of education.

"Well, Jessica," I replied. "What have you learned from this situation?"

"Not to get a criminal record," she answered, without hesitation.

Her response touched my heart and confirmed that I was doing a good job teaching her about living like the average person who doesn't believe in breaking the law.

"Exactly, I replied. "If you don't break the law, you never have to worry about being denied employment because of a criminal record. I've always told you that you have to be careful about how you behave today because your conduct will surely impact you tomorrow. There are always consequences. Some slipups you can correct, but sometimes, because we're young and misguided, we do things that are beyond repair and there's nothing we can do to fix those mistakes. Those errors will haunt us for the rest of our lives. Just like my past hangs over me like a dark cloud now. But don't you worry; I'm going to get a job." I told her, with more confidence than I felt.

"Okay, Dad."

After that, I was even more resolved to prove ex-cons could change. I understood that I would have to work harder than the person without a criminal record, but I didn't mind working hard. I also realized that I would encounter many disappointments, but I was determined not to let anything defeat me in my quest to enter the professional world. I convinced myself that what I was going through was nothing more than a temporary hindrance.

On days when I thought about running into a store and grabbing a whole rack of clothing, or robbing some innocent chump, and buying heroin to shoot up, I would be bombarded with poignant memories about things that had taken place in my life. Events that showed me everyone has a choice. Back in the day, I hadn't seen that I could have chosen another path because I had been so blinded by drugs, alcohol, and hate that the messages had never registered in my brain.

One particular memory remains conspicuously stamped in the recesses of my consciousness to this very day. I had been gone from my neighborhood for over six months and had recently married Jessica's mother when I decided to drive down to my 'hood' to visit my homeboy Alex who had been my friend for years. He had also been instrumental in persuading the main witness on a robbery charge the year before I moved out of my neighborhood not to give evidence against me in court. As a result, I had only been sent back to prison for a twelve-month violation as opposed to the thirty-seven year sentence I would have surely gotten had the witness testified.

When I arrived to Alex's house, his brother Sammy was sitting in front of their house.

"What's happening, Homeboy? You want a drink?" He held out a bottle of Thunderbird Wine.

"No, I'm good Bro."

Sammy took a deep breath, chugged a drink, then made a face as though he'd just drunk urine.

"Alex is in the hospital," Sammy said sadly. "He's in the last stages of cirrhosis of the liver and isn't expected to live much longer."

I didn't know what to say. Shit, what do you say to someone when they have a loved one on the brink of death? So I simply shook Sammy's hand and took off to the hospital to visit my homeboy.

Alex was seated in a chair when I walked into his room. He'd always been a large man, with wide shoulders, big arms, and a small waist, but this disease had shrunk his frame and made him look diminutive and fragile. The only thing big about him now was his stomach, bloated so that he looked nine months pregnant.

His eyes had withdrawn deep into his eye sockets and his teeth jutted out of his mouth. His long shiny hair, which he'd always worn in a ponytail, had turned a listless gray and the whites of his eyes were now a dull yellow. His once healthy caramel colored complexion had changed into a poisonous blackish purple color. His sister Angie was in the room with him when I stepped inside.

"Hey, Alex," she said. "Your friend's here." Alex turned slowly to see who it was. When he saw it was me, a thin smile crossed his face.

"Do you know who it is?" his sister asked.

"Of course I know who it is," he replied indignantly. "I'm not stupid. Hey *Dragón*, help me to the bed, Homeboy," he whispered faintly.

I wasn't a doctor by any stretch of the imagination, but I clearly saw that Alex was on the brink of death. He placed his arm around my shoulder and I helped him to the bed. Once he was comfortable, I looked down at him. Alex peered up and noticed I was weeping.

"Hey, *Carnál*," he said, his voice breathy. "We make of life what we want, *que no?*"

"Yeah," I answered sadly.

Alex shrugged his shoulders as if to let me know this was the life he had chosen. It had troubled me to see my Homeboy in such a critical state, but there was nothing I could do to help my friend. He had made his choices and now lay waiting to die.

I never saw Alex again. He passed two weeks later.

Not long after I had spoken with Jessica about not being able to get a job, I bumped into Jackie at one of the many Taco Trucks located in South Stockton, the low-income area where many Chicanos lived.

Jackie, an extremely smart guy with the gift of gab, was considered a con man in the neighborhood. Nevertheless, his intellect and conversational skills had not been enough to keep him out of prison, and he had been in and out since the 60's.

During the mid-seventies, after he completed his first prison term, Jackie had been involved with the development of a program funded by the federal government. The intent of that program was to teach guys who had spent years confined in the penitentiary the necessary skills to survive on the streets without reverting to crime. But the problem with guys like Jackie was that they never changed their criminal thinking. Instead of using the opportunity being given to improve their lives, these wiseguys simply stole everything they could. Jackie was one of the guys caught with his hand in the cookie jar. Ultimately, the program was discontinued and Jackie lost his job. Twenty years later Jackie was still pissed about losing his job and blamed the system for all his problems, never acknowledging that it was his thievery that had gotten him fired.

"What's up?" he asked when I ran into him that afternoon.

Not in the mood for conversation, I simply nodded.

"You find a job, yet?"

I shook my head.

"So getting a Masters doesn't really mean all that much for guys like us, huh?" he asked sarcastically.

I knew he was trying to get my goat because he was jealous that he couldn't stay off drugs and out of prison as I had done for the past seven years. I turned slowly to look at him with eyes blazing. Jackie saw my angry stare and realized he had let his mouth overload his ass.

"Hey, *Dragón*," he said meekly. "You know I'm just jiving."

"Bullshit!" I said. "I know you mean everything you're saying. But you know what punk; today's your lucky day because I know you don't have a fucking clue about what I've just pulled off and for that reason I'm going to give you a pass. But the next time you talk to me like I'm a chump, I'm going to forget I'm working on change for a few minutes and beat you like I own you, you dig?"

Jackie didn't say anything. He simply bowed his head like a puppy dog. So I rapidly walked to my car and split the spot before I changed my mind about beating him. As I drove to my house I tried to keep my emotions from going up and down like a teeter-totter. On the one hand, I was upset because I had let Jackie get to me, yet I was also relieved that I hadn't kicked his ass as I would've done in the past when I felt disrespected. Just as I was about to pat myself on the back for walking away without smashing on Jackie, I remembered a discussion that had taken place between an administrator who worked at San Joaquin Delta College and me a few weeks before and I got upset all over again.

At that time, I had been trying to get a job for months, but whenever I came to the proverbial question, "Have you ever been convicted of a felony" and answered yes, I wasn't even given an opportunity to interview. Sometimes

I thought about not telling the truth, but I knew that wouldn't work. One fib only led to more lies. I had played that game most of my life and in the end, my dishonesty had always come to light. What's more, I wasn't living dishonestly anymore. I was living a law-abiding life. I was plenty frustrated though and caught in a sort of 'damned if you do and damned if you don't' situation. I believed I had earned the right to a decent job, but as it was I couldn't even get to the starting gate. Everywhere I went doors were being slammed in my face. Not doors to keep me locked inside a prison cell isolated from civilization, but doors, nonetheless, that kept me out of the professional world, away from an opportunity to earn an honest living to support my family.

"What's the matter, Jess?" Mr. Smith asked that morning seemingly with genuine concern as I sat at his table in the staff lounge. Mr. Smith was Vice President of Student Activities at San Joaquin Delta College.

"I can't get a job and I just don't know how I'm going to pay my bills this month," I said, shaking my head in total frustration. "I knew it was going to be difficult to overcome my past, but I really thought that if I quit breaking the law, stopped hanging out with the wrong crowd, and let time lapse between my last arrest and what I'm doing now that I would be given a chance to prove I've changed. One of the reasons I put so much effort into getting a Master's Degree is because I knew I would have to do something extraordinary to show that I have changed."

"Well, Jess," Mr. Smith replied. "There's no doubt that what you've accomplished is huge. I can only imagine the difficulties you've been confronted with, having to overcome drug addiction and everything else. And obtaining a Master's Degree is a tremendous feat for anyone, but much, much, more difficult for someone with a background such as yours. On the other hand, you've admitted to breaking the law for most of your life and it seems you expect people to forgive you for your previous endeavors. Unfortunately, that's not the way it works. In fact, I've never heard you say you're sorry for what you did in your past life."

I was so completely surprised and offended by Mr. Smith's remarks that I almost gave him a piece of my mind right then and there. Instead, I held my tongue and kept my anger in check. I had to be very careful here so I gave myself a few seconds to compose myself before I responded. I had known this man for a few years now and had allowed him to get to know me so he wouldn't be afraid of people with criminal histories. I understood the images people had of ex-cons were negative and I had tried to change this man's perception by helping him see the ex-offender as a human being and not as some sort of deranged animal. I'd tried to demonstrate to him that the ex-offender could turn their lives around if given a chance. I had shared my life experiences with him and he'd led me to believe that he understood my dilemma, yet there he was saying people with criminal backgrounds needed to express regret in order to be given an opportunity to live prosperous lives.

"I can't believe you said something so cynical!" I responded, angrily after composing myself somewhat. "But now that I know how you truly feel, I want to make one thing perfectly clear. I'm not asking for absolution. I'm merely asking for a break to prove I'm someone who can be trusted to do the right thing. I've done everything I was asked to do. I quit using drugs and stopped breaking the law. I've served my time and paid my debt to the citizens of this state. How long will society keep its foot on my throat?" I asked heatedly.

"I don't think the general public has its foot on your throat, Jess, but people just don't forgive so easily."

"Yeah, I guess you're right, but what really irks me is that men like you, in positions to make changes in our system, don't step up and speak out against unfairness," I said looking at him intently.

With that I got up and left the room without giving him a chance to reply. I had to leave because I was livid and knew that if I didn't go right then, I was going to say some nasty things to this man, stuff he could use to support that I hadn't changed at all. I had also seen the fear on Mr. Smith's face when he noticed how angry I had gotten over his comments. By now I had learned that I could intimidate people without saying or doing much. My facial expressions and the manner in which my body language reacted to anger came involuntarily and were programmed into my psyche as a result of serving so much time in prison.

Once I got to my car and had time to cool off, I reminded myself about all the work I had ahead of me if I wanted to succeed. I told myself that I had to stop blaming others for my predicament because it had been me who had created the problems I was having today because of what I had done in the past.

As I drove off of the college parking lot I decided that I wasn't going to let frustration bog me down, or throw in the towel after everything I had worked so hard to achieve. I had read somewhere that every journey begins with the first step and I had taken many steps already. I was determined to work harder. I had a Masters Degree and even though it didn't seem to be worth much just now, I knew it would eventually pay off.

I went five months without work, living off my SSI check, maxing out my credit cards. Then one day in late October, I was offered a job by Tom, the man I had met during the time I attended Delta College. Tom had hired me to manage the student operated Flea Market while I had been a student at Delta and he had helped me maneuver through many of the situations I was experiencing in this new way of living. Like the time Jessica's mom kidnapped her. I called Tom and asked him what I should do? He advised me to call the police and file a report against Jessica's mom.

"I can't call the police," I said.

"Look, Jess," he replied. "You have to use the system that has been put in place to help you resolve these types of situations. The system is there to help you, too. You can't take the law into your own hands."

He was right. I had wanted to get a gun and go after Jessica's mom and her boyfriend and get my daughter back, but I did as Tom suggested and called the police.

The officer dispatched to my apartment was a female. When I answered the door, I noticed she made a disgusted expression when she saw the tattoos on my arms. After that she treated me with a subtle coldness and asked me questions as though I was the prime suspect.

"How long have you been out of prison?" she asked after she had run a warrant check on me.

"It's been about three years," I answered.

"Are you still on parole?"

"Yes."

"Why were you sent to prison?"

"Can I ask what my going to prison and being on parole has to do with my child being taken by her mom?"

"I'm just trying to get some background information."

"Do you always ask people these types of questions? After all, I'm the one who called you. I didn't want to call you, but the guy who mentors me said I should learn to use the system to assist me with situations like this. He said that's what regular people do. But it seems as though you think I had something to do with what happened and to be perfectly honest, I don't appreciate you treating me as though I'm a criminal."

Suffice to say that it wasn't a good experience for me. I did get my child back, but not as a result of any help from the police department.

NOT LONG AFTER this situation with the police, Tom, the Student Activities Supervisor at Delta convinced the San Joaquin Delta College Associated Student Body Government to hire me as the Flea Market maintenance man. Since I had managed the overall operation of the Flea Market before, I was familiar with the setup. In fact, I had come up with many ideas that had increased the annual income from $123,000 to $196.000 during the year I managed the Flea Market and was excited about working there again for a number of reasons. For one, I enjoyed working with people and thousands of people from every ethnic and social economic status went to the Flea Market every weekend. Additionally, I only had to work weekends, which would give me plenty of time to look for permanent work.

After I had been working at the Flea Market for approximately six months, I was contacted by Bill, the Executive Director of Central Valley Low-Income Housing Corporation, (CVLIHC) the same agency that was supplementing my rent, concerning a possible job.

When we met, Bill told me he needed an onsite manager for the Mayfair, a historical apartment building located in downtown Stockton. The owners of the Mayfair had been contracted by San Joaquin County Mental Health to provide housing for individuals with mental health issues and CVLIHC had recently been subcontracted to manage the program portion and was to take over operations on July 1, 2004.

"The city wanted to close the Mayfair because of the excessive police and Fire department calls associated with the complex even before the big fire last year. You remember the fire?" Bill asked.

"I read about it in the newspaper."

"According to the information I got about that incident, a female resident got angry with her live-in-boyfriend, doused him with gasoline and lit him on fire. The guy nearly died. We don't want that happening again especially now that CVILCH is responsible for the management of the complex. Nicky recommended you for the job and I think you fit perfectly for this position, too. You know the population and I believe you have the skills to keep the place running smoothly. You interested?"

"Sure!" I replied excitedly.

Here was the opportunity I had been waiting for so I jumped on it. Afterward, I went down the hall and thanked Nicky for recommending me. Nicky had been my counselor during the time I had been a CVLIHC client and had always encouraged me to keep pushing ahead.

"Don't give up," she would often tell me.

Jessica and I moved into the Mayfair in late June of 2004.

"You see, Baby," I said to Jessica when we finally settled into our apartment. "I told you I'd get a job."

Jessica simply smiled and gave me a tight hug. It was great to show my daughter that if you did the right things, most of the time the right things would happen to you.

WORKING AT THE MAYFAIR didn't pay much, but when I combined my Flea Market salary with the Mayfair income, I was doing pretty dang good. Most important, I had plenty of time to work on establishing a nonprofit and developing a program that would provide housing for ex-offenders. The goal I'd been working toward since my transformation.

One day in early January 2006, I got a phone call from Bill. He told me a representative from a company—let's call them Transitional Help Inc., or T.H., for short—involved with providing reentry services for ex-offenders, had called asking if he was interested in providing sober living housing for clients of a program that was to be established in Stockton in the near future.

"I told the gentleman CVLIHC didn't offer those types of services but that I knew someone who did. You want their number?" Bill asked.

"Yes, sir!" I replied excitedly. "And thanks for thinking about me, Bill. I appreciate it."

"It was nothing."

Bill gave me the number, and I contacted T.H.'s West Coast Regional Manager who was responsible for putting the Stockton Day Reporting Center (DRC) into operation.

The following morning I called the man. When he answered the phone, we exchanged pleasantries and set a meeting for later that week to discuss my interest in subcontracting sober living to their clients. I was ecstatic. Here was a chance for me to move forward and one more step toward my ultimate goal of developing a program for the ex-offender population.

"Hey," he said, as he stuck his hand out the morning we met.

"Glad to meet you." I replied.

"You want to get some breakfast and talk?"

"Sure."

T.H.'s rep drove to Susy's, a Mexican restaurant located in central Stockton. Once we were seated he began to give me a brief history about his company and an overview about the theory behind DRCs.

"Our company developed the Electric Monitor approximately 30 years ago and in 1997 ventured into the ex-offender reentry industry. We opened our first DRC on the Southside of Chicago at that time. Since then, T.H. has replicated what we do in Chicago in every DRC we operate across the country. DRC's offer parolees a myriad of cognitive-based services and provide state agencies an alternative to incarceration. They reduce overcrowding in our prisons, and increase public safety. It's a win, win situation for everyone.

"Sounds exactly like the type of work I want to be involved with."

"I've been working with this population for over twenty years and I find it very satisfying to see the light appear in a client's eyes. You can actually see when it happens. Their eyes begin to sparkle. It's a slow process to get the client to that spot, but really amazing to help them get there if you ask me."

I knew what he was talking about. I had seen that glitter in my eyes when I crossed from the dark side into the light. I told him I would sign a contract to supply sober living for their clients, but that I would have to consult with my potential partner first. I rushed over to Delta College and met with Tom and told him what the Regional Manager had said and what this could mean if we agreed to sign a contract and furnish sober living to their clients.

"This is the beginning, Tom," I said. "If you say yes, this contract can very well kick-start our program."

For the past couple of years, I had been discussing with Tom the development of a program for ex-offenders, but up to this point he had always been hesitant. I think he was worried about jeopardizing his position at the college. However, I didn't think his job at the college would be a concern anymore given that college administration had begun the process to terminate his employment. Tom and I had done plenty of research on what was needed to apply for a non-profit number and had even developed a business plan. It looked as if things were finally falling into place.

"Let's do it," Tom said. Pulling out my cell phone right then and there, I called T.H.'s Regional Manager and told him I would sign a contract to provide sober living. A few weeks later the California Department of Corrections and Rehabilitation awarded T.H. a contract to provide cognitive-based programming to parolees in San Joaquin County. At this time, I was a member of the Mayor's Blue Ribbon Crime Prevention Committee which had been formed by Mayor Ed Chavez to tackle address the high crime rate in Stockton. The DRC seemed a God-sent solution to the specific problem the committee was addressing. Every member of the committee agreed that lack of funding was an issue, but here was an opportunity for Stockton to deal with this crisis with free money from the State. I honestly believed it would be a walk in the park to obtain the Conditional Use Permit needed to operate the DRC since Stockton had the second highest crime rate in the nation.

Not long after the contractual award, I met with the Mayor's executive assistant to explain that this money was to be used specifically to address recidivism in San Joaquin County. The Mayor's aide was ecstatic and said he would speak to the Mayor about getting his support to get zoning for the building needed for the DRC.

A week or so later, T.H.'s Regional Manager, the Vice President of Reentry Services and I met for a Planning Commission meeting at City Hall. There were bigwigs from every department of the city at the gathering. I looked around at all the men present and was reminded of the times we had meetings when I was in the NF. It was the same type of scenario with all the big shots being assembled to make decisions that would impact people's lives. The only difference here was that these men hid behind their titles, wore suits, and supposedly made their decisions for the betterment of the populace. Like shot callers in prison, these men and women never bothered to get input from the people who were being impacted by their decisions.

Every member present at the board meeting was of the same opinion concerning ex-offenders. They did not want this type of program in their city. The Program Development Director for the City of Stockton, Steve Erickson, summed it up by asking; "Why should I care that you folks want to help these people?" he asked.

I wanted to respond to his question, but I let the Regional Manager answer instead. After he finished, I realized the local politicians had made up their minds to reject T.H.'s request for a Conditional Use Permit long before the meeting. This discussion had simply been a formality.

Before the meeting adjourned, I was asked by the Commission Chairman if I had anything to say. I took a deep breath and tried not to let my emotions get in the way of business.

"I want to reply to the question asked by Mr. Erickson."

"Go ahead," the Chairman said.

"You have children?" I asked Mr. Erickson.

"Yes, I do," he replied looking at me skeptically.

"Well, Sir," I replied looking at him intently. "Your children are the reason why you should care about helping these people. You see, the individuals we've been discussing here this morning have children too. And their children shop in the same shopping centers, travel down the same streets, and go to the same theaters as yours do. However, there is one very different factor between their children and yours. Kids who come from the broken homes of ex-offenders are generally pretty angry about the hand life has dealt them. They don't understand why life is so unfair or why they have nothing while your kids have everything. Therefore, they hate kids like yours because they believe they don't get the same opportunities as your kid's do. And so they lash out and hurt people. How many of you remember the murder of Kelly Freed?" I asked.

Everyone in the room nodded, with the exception of the T.H. Regional Manager and Vice President.

"I'm sure most of you read the newspaper stories concerning that tragic event. However, what most of you probably don't know is that the teenager who committed that senseless crime was one of the angry kids I'm talking about. He was mad because a few years prior to the Kelly Freed shooting, he witnessed his older brother's killing after he got shot in the head as they stood outside on the front porch of their house. His brother died on the spot. He was only thirteen when he witnessed his brother die in front of him. Afterward, no one offered him counseling or even bothered to find out how he was doing. He was left to deal with his loss on his own. His mother, who didn't have a clue about dealing with this type of situation tried in her own futile way to make things better for her family, by moving them away from Stockton. But she eventually returned, and it wasn't long after, at the age of 16, that this youngster shot and killed Kelly Freed.

"It's very possible that if his mother had been provided with information through a program such as the one we're discussing here today, this young boy could have gotten the right guidance from his mother and the outcome might have been different and this teenager wouldn't have to squander the remainder of his life in prison at taxpayers' expense? It very well could be that maybe, just maybe, Kelly Freed might still be alive today? But that we'll never know, now will we?"

In the end, it didn't matter what anyone said and the zoning permit was denied. Eventually, the state nullified the contract and T.H. went away.

In the meantime, Tom and I continued with our plans to open a sober living home for ex-offenders and on May 10th, 2006 The Jonah Foundation opened its doors. A friend of mine helped me come up with the name. We both agreed that the name was appropriate because in many ways the Biblical story of Jonah fit this population perfectly. Like Jonah, ex-offenders are always running from their problems and seldom, if ever, follow instructions designed to help them. They often wind up being swallowed by the whale, which is, in the case of the ex-offender, the CDCR.

Tom and I started the Jonah Foundation in a two bedroom house belonging to Tom, but soon realized that the house was way too small for what we had in mind so a few months later we bought a four bedroom house located on Stella Court in north Stockton. By then I had obtained a contract to provide housing for ex-offenders from San Joaquin County for a small fee of twenty dollars a day through the county's Prop 36 Program. The Jonah Foundation provided two hot meals, a sack lunch, and housing. I also started a landscaping business and acquired a number of contracts to supplement our income and help make the house mortgage and operational expenses.

One day, in early fall of 2006, I drove to Recovery House to attend to Jonah business. A young man approached me.

"Hello, my name is Nate Summers. I heard you speak at the Mayor's Blue Ribbon Crime Prevention Committee meeting not long ago. I also heard you have a Sober Living House. I'm living in a halfway house right now, but I don't like the atmosphere there and I was wondering if I could move into your place? I don't have any money, but I'm willing to work to pay my way."

"Are you ready to work right now?" I inquired.

"Sure enough!" he replied excitedly.

I liked this young man's enthusiasm. His passion was a lot like mine when I first started my recovery.

"Alright," I said. "Jump in my truck and let's go dig a ditch for one of my landscape customers."

Just the day before Bill's father had asked me if I could locate a leak in one of the water pipes in his backyard. Finding the leak would involve digging a ditch, something I didn't want to do myself, but I told the gentleman I would try to find someone that would do the job. Luckily Nate was a big, strong, young man who could dig ditches all day long if need be.

When we arrived to Bill's father's house, Nate grabbed a shovel and proceeded to dig where he was instructed. He didn't complain or let on that he didn't like doing the work. He just got busy shoveling and in less than an hour found the water seepage.

After we left, Nate broached the subject about moving into The Jonah House again.

"Like I said earlier,' he said. "I don't have any money, but I'll work for my room and board if that's okay with you."

I didn't doubt Nate would be an asset to The Jonah Foundation.

"Listen, I don't have any reservations about you moving into the house, but I have to ask my partner if it's okay with him. I don't think he'll have any problem with you moving in either and I'm sure we can find plenty of work for you to do as payment, okay?"

"Great!" he exclaimed.

Two days later we loaded Nate's meager belongings onto my truck and moved him into The Jonah Foundation Sober Living House. It was a good move for him as well as for the Foundation. Nate brought with him an eagerness that was contagious. He never objected to helping me maintain the landscaping contracts although there were times he did get angry. Whenever he got pissed, he would politely excuse himself for ten or fifteen minutes. When he returned, it was always with a completely different attitude. I never asked him what he did while he was gone, but whatever it was it worked for him.

One morning, about a month or so after Nate moved into The Jonah House, I arrived to pick up him up for work. When I entered the house to get a cup of coffee, I saw one of the residents sprawled on a couch with one of his legs slung over the armrest and his shoes and socks scattered in the middle of the main room. I got a little peeved at what I saw, but I didn't jump on the guy. I simply asked him politely to pick up his stuff and put them in their proper place.

"Fuck you!" he replied heatedly. "I'm not picking up a goddamn thing! I'm tired of you telling me what to do. Who the fuck do you think you are anyway!? You ain't my father. And if you don't like what I'm saying, then take off on me motherfucker!" He jumped up ready to fight.

I didn't know where this guy's outburst had come from, but his flare-up stopped me dead in my tracks and a very dangerous calm came over me. I recognized the stillness. I'd had it each time I had hurt someone in my past. I had to fight back with great effort the urge to snatch a knife from the kitchen and shove it down this guy's throat. I knew violence wasn't the way to deal with antagonistic situations, but there was still a small part of me that believed there were times brute force was necessary, especially when dealing with guys who came from the criminal lifestyle. This, I believed, was one of those times.

During the guy's outburst, I repeated silently over and over in my mind "don't feed into his bullshit, Jess, don't feed onto his bullshit Jess." When I didn't say anything to the guy, he spun and stomped off leaving me so severely angry that my hands trembled and my insides shivered. I took deep breaths to regain my composure.

Nate had been standing next to me while the client spewed his malevolence, but he hadn't said anything during the entire confrontation. Once the resident walked off, Nate followed the guy into his room and told him he had to leave the house. The guy didn't argue with Nate. He just packed his stuff and in minutes he was gone. I think he was afraid of Nate because he had a reputation of being a good fighter. He probably thought Nate was going to kick his ass.

"That guy's really dumb," Nate said after I calmed down. "He should be afraid of you way more than me. The only thing I'll do is beat him down, but you'll put steel in him. I saw how you were looking at him. I was ready to step in if you had made a dash for the kitchen."

I was so thankful to Nate for what he did that day, that I told Tom we needed to hire him as the Jonah House manager. Tom readily agreed and from then on Nate was in charge of the operations of Jonah. He made sure everyone living at the house was out of bed by 7:00 each morning and that each resident completed their assigned chores before they left the house at 8:00 to attend school or work. He made sure the landscape equipment was ready for the day's work schedule and handled unexpected situations that occurred at the house on a day-to-day basis.

CHAPTER THIRTEEN

AT FIRST, like any other businesses, the Foundation struggled, but we pressed forward with our plans to expand. In May of 2007, we bought a bigger place on the east side of Stockton and moved our operation there. The building had formally been used to house foster kids and was already ADA approved. It had a long, wide hallway, with custom built doorways. There were three big bathrooms, nine bedrooms, a huge kitchen, a large recreation room, and an expansive backyard for possible growth.

It was an excellent move and Tom and I began the process of obtaining a Conditional Use Permit from the county that would allow sixteen people occupancy at The Jonah Foundation. It took over a year before we were able to obtain the permit, but when we got approval from the County Planning Commission, I felt great! The Jonah Foundation was finally legit and I believed we were on our way to bigger and better things.

In January 2008, I got a call from T.H.'s Regional Manager notifying me that the contract for a DRC in Stockton had come out for bid and that T.H. was going to apply for the contract again.

"Are you still interested in subcontracting to provide sober living for our clients?" he asked.

"Sure!" I replied enthusiastically.

I called Tom to give him the news. Tom was excited, too.

From our previous dealings with the City of Stockton we knew it would be tough to get zoning so I enlisted the help of Wayne Hose, the Chief of Police during that period. I called his office and left a message with his secretary asking to meet with him. A few days later the Chief returned my call.

"How are you doing Jess?" He asked.

"I'm good, Chief."

"I got your message that you want to meet."

"That's right," I replied. "You remember last year when the city rejected the application for zoning to set up a DRC in the city?"

"Yeah, I recall the controversy surrounding that application."

"Well, Chief, we've shared our views about reducing crime in Stockton and I know you can't hang yourself out to dry by supporting what we're trying to do, but I would like to have a meeting with you just to brainstorm ideas and get your opinion about what we can do to get zoning?"

"Who will be at the meeting?"

"T.H.'s Regional Manager, a realtor by the name of Lloiden Gaza and me."

"Does Thursday at 1:00 p.m. sound okay with you?"

"Whenever it's convenient for you is fine with us. The Regional Manager already told me to let him know the time and he'll be here."

"Great. I'll see you folks then."

When Thursday came, the Regional Manager and I met outside police headquarters. As we waited for Lloiden to get there, I thought about all the changes taking place in my life. I found it ironic that throughout much of my life I had despised cops, yet here I was about to walk into police headquarters on my own accord to meet with the Chief of Police! A mind-blowing turnaround and an extraordinary conversion of the way I looked at police officers today.

A few minutes later Lloiden arrived and we walked to the front desk and announced to the receptionist who we were. A few minutes later a policeman escorted us upstairs to the conference room where the meeting was to take place. Walking down the hall made me uneasy and reminded me of the many times I had been lead into police interrogation rooms after being arrested. I wondered if I would ever be free from those disturbing emotions.

Entering the room, I saw the room was much nicer than the ones used to interrogate me back in the day. This room was painted sky blue and had a number of paintings in elaborate frames. There was also a huge redwood oval table with comfortable cushioned chairs and set of glasses and crystal pitcher filled with ice water.

"Good afternoon, Jess," the Police Chief said as he entered the room. "This is Captain Belso. He's with the San Joaquin County Sheriff's Office. I asked him to join us because I think he might have a solution to the problem you folks are having obtaining a building for your program."

Captain Belso was so tall it hurt my neck looking up at him. Introductions were exchanged and the Regional Manager started to explain what his company was trying to accomplish. Captain Belso listened closely and asked questions throughout the Regional Manager's exhaustive account. When he finished, Captain Belso seemed genuinely interested.

"First, I want to thank you for allowing me the opportunity to join you folks," Captain Belso said. "When Chief Hose called me about this, he said your program sounded as though it would benefit the Sheriff's Department since our agency handles the incarceration of the criminals in our county. And after what you just said, I think we might be able to accommodate your program on the Honor Farm complex. I don't believe we'll get any opposition if we put it out there. Will that work for you folks?" he asked the T.H. Regional Manager.

"That would be awesome. When do you want to show us the building?" The Regional Manager asked.

"We can go right now if you'd like?"

"Great. We'll follow you."

We bid the Chief goodbye and drove out to the Honor Farm complex located in French Camp, a few miles outside Stockton. Once there, Captain Belso gave us a tour of the building after which the Regional Manager told him that although the building would require some build out, the structure appeared to meet the standard requirements by CDCR for a DRC.

A few weeks later, a meeting was held with the county sheriff to get his authorization. It took a few weeks, but things worked out and building modifications to meet the state's requirements were quickly underway.

In the meantime, the Regional Manager and I spent lots of time together working on issues related to the actual implementation of the DRC. During one of our get-togethers I broached the subject about applying for the DRC Program Management position.

"Well," the Regional Manager replied. "I think you could do well. Go ahead and apply, but you'll have to go through the interview process. I can't promise you'll get the position, but I know our firm appreciates people who help create opportunities for our company and you have definitely been instrumental in getting us where we are here in Stockton. As far as I'm concerned, I can tell you that what I'm looking for in a manager is not how smart he or she is, but if they're willing to learn. I definitely think you meet that criterion."

When the job was posted on the company's website I applied. A few days later a phone interview was scheduled. On the date of the interview, I called the 1800 phone number that had been emailed to me by the Regional Manager. I was subjected to a comprehensive interview process, but in the end I landed the job. When I got the call that I had gotten the job, I was on the road and had to pull over to keep from causing an accident because I was in such awe of what had just happened. I sat in my car for a long period of time absorbing the enormity of it all. I wondered how I had come from the bowels of the California prison system to being the manager of a program where I would be an example to guys who had come from the same place as me and give them hope. It was an emotion unlike any I had ever had. I felt tears run down my cheeks and instinctively looked around to see if anyone was watching me. I didn't want anyone to think I was getting weak by crying. Cleaning my face, I laughed out loud.

After I drove off, I wondered if I would ever be able to cry without feeling as though I was less of a man. I still remembered what my Mama would say to me as a boy when I cried, "*Los hombres no lloran*" (Men Don't Cry).

I started working on April Fools Day 2008. I was instructed by the Regional Manager to drive to San Diego so I could attend a conference being held there for Western Region Office Managers. I was nervous, yet excited. During the drive to San Diego I got a call from the Vice President of the company.

"Hey, Jess," he said. "I have some terrible news. You need to turn around and head back to Stockton. We made a huge mistake and can't hire you after all."

My initial reaction to what he said was one of sheer shock. It felt as though I'd been hit upside my head and forced to wake up from an incredible dream, which in a split second, had turned into a nightmare.

"April Fools," he guffawed. "I got you, huh?"

"Yes sir, you sure did," I replied relieved to hear he had only been joking.

I felt my body relax, yet I got angry. I'd never been on the receiving end of an April Fool's Day joke before and I didn't like being anyone's sucker. Where I came from you could get killed for playing this type of joke on someone. I wanted to let him know I didn't appreciate being his sap no matter if he was only playing. Instead, I went along with his practical joke. I figured this was what people in the real world did sometimes, play games on each other.

On April 14, 2008 I met the employees who had been hired to work under my supervision at the DRC. Human Resource personnel hired an older White lady as our Substance Abuse Counselor, a retired White man who had taught in prison was brought on board as Employment/Education Coordinator. A young White woman and an older Black man were hired to service as Client Services Specialists (CSS's), and a Mexican friend of mine whom I had recommended was employed as a Case Manager. The ethnic diversity of each staff member gave the DRC mixture of different cultures and perspectives. Three other staff were scheduled to be hired after we ramped up to our full capacity of one hundred clients.

We met at the Marriot Hotel that morning to begin two weeks of rigorous training and were introduced to Moral Reconation Therapy (MRT).

"MRT," the trainer said, "is the essence of this program. It is designed to challenge participants to dig deep into their inner-core and helps them expose issues hidden in the recesses of their unconsciousness. Each of you must undergo this process too, so that you may get a better understanding of what the client experiences when they go through this course."

MRT training consisted of four days of comprehensive instruction on the techniques needed to facilitate this particular subject matter. We were also taught how to use the company's Group Model and how to record vital client information into the company's database. We did mock interviews and learned how to complete a Level of Service Inventory Revised (LSIR) assessment—the tool used to measure client's crimino-genic risk/needs. Everyone completed a series of Level I training modules on the company's webpage. It took staff months to wrap up the extensive training requirements.

In the meantime, the Stockton DRC opened for business on May 5, 2008. We got our first client on May 7th. He was a really tall gentleman who appeared to be just as nervous as me when I greeted him in the lobby.

"How are you, Sir?" I asked, looking up at him while we shook hands. "And your name is?"

"I'm Timothy White," he replied apprehensively.

"Welcome. I'm Mr. De La Cruz, the program manager. Behind the counter there are Mr. Jones and Ms Williams. We're glad you're here. By the way, you, sir, have the distinct honor of being our very first client. Congratulations!" I exclaimed as Mr. Jones, Ms Williams, and I applauded.

I saw small beads of sweat on Mr. White's forehead and his facial expression indicated he was nervous.

"Don't worry Mr. White," I said, attempting to ease his anxiety. "You don't have anything to fear but fear itself. Everything's going to be fantastic. This is the first day of the rest of your life. You want a cup of coffee?"

"That would be good."

I poured him a cup and handed it to him. I let him take a drink and then proceeded with the intake process. I tried to remember all the things I'd learned during the training and dived in feet first.

"Let me begin by giving you a brief overview about what you can expect while you're at the DRC, okay?"

The pinched expression on his face told me he wasn't comfortable with this type of interaction. This type of treatment was completely foreign in his world. He had every right to be suspicious. No one gave up anything unless you had something to give in return and no one was genuinely happy to see you unless you were giving them money, dope, or sex.

"Sure," he replied hesitantly.

"Very well," I said. "The first thing I'd like to make perfectly clear is that you will always be treated with respect and dignity. You don't have to earn respect here. It's freely given. You'll always be addressed as Mr. or Sir. That being said, we also expect you to treat us with the same respect. Is that cool?"

"Okay," he answered.

"You see those words on the walls?" I said pointing to the words stenciled on the walls throughout the facility.

He nodded.

"One of those words will be assigned to you. In fact, let me find out right now. Yeah, here it is. Your word is Achievement. From this point on, whenever you see Achievement posted on that bulletin board, you'll be required to drop a urine sample. A urinalysis will be conducted randomly on a weekly basis and you'll be breathalyzed each time you check into the DRC. So if you drink alcohol, please don't drink before you come here ok? It just complicates everything if you blow positive for alcohol." "I don't drink," he said. "My problem is Rock Cocaine."

"Your drug issue will be addressed here too," I replied. "There are three Phases and an aftercare component to this program. Phase I, II and III. In Phase I you will be expected to report seven days a week. In the course of this phase you will complete a number of assessments that will aid us in the development of a treatment plan specific to your needs. During Phase II you will only have to report to the DRC five days a week. You'll attend a number of groups, depending on your needs, and complete ten hours of community service before you can move onto Phase III. In Phase III you only report three days a week to the center, but you have to do a little more in order to transition into aftercare. You must complete another ten hours of community service, be employed, or be enrolled in school, and have stable housing before you can complete the program."

When I finished, the client looked at me as though I was crazy. I knew exactly what he was thinking. I had had that same expression when my parole agent had given me the conditions of my parole the last time I had been released from prison. I remember thinking she was crazy. Afterwards, I had rushed straight to my heroin connection and bought myself a shot to get relief from the pressure she had imposed on me. I didn't want Mr. White to go get a hit to ease his anxiety. We would lose him for sure if he did that, so I tried to reassure him that things would be fine.

"Hey, Sir," I said soothingly. "I know what's going through your mind right now. I've been there. Trust me. And I'm not going to lie. It's going to take lots of work on your part to change how you think because it's you're thinking that has kept you stuck where you are today. When I started my journey of change, there were many days I wanted to throw in the towel and go back to my old ways because it was familiar. I wasn't used to living without breaking the law, but I hung in there, and now I live a life second to none. My very worst day now is a whole lot better than my best day back then. Living according to societal rules will require tremendous strength, a quality you have plenty of or you wouldn't be here right now. You have a source of power you haven't even begun to tap into. You didn't get to where you are today by being weak. The problem is that growing up, you learned to use your strengths in the negative. Can you imagine what would happen if you redirected that same energy into a positive? That's what we're here to do, assist you in doing just that. This program is not here to change the world Mr. White, we're here to give you new information that will bring to surface the real Mr. White so that you can change your world, okay?"

"Whew! You said a whole lot right there," he said. "I suppose I should give it a shot. After all, what do I have to lose? I've already dug a hole so deep I can't see any light. I've tried numerous times to get straight, but for one reason or another always get sucked back into using drugs and crime."

"Then try again, Mr. White."

"I don't even have a place to live right now."

"You need a place to live?" I asked.

"I need the works. I lost everything again when I went to prison. What I'm wearing is all I have right now."

"Well, Mr. White, you've come to the right place. All you gotta to do is suit up and show up."

I called Tom and The Jonah Foundation had its first T.H. client. Things were beginning to look optimistic for the future of the DRC and The Jonah Foundation.

DURING THE NEXT FEW DAYS we received two more clients and by the end of the first month of operation, clients were being referred to the center in droves by the parole department. The office pace was extremely hectic. T.H. had never experienced such a rapid ramp-up. Therefore, all staff, including me, were involved in processing the intakes. In the midst of all the admissions were lots of questions from my staff that I couldn't answer. The truth was I had a huge learning curve, although I never thought I couldn't manage the program once I got some training. I had always been a leader so I pushed myself hard with the sole intent of eventually becoming a topnotch manager.

One thing I did need to do was ease up on was my unyielding directness. I didn't even realize I was managing my staff with an iron fist until the District Manager called me into his office and told me I had to cut them some slack. He said I was being too harsh with them, that I needed to use tact and stop being so insensitive.

At first I didn't agree with him, but when I got home that evening, I took a closer look at what he had said I was doing and had to admit I was using a "go for the neck" approach as I used to do with gang members back in the day. Coming to this realization made me feel ashamed and I quickly decided to modify my management style to fit the professional position I held. By now I knew I could revise whatever needed to be changed. All I had to do was put in the work.

The following Monday I started the process of shifting my approach toward my staff. I began to listen to what they had to say. I quit reacting to situations without thinking about the affect my responses had on them. Most importantly, I paid close attention to what I said to them and after a few months things began to run more smoothly.

One big difference between the DRC and other programs was that there weren't any exclusionary rules based on the type of crime the client had committed. This meant that all parolees at high risk to recidivate, including sex offenders, had to be given an opportunity to participate. This was a real challenge for me. Like most people, the term sex-offender automatically created images of child molesters; of perverted old men that preyed on our children. I had always despised them while I had been in prison and if it had been up to me back then, I would've enjoyed watching them hang by their nuts.

The problem was that many men labeled sex-offenders weren't child molesters at all. Some had done nothing more than have consensual sex with their girlfriends as far back as thirty years before when they were young too. Others had been convicted of urinating in public. I fully agreed that anyone who exposed themselves in public was a pervert, but I wasn't too sure about someone being labeled a sex-offender for taking a leak behind a car or tree? I couldn't believe this was happening until a client told me that was exactly what had happened to him.

"I wasn't exposing myself, Mr. De La Cruz," he said. "I was drunk and couldn't hold my piss anymore. So I went behind a tree to relieve myself. I made sure there was no one around before I pulled my dick out, but a cop drove by while I was urinating. Talk about bad luck. If it wasn't for bad luck, I wouldn't have any luck at all," he said glumly.

The intense focus on sex-offenders was brought about as a result of Jessica's Law being passed by Congress in 2005 after the sexual molestation and murder of Jessica Lunsford in Florida. California followed suit and adopted the decree in 2006. I read the language of the document and agreed with everything it said concerning a child molester or rapist, but the criteria used in the bill to label someone a sex-offender seemed way too expansive as far as I was concerned.

One day, Ms Williams, one of my receptionists called to tell me there was an older gentleman in our lobby requesting to speak with me. It wasn't unusual for a new client to want to chat with me when they first arrived to the DRC. After all, I was acquainted with many of the men being referred to the center by parole agents. When I walked into the lobby I saw it was *Chuco*, my old friend from back in the day. I hadn't seen him since the last time I had been released from Folsom prison twelve years before.

"How are you, Sir?" I asked him.

Without giving him an opportunity to respond, I signaled for him to follow me to my office where we could talk in private.

"Have a seat," I said to him.

"This is nice," he said enthusiastically. "I heard through the grapevine in the neighborhood you were the shot caller out here."

"Listen," I replied humbly. "I'm not a shot caller. I'm the Program Manager."

"I hear you, Bro."

"And you can't call me Bro," I replied apologetically. "You have to call me Sir or Mr. De La Cruz."

"Yes, Sir," he replied smiling brightly. "I'm not trying to be a smartass. I'm just amazed to see how far you've come. Wow!" he continued as he shook his head. "It blows my mind to see you sitting behind that desk."

I was touched by his sincerity. *Chuco* was familiar with my reputation from back in day and he knew how difficult it was to live right after being involved in crime for as long as I had been.

"Man, I can only imagine how tough it's been for you to live like a square."

"It's not really that difficult, but let's quit talking about me. What can I do for you?"

"Well," he began. "You know what my motherfucking parole agent did!?"

"No, but you can't cuss here, okay?" I told him gently.

"*Despensa,* but I'm really pissed at that punk right now, you know."

I wasn't surprised to hear *Chuco* blame his agent for the situation he was currently in. Blaming others was what parolees did. I used to do the same thing when I was on parole.

"Hey listen, I know you're heated right now, but you have to control your anger or you're going to get yourself into more trouble."

"Yeah, you're right, it's just that having this gadget strapped on my ankle makes me feel like I'm some type of sicko, you know." He lifted his pant leg to display the monitoring device strapped around his ankle. "When that punk told me he was gonna put it on, I thought about jumping out of my chair and knocking him out and taking off. It was hard to hold back from laying him out, believe me. Shit, I ain't no Fu…" he stopped himself. "Sorry, but I ain't no damn child molester!"

I nodded.

"Hell, I didn't even know what he was talking about when he brought this bullshit to my attention. I righteously had to think way back, but then it came to me. The sex crime he was talking about happened thirty years ago. Can you believe it!? Thirty years ago!" He shook his head despondently. "It wasn't a sex crime either. I mean there was sex involved, but she was my girl-friend at the time and she gave me her booty willingly. I didn't force her. In fact, everything was cool between her and me until she got pregnant. That's when her dad told me I had to marry his daughter. He wanted to save her reputation, but I refused to get hitched. Since she was a minor, the prick went to the DA and pressed charges against me. I had just turned eighteen years old when all this happened. I don't think I would've been charged, but I had just gotten out of Youth Authority so the DA made sure I was sentenced to a year in the County Jail. I didn't complain. I did my time and forgot about it. Now, I'm being treated like a leper, as though I run around molesting kids. I can't live at my sister's house cuz my nephews and nieces live there too. I can't stay at the homeless shelter cuz there's a child-care center located on the grounds. I literally have to live on a campsite located under a bridge with other sex-offenders some of which are child molesters. Can you believe it!?"

I didn't know what to say to *Chuco*. After all, he wasn't complaining about having to serve time. He just didn't like being treated as though he was a pervert and being forced to live with depraved men who were considered the lowest form of life, not only by societal standards, but in the criminal world as well.

"I understand normal people hate child molesters," he went on. "I hate them too. But don't put that label on me."

I understood *Chuco*'s predicament, but I also understood society was mad and wanted revenge on men who raped and murdered our children. In their unappeasable quest for vengeance, society had pressured Congress to implement laws that removed predators from our streets. The problem was that when people reacted out of anger (and their anger was surely legitimate in this type of case), laws were usually written in a language that effected guys who weren't child molesters or rapists, guys who had never harmed, nor would they ever injure a child. But most people didn't care, their only concern was to rid the streets of predators and if other types of criminals got hurt in the process, too bad.

Chuco's despair filtered through to the core of my being as I recalled having that same look many times at the end of my criminal career when I wanted to change but didn't know where to start.

We sat in my office without saying a word for what seemed a long time although it couldn't have been more than ten seconds at most. I finally broke the silence and gently told him we would provide him with whatever services we had available to make his transition as smooth as possible.

Chuco nodded somberly. He got up and left, never to return to the center. Later, a client told me *Chuco* had been returned to prison after he cut the electric monitor off his ankle and went to live at his sister's house anyway.

Not long after, while facilitating a Program Orientation group for new clients, a parolee asked me what I would do if a child molester sat across from me and my daughter on an RTD bus and looked at her lustfully.

"Nothing," I replied. "What do you think I should do?"

"Beat him down!" he answered.

"Why?"

"Because he's a sexual pervert and he's looking at your daughter in a depraved way!" he exclaimed.

"How would I know what he's thinking? After all, I can't read minds? Can you?"

"No, but that's what child molesters do. They devise ways to molest kids. Those dirty S.O.B's shouldn't be allowed to live."

"How do you know what they think? I mean, I know you're not a child molester yourself so you couldn't have firsthand experience as to what they think. Maybe you know how they think because you've studied them?"

"No, I haven't done what you mentioned. I just know that's how they think."

"I think you're just making assumptions as to how they think like a lot of people do and your suggestion that they shouldn't be allowed to live is really dangerous too."

"Why? All they do is hurt and kill our children. We should get rid of them!"

"I don't think you understand what you're saying. That type of barbarism leads to uncivilized conditions. The next thing you know, society might decide to exterminate all criminals which includes you."

The client never did grasp what I was trying to explain to him, but those types of discussions were always more helpful to me than anyone else. It was during these debates that I was able to measure my emotional and psychological growth of the past twelve years. I realized I still needed to improve on how I reacted when someone said something I disagreed with or found disrespectful. But the fact that I was even in the same building with child molesters much less working with them was utterly unbelievable to me sometimes.

"HOW MANY OF YOU believe you'll never go back to prison?" I asked during another Program Orientation group.

"I'll never return because I'm not living with my crazy ass ex-girlfriend. She was the reason I kept getting violated," one client replied.

"I won't go back because I don't use drugs anymore," said another.

Still another client indicated he wouldn't return to prison because he was now working.

"Did you have a job the last time you went to prison?" I asked.

"Yeah, now that I think about it, I did."

"So a job isn't really your problem. In fact, getting rid of an ex-girlfriend or using drugs are not the reasons people go to prison in the first place. What you men are talking about are simply symptoms of hidden causes and conditions as to why you break the law. You guys want to know why I'll never go back to prison?"

I had captured their attention and every man in the room nodded.

"Because I altered my thinking, which changed my behavior and because I don't break the law anymore, So I don't get arrested anymore. It's really simple. The problem is that most of you don't know how to live without committing crimes."

"That's it!?" one client asked completely perplexed.

"That's it in a nut shell," I replied. "There's no scientific formula, but if you stick around and participate in this program, I guarantee you'll learn how to live crime free just like I did."

I could see by their puzzled expressions that they'd never thought it was that easy. Not breaking the law equaled not going to jail. I remembered how confused I had been back in '96, when Frank told to me that if I stopped breaking the law I would never get arrested again. That concept was completely unfamiliar to me at the time. I couldn't imagine how I was supposed to survive without committing crimes, using drugs or alcohol. It was inconceivable that anyone could live without using substances or breaking the law. But I had learned and found that living crime free was the ticket to real happiness. Now it was my job to do whatever I could to help these guys see that there was another way to live.

ABOUT A YEAR after the DRC opened, two representatives from a local postsecondary college came to the center to provide information to our Community Connections group. The purpose of this particular assemblage was to bring agencies that provided services into our center so our clients could learn what was available to them in the community. The college was a proprietary educational institution that offered unconventional students educational opportunities in Office Information Technology, Medical, Dental or Criminal Justice fields. I met with the two representatives after their seminar and gave them an explanation about what we were doing at the DRC. In the course of our conversation, my checkered past came to light and the lady representative suggested I contact the Criminal Justice Program Director at the college about possibly teaching on a part time basis. I had often entertained the thought of teaching, but I never thought I would be allowed to teach because of my criminal history. So I never called the Program Director and shelved the thought of teaching.

One day, about two months later, I got a call from a gentleman who said he was the Program Director of the Criminal Justice Department at the college. He told me the lady who suggested I call him had given him my name and number.

"She spoke very highly of you and said you're doing extraordinary things where you work. I'd like to meet you and explore the possibility of bringing you on board as an adjunct instructor here at our college. Can we have lunch tomorrow?"

"Sure," I replied.

I was ecstatic, but didn't let my emotions get out of control. I didn't want to get too excited in case things didn't pan out. I had often gotten my hopes up in the past after applying for a job I believed was tailor-made for, only to be notified I didn't get the job because of my criminal history.

The following day, Mr. DiSomma, a retired Judge and I met at the Elephant Bar Restaurant. He was about my age, of Italian decent, and talked with a New York accent.

"How are you, Sir?" I said. "I'm Jesse De La Cruz. It's good to meet you."

"The pleasure's all mine," he replied. "Let's go inside and talk, okay?"

A waitress led us to a table where we both ordered iced tea.

"My coworker was very impressed with what you've done to turn your life around. Would you mind telling me a little about yourself? I'm interested in hiring good people; people who bring different perspectives to our Criminal Justice Program. You have a Bachelors Degree, right?"

"I have a Master's Degree."

"You have a Masters?"

"Yes, sir, I do."

"In that case, there shouldn't be any problem hiring you, but I do need to know about your past in case someone from administration argues against your employment, you know what I mean?"

"I understand perfectly. That's one of the reasons I always bring up my past up front. I don't want people to say I tried to keep my extensive criminal background hidden. I was deeply involved and committed many types of crimes during my criminal career. There are too many crimes to name them all, so suffice it to say that I never molested children."

I told him I had been in and out of prison for thirty years and that the last time I had gotten out I had started using drugs the first day of my release just as I had done every other time I had been released. The difference this time was that I genuinely didn't want to be a drug addict/criminal anymore, but didn't know how to live any other way. I didn't know there was another way of living.

"One day," I went on, "after two months of living in a homeless shelter and using drugs, I bumped into a guy who was the liaison between the Courts and drug treatment centers in San Joaquin County. I didn't know him, but he knew me. He suggested I admit myself into a ninety-day residential drug treatment program. I took his advice and he helped me get into treatment the following day. It was there that I started to gain the knowledge to live drug and alcohol free and where my journey into a new way of living began."

I went on to tell him that in January of '97, I enrolled in San Joaquin Delta College where I started my educational journey and obtained an Associates of Arts degree, which had culminated with a Masters of Social Work Degree from California State University, Stanislaus in Turlock, California in 2003.

"Truly amazing, sir," he said. "From what you've told me, you have done a remarkable job of turning your life around. Can I tell you something else?"

"Of course," I answered.

"You're a Judge's dream come true. What I mean is that most Judges want people who come before them to succeed, to quit appearing before them like so many of them do. Sadly, what you have done doesn't happen very often. Most of ex-prisoners keep going back time and time again. So it is satisfying as a judge to meet someone who has succeeded. I commend you."

"Thank you, sir."

"What I'd like you to do now is to prepare a PowerPoint presentation for a committee I'll choose to hire you as an adjunct instructor. Can you do it?" he asked.

"Of course," I said. "In fact, I created a PowerPoint awhile back that fits perfectly with this subject. When do you want me to present?"

"It will probably be next week. I want you to start teaching next quarter. I'll call you with the time and date of the presentation in the next few days, okay?"

I nodded, too excited to answer with words.

Mr. DiSomma seemed just as happy as I was. He had a smile from one side of his face to the other. I had a deep respect for this man who was going out on the limb for me, putting his reputation on the line even though he barely knew me. I promised myself that I would never to do anything to disappoint or make him look bad in front of his peers because he had hired me. I knew there were people who couldn't wait for me to make a mistake so they could say, "You see, those people never change. Once a criminal, always a criminal."

I was on a mission to prove that statement false, to show that some of us did change. I was living proof.

The following week I presented my PowerPoint to a panel chosen by Mr. DiSomma to determine if I met the qualifications to teach at their institution. I presented a historical overview of the California prison system that showed the immense population growth between 1974 and 2010 and how CDCR had gone to a strictly retribution system without offering rehabilitation. During my presentation one committee member got heated.

"Are you suggesting we give them whatever they want? My ex-wife, who's a warden at one of our prisons, recently told me that all inmates are nothing more than liars and crybabies. She says they complain about everything and expect citizens to pay for their educational/vocational training. Why should we provide them with a free education while law-abiding citizens have to pay for theirs? I think someone who breaks the law should get nothing but hard labor!" He stormed out of the room.

I didn't get an opportunity to respond to his remarks, but I didn't allow myself to get flustered. I figured he had the right to his opinion. Besides, I was sure I would encounter students who would behave a lot worse than he did if I started teaching. I ended my presentation by saying that if we wanted to keep incarcerating people without providing them any type of treatment for their substance abuse issues or educational deficits, then society had to suck it up and quit complaining about the enormous amount of tax revenue that went into the CDCR budget.

"As you saw during my presentation, the number of inmates has grown three hundred percent during the last thirty years which clearly shows that the approach we've been using to impact our nation's current crime crisis isn't working. And unless we do something different, crime will continue to increase."

Afterward, every committee member thanked and congratulated me for my insightful presentation and I was asked to step outside. About thirty minutes later Mr. DiSomma came out to meet with me.

"Everyone on the committee voted to hire you," he said smiling brightly. "All we have to do now is verify your employment and educational background information. Don't worry about your criminal history, I'll take care of that, but I don't want you talking freely about your past. People don't need to know. If you run into someone who knows about your past, there's nothing you can do about that, but try not to bring up, okay?"

"Sure," I replied with more confidence than I felt. I wasn't sure I would be able to speak having to omit such a large portion of my life. Besides, I was sure some students, the ones who had been locked up themselves, would know by the manner in which I carried myself that I had served time in prison. After all, the old adage "you can take the man out of prison, but you can't take the prison out of the man" is very true. I decided to use this opportunity to purge the residual prison gestures that had been a part of my life for many years, a task that would require lots of skill and work.

Apart from not being able to discuss my past, I was elated that I'd been hired and I rushed home to tell Jessica about my new position as a teacher. "Wow, Dad, I can't believe it," my daughter said when I told her.

"You see baby, anyone can achieve their goals as long as they do the work. It's more difficult for people with criminal backgrounds, but it can be done."

I started teaching in January 2010 and quickly realized I had the knowledge, but that I needed to learn the skill of delivering the information to students. I also found myself fluctuating between the old and the new me whenever students misbehaved in class. On the one hand I wanted to go ballistic on them, yet I realized being hardcore wasn't the way to respond to students who acted out. I had already learned that I could be fair, firm, and consistent with understanding and compassion. I also kept in mind how I had been impacted by teachers when I had been in school as a young kid. I knew it was my responsibility to look beyond their behavior and find out why they were being disruptive. I began to take time to speak with them privately after class. It was during those sessions that I would learn the student being disruptive was experiencing some type of distress in their personal life that they didn't know how to handle. Sometimes I was able to give suggestions that helped, other times I was simply a sounding board for them to get stuff off their chest. By and large, those talks were helpful to the student and definitely useful for me. I always walked away from those discussions with a new perspective about other peoples' lives.

In June 2010, I began the last portion of my educational journey. I finally got enough courage to go back to school and obtain my Ed.D (Doctorate in Education). I had put if off since 2003, because truth be told, I was afraid of taking the GRE (Graduate Record Examine) in order to be accepted. Ultimately, I got the courage and started the process to get into California State University at Stanislaus, the place where I earned my BA and Masters Degrees. I know I can do it and that I will be pushed to my limits, but I have no doubt I will complete it by 2013. Then I'll be known as Dr. De La Cruz.

NOT LONG AFTER I enrolled in the Doctoral program, I traveled to my neighborhood to visit Mama. Before I headed home, I went to visit my homeboy Steve. I often visited him whenever I was in Woodlake. Steve was one of the few guys who grew up with me who was still alive and not in prison. He had also made some positive changes in his life and was no longer drinking. He was on Methadone, but he wasn't using illicit drugs anymore. These were huge changes for Steve.

That day, he talked about his health and what was happening in the neighborhood. Like most times I went to see Steve, I didn't say too much. I mostly listened. I didn't mind. When it was time to go, I told him I had gone back to Cal State.

"You did?"

I nodded.

"That means you're getting a Ph.D., right?"

"I'm getting an Ed.D. A Doctorate in education, similar to a Ph.D."

"*Oralé!*" Steve stuck his hand out and shook my hand vigorously. "Hey, homeboy, you remember when we were growing up how the older folks in the neighborhood didn't want their kids hanging out with us because they said we were bad influences?"

I nodded.

"You remember how our teachers told us we would never amount to anything when we grew up?"

I nodded again.

"You proved them wrong, huh?

CHRONOLOGICAL ORDER
OF CHARACTER'S LIFE TRAJECTORIES

Alex: Died from cirrhosis of the liver.

Bella: Still lives in the neighborhood.

Benita: Died from cancer at the age of ﬁfty-four.

Big Indio: Found hanging in his cell at Vacaville State Prison.

Blue: Lives in San Jose and is currently on Methadone.

Caboobie: Last time I saw him was in 1986 at California Men's Colony in San Luis Obispo, CA.

Cerrillo: Found in the park restroom dead from a heroin overdose.

Chicken Man: Serving life for the murder of my brother Neto.

Chipmunk: Died from cirrhosis of the liver at the age of forty-six

Chapo: Found slumped on the steering wheel of his car with his head blown off by a shotgun blast in San Jose, California.

Claw: Died from cirrhosis of the liver at the age ﬁfty-one.

Frank Lopez: Moved out of the neighborhood. Whereabouts are unknown.

George: Shot in the head with a Forty-Five-caliber pistol while out on bail litigating his conviction after it was overturned by the 5th District Court of Appeals.

Gibby: Currently lives in Modesto California. Last time I seen him was in Folsom State Prison in 1996.

Hollywood: Died in 1990 from cirrhosis of the liver at the age of ﬁfty-two.

Huéro: Died in a car accident. The medical examiner determined he was drunk.

Jackie: Found hanging in his cell at San Quentin State Prison.

Leonard: Lost contact with him after he was released from prison in the early 1980s.

Lil Joe: Lost a leg from an infection caused by an abscess after injecting heroin. Currently lives in the Bay Area.

Old Man Mike: Died in 1994 from emphysema at the age of eighty-two.

Palio: Stabbed eighty-six times. His body was discovered by a passerby in an alley next to a garbage bin in Stockton, California. Pato: Stabbed to death in Folsom State Prison in 1984.

Perico: Convicted of six counts of conspiracy to murder and sentenced to six life terms. He dropped out of the NF and is currently at Sacramento State Prison.

Puppet: Lives in San Jose, California and is currently on Methadone.

Pancho: Finally got straight and is currently clean and sober. He still lives in Stockton, CA and is working as a barber.

Poncho: Still going in and out of prison.

Sach: Died from cirrhosis in 1995 of the liver at the age of thirty-nine.

Shark: Died from cirrhosis in 1984 of the liver at the age of thirty-six.

Steve: Still lives in the neighborhood.

Quate: Died in 1991 from cancer after deciding to change his life.

Vek: Died in 1984 from cirrhosis of the liver at the age of forty-four.

GLOSSARY

Bella: Beautiful

Brujo: Male Witch

Caballo: Horse

Cabrón Mion: Pissing Goat

Carnal: Brother

Carnalito: Lil Brother

Chapo: Slang for Asian Eyes

Currandero: Healer

Diablo: Devil

El Caballo Blanco: The White Horse

Ella: Her

El Venadito: The Small Deer

Ese: Dude or Guy

Es tu hermanito: He's your little brother

Flaco: Skinny

Gabacho: White Guy

Hueró: Light Skinned

Jéfita: Mother

La Rana: The Frog

Las Rejas No Matan: The Bars Don't Kill

Los Hombres no lloran: Men don't cry

Mayate: Black Guy

Menso: Dummy

Mijo: Son

Norté: North

O. G. : Original Gangster

Oralé: Okay

Otra: Another

Palio: Stick

Pan Dulce: Sweet bread

Pato: Duck

Pélon: Bald

Pendejo: Stupid

Pepino: Cucumber

Prieto: Dark Skinned Guy

Quate: Twin

Sabes que: You know what?

Simón: Yes or Yeah

Técato: Heroin Addict

Tú Sabes: You Know

Trampa: Tramp

Vato: Dude

Vétéranos: Veterans

ACKNOWLEDGMENTS

THE MOST REWARDING PART of writing my memoir was getting to know the many people who helped me along the way. In a world where few us find enough time for our closest friends and family, many of the folks mentioned below made time to share their invaluable experiences with me.

Special thanks to Richard Rios for providing the key suggestions that got this memoir started. Without his guidance I never would have known how to imagine this book, much less finish it.

Thanks to Sam Hatch for reading my work in progress, and helping me articulate important points in the book.

Thanks to the countless people who helped me along the way to change how I looked at the world, and for having patience with me when I was completely behaving as though I was still on the prison tier.

Special thanks to Rachel Zapien, Renee Gomez, Lloiden Gaza, and Loretta Alvarado, for being patient and teaching me how to treat women when I didn't have a clue.

In the same spirit, I wish to express my profound gratitude to my best friend Joe Loya. He believed in me from the very start. Without his countless hours of help I never would have completed this project. He listened when I needed someone to hear me. He was there at the drop of a hat whenever I needed him. Joe and I are ex-cons and hold a special bond that goes beyond most people's understanding. I will always be grateful to him for being my friend.

Last but not least, I want to thank the many, many, people in A.A. who helped me learn that I could live without the use of drugs and alcohol. I owe them a debt I can never repay.

ABOUT THE AUTHOR

JESSE DE LA CRUZ was raised in the *barrios* of California. At the early age of twelve, Mr. De La Cruz began a journey that would eventually lead him to become an ex-convict, ex-drug abuser, and former gang member who served approximately thirty years of his life at California prisons like Folsom and San Quentin. He has experienced firsthand the hatred, misery, and despair brought about by a criminal/gang lifestyle.

After his final release from prison, Mr. De La Cruz enrolled in college, graduating with a Baccalaureate Degree in Sociology in 2001 and his Masters of Social Work Degree from California State University, Stanislaus in 2003. He is currently working on his Ed.D.

Mr. De La Cruz truly exemplifies the phrase 'chosen a new path,' and has risen from the 'pits of hell.' He has withstood the ordeal and rigors of the system and has managed to transcend these experiences, adopting acceptable patterns of social behavior to reach success in his relationship to family and community.

He is the founder of The Jonah Foundation, a sober living house that provides housing to ex-offenders transitioning from prison to the streets. He also established the first Criminals & Gangs Members Anonymous fellowship in California. The group is made up of individuals who have come to realize the tragic effect of their lifestyle and come together to address the causes and conditions as to why they continue to hurt themselves and others.

He lives with his daughter in California.